Women in the Bible For Dummies®

Cheat Sheet

Five Bad Girls of the Bible

Five gals with whom you wouldn't want to cross paths:

- **Jezebel:** A notorious evil queen who encouraged her husband to falsely denounce their neighbor Naboth, which results in Naboth's unjust execution merely to acquire his vineyard. She dies a gruesome death. See 1 Kings 16:31, 18:4, 19:1–2, 21:5, 23, and 2 Kings 9:30–37.

- **Herodias:** The wife of Herod Antipas and mother of Salome. After marrying her uncle Herod Philip, she dumps him for his brother Herod Antipas and collaborates with her daughter, Salome, to have John the Baptist beheaded (because he denounced Herodias's adulterous marriage). See Matthew 14:3–11 and Mark 6:17–25.

- **Athaliah:** The daughter of Jezebel who killed her own grandchildren to secure the throne for herself. See 2 Kings 8:26.

- **Delilah:** The mistress of Samson who betrayed him to the Philistines by revealing the secret of his strength. See Judges 16:4–20.

- **Maacah:** The mother of King Asa who was deposed by her own son for promoting idolatry. See 1 Kings 15:13.

The Bible's Top Moms

Mommy Dearest, they weren't. These ladies are considered some of the best mothers from the Bible:

- **Jochebed:** The prudent mother of Moses, Miriam, and Aaron. She saved Moses' life by floating him down the Nile River, where he was later discovered by the daughter of Pharaoh, who raised him as her own. See Exodus 6:20; Numbers 26:59.

- **Hannah:** The thoughtful mother of the prophet Samuel who dedicated him to God after praying for a child for many years. Each year, she made him a new robe that she brought faithfully to her son when she and her husband visited the Temple. See 1 Samuel 1:2-2:21.

- **Virgin Mary:** The devoted mother ... t his first public miracle (the wedding feast ... o wine, and at the crucifixion, death, and b ...

D1402003

Women in the Bible For Dummies®

Cheat Sheet

The Bible's Visionaries

- **Miriam:** The first prophetess and the sister of Moses and Aaron. See Exodus 15:20.
- **Deborah:** She prophesied the Canaanite defeat by Barak (Hebrew General of the Army who, with the help of Deborah, conquered the troops of Sisera, the Canaanite Commander). See Judges 4:4–9.
- **Huldah:** Her prophecy brought about a religious revival under King Josiah. See 2 Chronicles 34:22–28.
- **Anna:** The only prophetess in the New Testament. She lived to see the infant Jesus. See Luke 2:36–38.

Little-Known Facts about Biblical Women

Want to sound really smart? Throw these little bits of trivia into any conversation:

- Sarah is the only woman in the Bible to have her name changed — from Sarai to Sarah.
- Deborah is the only female Judge.
- Athaliah is the only woman to rule the Kingdom of Judah.
- Seven hundred women became wives of Solomon.
- The daughter of Herodias is never identified by name, but historians believe she was called Salome.

Important Songs of Women

Three songs (hymns or poems) of significant women appear in the Bible. They are expressions of the deep faith, gratitude, and trust these ladies had in God and in his love and mercy. Though their stories were written by someone else (the sacred author for each book), the particular song attributed to them is considered their own and merely retold by the scripture writer.

- **Song of Hannah:** Recited at the dedication of her son, Samuel. It expresses enormous gratitude for the blessings that come from God. See 1 Samuel 2:1–10.
- **Song of Deborah:** An epic poem that retells the victory of the Hebrews over their enemy the Canaanites while Deborah was Judge of Israel. See Judges 5:1–31.
- **Song of Virgin Mary:** This song is called the Magnificat, from the first word in the Latin Vulgate Bible of St. Jerome. Similar to Hannah's maternal song of gratitude, it was said by Mary, the mother of Jesus, after she visits her cousin Elizabeth. Both women were pregnant at the time, Mary with Jesus and Elizabeth with John the Baptist. The song expresses profound appreciation for the goodness of the Lord. See Luke 1:46–55.

For Dummies: Bestselling Book Series for Beginners

Women in the Bible
FOR DUMMIES®

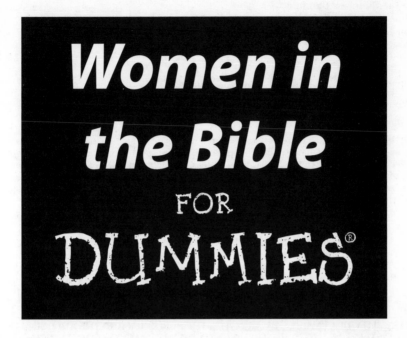

Women in the Bible

FOR DUMMIES®

by Rev. John Trigilio Jr., PhD, ThD,
and Rev. Kenneth Brighenti, PhD

WILEY

Wiley Publishing, Inc.

Women in the Bible For Dummies®

Published by
Wiley Publishing, Inc.
111 River St.
Hoboken, NJ 07030-5774
www.wiley.com

WILEY

About the Authors

Rev. John Trigilio, Jr., PhD, ThD, a native of Erie, Pennsylvania, serves as the pastor of Our Lady of Good Counsel (Marysville, Pennsylvania) and St. Bernadette Catholic Churches (Duncannon, Pennsylvania). He is the president of the Confraternity of Catholic Clergy and executive editor of its quarterly journal, *Sapientia* magazine. Father Trigilio is a co-host of two weekly TV series on the Eternal Word Television Network (EWTN): *Web of Faith* and *Council of Faith.* He also serves as a theological consultant and online spiritual advisor for EWTN. He's been listed in *Who's Who in America* in 1993 and *Who's Who in Religion* in 1999 and is a member of the Fellowship of Catholic Scholars. He was ordained a priest for the Diocese of Harrisburg (Pennsylvania) in 1988.

Rev. Kenneth Brighenti, PhD, a native of New Britain, Connecticut, serves as pastor of St. Ann Catholic Church (Raritan, New Jersey). He is the managing editor of *Sapientia* magazine, a member of the board of directors for the Confraternity of Catholic Clergy, and co-host of *Council of Faith,* a weekly TV series on EWTN. Father Brighenti also served as a U.S. Naval Reserve Chaplain for ten years and was ordained a priest for the Diocese of Metuchen (New Jersey) in 1988. He and Father Trigilio co-authored *Catholicism For Dummies* (2003) and *The Everything Bible Book* (2004).

Dedication

This book is dedicated to the important women of our lives who greatly influenced us and our faith:

Reverend Mother Angelica, PCPA, founder of Eternal Word Television Network (EWTN) and Abbess of the Monastery of Our Lady of the Angels. She has been a shining example of a strong woman of faith.

In particular we dedicate this book on the women of Scripture to our two beloved and dear mothers:

Elizabeth Trigilio and **Norma Brighenti,** whose great love and deep faith have been a great source of comfort and inspiration to us as their sons.

And finally, we dedicate this work on biblical women to the star of scripture, the **Blessed Virgin Mary,** mother of Christ and mother of the Church.

In memory of the Most Rev. Nicholas Carmen Dattilo, D.D. (1932–2004), former bishop of the Diocese of Harrisburg, Pennsylvania, and the Most Rev. Vincent de Paul Breen, D.D. (1936–2003), former bishop of the Diocese of Metuchen, New Jersey.

Authors' Acknowledgments

Father Brighenti and Father Trigilio are grateful for the assistance, guidance, and advice we received from:

Rev. Dr. Robert J. Levis (Gannon University), Rev. James M. Cafone (Seton Hall University), Jennifer Rung, the Poor Clare Nuns of Perpetual Adoration (Hanceville, Alabama), the Religious Teachers Filippini (New Jersey), the Discalced Carmelite Nuns (Erie, Pennsylvania), and the Dominican Nuns of the Perpetual Rosary (Lancaster, Pennsylvania) for their prayers and support.

We also wish to thank our bishops, the Most Rev. Kevin C. Rhoades, DD, STL, JCL (Bishop of Harrisburg, Pennsylvania), and the Most Rev. Paul Gregory Bootkoski, DD (Bishop of Metuchen, New Jersey) and the people of our parishes where we serve as pastor (St. Ann, Our Lady of Good Counsel, and St. Bernadette) for their prayerful support.

Finally, a special word of appreciation to His Holiness Pope John Paul II for his example, teaching, and leadership.

Publisher's Acknowledgments

We're proud of this book; please send us your comments through our Dummies online registration form located at www.dummies.com/register/.

Some of the people who helped bring this book to market include the following:

Acquisitions, Editorial,
and Media Development

Project Editor: Sherri Cullison Pfouts

Acquisitions Editor: Stacy Kennedy

Senior Copy Editor: Tina Sims

Technical Editor: Todd Alexander

Editorial Manager: Christine Meloy Beck

Media Development Manager:
Laura VanWinkle

Editorial Assistant: Hanna Scott,
Melissa Bennett, Nadine Bell

Cover Photos: © The Palma
Collection/PictureQuest/Photodisc

Cartoons: Rich Tennant, www.the5thwave.com

Composition Services

Project Coordinator: Maridee Ennis

Layout and Graphics: Andrea Dahl,
Joyce Haughey

Proofreaders: Leeann Harney, Jessica Kramer,
TECHBOOKS Production Services

Indexer: TECHBOOKS Production Services

*Myria*Tracy Barr, Jennifer Bingham,
E. Neil Johnson

Publishing and Editorial for Consumer Dummies

Diane Graves Steele, Vice President and Publisher, Consumer Dummies

Joyce Pepple, Acquisitions Director, Consumer Dummies

Kristin A. Cocks, Product Development Director, Consumer Dummies

Michael Spring, Vice President and Publisher, Travel

Kelly Regan, Editorial Director, Travel

Publishing for Technology Dummies

Andy Cummings, Vice President and Publisher, Dummies Technology/General User

Composition Services

Gerry Fahey, Vice President of Production Services

Debbie Stailey, Director of Composition Services

Contents at a Glance

Table of Contents

Introduction

● ●

*T*he Bible has been and continues to be one of the oldest and longest best-
selling books in the history of humankind. Within the pages of this epic
piece of literature, and what believers consider to be the inspired and revealed
Word of God, are the fascinating stories of human beings on their journey of
faith. Women play an important and vital part — not only in salvation history
itself but also in the journey of faith.

Women in the Bible are prominent and obscure: the Bible mentions women
by name, by title, by familial relationship (wife, mother, daughter, widow),
and sometimes just by geographical location. Famous women like Eve (the
first woman), Sarah (wife of Abraham), Mary Magdalene (follower of Jesus),
and Mary of Nazareth (mother of Jesus) are discussed, but so are lesser-
known women like Judith, Dinah, Jochebed, Huldah, Dorcas, and Lydia.

About This Book

Although it's not a substitute or replacement for the Bible, this book serves
as an introduction for those who may never have read the Bible, or it can be
a help for those studying the Bible. If we're lucky, it can also serve as an eye-
opener to some who never realized how many or how vital women have been
in scripture. Some of these women may inspire you. Some may impress you.
Some may just make good reading. Many questions, mysteries, and unknowns
remain about several of these women. We may not answer every question,
but that's because the Bible often doesn't give all the details. Unlike mystery
novels in which the mystery is resolved at the end, the Bible usually unveils
more mysteries and unanswered questions every time you read it.

Conventions Used in This Book

We use the New Oxford Annotated Bible, New Revised Standard Version, for
most of the quotations taken from the Bible. We use the traditional dating
system of B.C. (before Christ) and A.D. (*anno domini,* which is Latin for "year

of the Lord") because it is better known and has been in use historically a lot longer than the newer designation of B.C.E. (before the common era = before Christ) and C.E. (common era = year of the Lord). There is merit in using the newer system because it respects the different calendars and dating system of non-Christian religions and cultures. However, the older system is still more familiar to people because many historical documents since the time of Christ until recently have used it. Many Bibles printed until the last part of the twentieth century use the older system in their commentaries and footnotes, so we chose for the sake of consistency to keep it.

The word *scripture* is used synonymously in this book with the word Bible, so when you read "it says in scripture" that means "it says in the Bible." The term Hebrew Scriptures is synonymous with the Christian designation of Old Testament in the Bible. The Hebrew Scriptures and Protestant Old Testament have the same 39 books, whereas the Eastern Orthodox and Catholic Old Testaments have seven more books (46). Those seven extra books are called the Deuterocanon (meaning "second canon," or official list of what books belong in the Bible) by Catholics and Orthodox Christians, whereas Protestants call them Apocrypha (meaning other or hidden writings). Read more about the explanation of these books in Chapter 2. God has many names in many religions — and even in the Bible. Some refer to him as "the Lord" or "the Almighty." Recognizing the Hebrew respect for the sacred name, we do not use the word "Yahweh" in this book as a few Bible versions do, but we instead use the more common translation of the Hebrew *Adonai,* "Lord," or the Hebrew *Elohim,* "God."

We often refer to idolatry in this book. *Idolatry* is considered a personal sin against God, but also a crime against the Hebrew nation because it violates the covenant between God and his chosen people. When someone worships false gods, as did the Canaanites, it is seen as an offense against the Lord and a breach of trust between the individual citizen and the Hebrew nation.

This book uses the traditional chapter and verse designation of a number followed by a colon. Genesis 3:15 is shorthand for the third chapter of Genesis, verse 15. Commas separate verses or chapters, while semicolons change from one passage to the next. Luke 1:28, 42 means you look at the first chapter of Luke's Gospel, verse 28 and verse 42. Deuteronomy 6:4–6 means you look at the sixth chapter of Deuteronomy from verse 4 all the way to and including verse 6. John 6:53; 15:5 means you look at the sixth chapter of John's gospel, verse 53, and at the 15th chapter, verse 5.

You'll notice that some words in this book are in *italic*. We use italic for emphasis and to highlight new words or terms that are defined. In addition, italic is used to help you identify foreign words and phrases.

What You're Not to Read

Well, maybe you shouldn't take it to that extreme, but we should let you in on a couple of things to know about this book:

- ✔ *Sidebars* contain information that you don't have to read to understand the Bible or the women mentioned in it. They serve as asides, anecdotes, or extended examples of what we discuss in the regular text.

- ✔ Order doesn't matter. That being said, you can read anything you want without hurting our feelings. Feel free to skip around. We use copious cross-references to help you understand anything you may have skipped over.

Foolish Assumptions

In writing this book, we made some assumptions about you. Want to know what they are?

- ✔ You want to know something about the women who are mentioned in the Bible, whether you're a woman or a man.

- ✔ You're curious about what the Bible has to say about women or how it describes women.

- ✔ You've heard or seen some of the names of these women in the Bible before — maybe you've even read about them in another book — but you want to know how much of what you know or have read is actually from the Bible, and how much is fiction.

- ✔ You want to know the actual stories about these ladies in easy-to-read-and-understand formats.

How This Book Is Organized

We've intentionally written this book in such a way that you can jump into it at *any* point and just go. You can read straight through, cover to cover, from Chapter 1 to Chapter 24, or you can go directly to the section that interests you. Here's a brief summary of our organization.

Part 1: Connecting with the Women of Ancient History

This part gives a brief background on the origin, history, and development of the Bible; the biblical, religious, social, and cultural roles and perspectives on women in general; and the impact of language, gender, and ideology on how women are treated. Because the Bible was written over a period of many centuries and by people influenced by various philosophies, cultures, and societies, this part also looks at how those factors affected what was written, what was intended, and how it is understood today.

Part 11: The Big Six: The Most Famous Women of the Bible

This section begins our actual look at the women mentioned in the Bible, and we discuss the six most famous for starters. Eve, the first woman; the Virgin Mary, the mother of Jesus of Nazareth; and Mary Magdalene, follower of Jesus, are the starting lineup here. We also discuss the only three women to have a book of the Bible named after them: Ruth, Judith, and Esther.

Part 111: Influencing Lives, Shaping History: Women of Faith and Power

This part deals with the women who were the movers and shakers of their time. We look at the matriarchs who helped shape the foundation of the Hebrew people, the women during the times of slavery and persecution, the powerful and influential women who helped establish the Hebrew kingdom (particularly those women who ruled), and the women who knew and followed Jesus, as well as the women who helped the early Christian church get off the ground.

Part 1V: Women of Public Debate . . . or Disdain

This part looks at the obscure, the intriguing, and the scheming women of the Bible. Their motives may not have been known, but what they said and/or did as recorded in the Bible is examined.

Part V: The Nameless: Wives, Mothers, Daughters, and Widows

This part zeroes in on the women of scripture who have no name. They're merely identified by their familial relationship (wife, mother, daughter, or widow), their location (the town or region they are from), or their situation (physical or spiritual health).

Part VI: The Part of Tens

Here's the fun part. We give you quick overviews of the most misunderstood women of the Bible, the most famous women of the Bible in art, and the most influential women of the Bible.

Appendix

Here we list the women in the Bible — even the ones we did not discuss in depth — alphabetically and with their corresponding biblical citation.

Icons Used in This Book

Throughout this book, we guide you toward important points by using the following icons:

Next to this icon, you find information that's good to keep in mind. This is just stuff we think is important to remember.

Lots of people have lots of different opinions about the Bible's stories. We use this icon to point out many of the points about which people disagree.

This icon signals that we're going to delve a little deeper than usual into an explanation or definition. We don't mean to suggest the information is too difficult to understand — just a little more detailed.

"Exactly!" That's what you'll think when you read this icon's info — because it quotes exactly what the Bible says about a woman or an event.

Where to Go from Here

Women in the Bible For Dummies is like an appetizer. You can get a taste of the women who are mentioned in the Bible, what they said or did, and maybe what impact they had. We recommend that you have a Bible of your choosing nearby as you read just in case you want to look up what the scripture says about these women. Otherwise, jump right in.

Part I

Connecting with the Women of Ancient History

The 5th Wave   By Rich Tennant

"Okay, but this remains between the three of us-right?"

In this part . . .

This part explains why we wrote a book about women in the Bible and why you may find it interesting, informative, and enjoyable to read about these ladies of scripture. In this part, we also discuss some important things you should know in order to appreciate the context as well as the content of what the Bible has to say regarding women. You see the background of how the Bible came to be, what makes it such a special book, and how women play a part in what is written on its pages. We also describe the religious, social, and cultural viewpoints on women during the time of the Bible and today and shed some insight on the roles of the only female Judge in the Bible, the prophetesses, and Lady Wisdom.

Chapter 1

Women of the Bible at a Glance

In This Chapter

▶ Understanding God's wish for unity of the sexes

▶ Becoming acquainted with women and biblical culture

▶ Turning to biblical women as good examples

The Bible contains many more stories of men than of women . . . and in much greater detail. Although most of you probably know the stories of biblical men — Adam, Moses, Noah, Jesus, and Peter, to name several — many biblical women remain mysteries. Yet women play critical roles in the Bible and in salvation history. Some are famous, and others are unknown; some are powerful, and others are powerless. Like their biblical male counterparts, some women used their gifts and abilities for good, and some for evil. But no matter what their individual personalities and contributions, their stories are often crucial to understanding salvation history. They also provide a multitude of examples for readers today. From the original woman on earth (Eve) described in the first book of the Bible to the "woman clothed with the sun, with the moon under her feet" (Revelation 12:1) mentioned in the last book, we discuss all the notable and noteworthy women in sacred scripture. Their examples provide a perspective on history, as well as enlightenment on the modern-day world.

Unifying Man and Woman

The best-selling book of all time isn't some John Grisham thriller. It's the Bible. But like any Grisham novel, the Bible is also chock-full of drama and excitement. Yes, the Bible has its fair share of adultery; it has sin, and it even tells many tales of love, romance, and kindness. The Bible has it all, and its importance throughout history can't be underestimated. Many world religions regard it as the inspired, inerrant, and revealed Word of God.

The Good Book, as it's often called, describes the words and deeds of the good, the bad, and the ugly of our species in their relationships with the Almighty and with each other. These stories and people cross every line — gender, race, class, ethnicity, age, and more. There is no good gender, class, or other group portrayed in the Bible, and on the flip side, there's no "bad" group, either. Even the Bible's greatest heroes are portrayed as real — and flawed — human beings.

The bigger picture in Genesis

The Bible tries to teach unity within diversity. Just as every man and woman is a unity of body and soul, and human nature is a unity of intellect and will, humankind is both male and female. Men and women are not inherently rivals, one against the other. According to Christian and Jewish theology, it was the devil (whose name means "adversary") who tempted Adam and Eve to commit sin, an action that brought disunity into the human equation. The Bible teaches that grace unites and sin divides.

This unity is shown in two passages in Genesis. Genesis shows that both genders are equally human and are equally made in the image and likeness of God.

Genesis 1

"So God created humankind in his image. In the image of God he created them; male and female he created them" (Genesis 1:27). This key passage from the first chapter of the first book of the Bible underscores the idea that both men and women are made in the image of God and that both genders together reflect the divine. Though the masculine pronoun is often used to describe God (he, his, and him), it isn't because men more resemble the Almighty than women do. (See Chapter 2 for more on translating what the Bible says.)

Because the scriptures also reveal the idea of God as both Father as well as Creator, the masculine is used in the same way we use the feminine to speak of mother earth (*terra mater* in Latin) or holy mother church. Yet, theologians point out that even the notion of God as Father is not to say that God is male. They say God is a spirit — pure spirit to be exact — and therefore has no gender in terms of divinity. Human beings, on the other hand, are either male or female, while at the same time both share the same human nature. Interestingly, though, the Bible does describe wisdom as if speaking of a woman by using the feminine pronoun (see Chapter 4 for more about Lady Wisdom).

Because of the human need to make God approachable, accessible, and lovable, people use a personal pronoun to describe him. Although the neutral "it" could be used to refer to God, that word sounds cold, unemotional, and disrespectful. Bible versions use "he" in reference to God, but that's not meant to demean or diminish women or femininity, because God made both "male and female" in his own image and likeness.

Cooperation, rather than competition, between the sexes is encouraged because both were created in God's image. Through the creation stories in Genesis, the Bible seeks to show that differences between men and women can be complementary and not necessarily adversarial or contradictory. For example, while there is a difference between how God created Adam (from the dust of the earth) and how he created Eve (from the rib of Adam), both are said to have been made in the image and likeness of God. Both father and mother are to be equally honored, as mandated in the Ten Commandments. Murdering a man or a woman incurs the same guilt and punishment.

Genesis 2

"Therefore a man leaves his father and his mother and clings to his wife, and they become one flesh" (Genesis 2:24). Whereas Genesis 1:27 (see the preceding section) speaks of male and female beings made in the divine image, this quote now speaks of unity, the two becoming one flesh. Scripture scholars point out that Genesis 1 has a slightly different Creation story than does Genesis 2. Both describe the same event, but each has a different perspective and purpose.

The passage from Genesis 2 shows that husband and wife are united in marriage in the same way that new skin is grafted to the old, the two becoming one. You experience the dual aspects of your human nature already as body and soul, flesh and blood, and mind and will. Male and female are just two more levels of ways to distinguish each other. The two passages together give the whole picture.

Two genders, one history

Both genders have a part to play in salvation history. When Exodus describes the Ten Commandments, both sexes are explicitly mentioned when it says, "honor your father and your mother" (Exodus 20:12).

Although most of the people listed in the Bible are men, the women aren't just window dressing or background scenery. Women like Sarah (see Chapter 9) are not just wives and mothers; they're also matriarchs, prophetesses, teachers, and leaders, as in the case of Deborah the Judge (see Chapter 10) and Esther the Queen (see Chapter 8).

The Lord worked through both women and men in the Bible to teach, to save, and to protect. They may have been assigned different roles and responsibilities in this ancient culture, but they were both given one objective: to serve the will of God as best they could.

Equal *dignity* doesn't always translate into equal duties and responsibilities, whether cultural or religious.

This book looks at the significant women of the Bible, including Sarah (Chapter 9) and Miriam (Chapter 10), controversial women such as Delilah and Jezebel (Chapter 16), misunderstood women such as Mary Magdalene (Chapter 7), and famous women such as Eve (Chapter 5) and the Virgin Mary (Chapter 6).

Societies have, over time, chosen to embrace, embellish, adapt to, or reject boundaries placed on men and women. (And some societies, as discussed in Chapter 2, have even misinterpreted the Bible in order to protect their perceived powers.) The Bible explains how humans were created with the same rights, and its tales describe many women who, united with their men, made quite a difference in the history of the world.

Getting to Know the Women

Though men outnumber women in the Bible's stories, the book doesn't neglect the importance and influence of women of faith and the invaluable contribution they have made. The Bible shows from the very beginning of creation that women are not incidental but instead essential to the main stories being told — in spite of the patriarchal system in which they lived.

A *patriarchal society* is characterized by the supremacy of the father in the clan or family, the legal dependence of wives and children, and the importance of carrying on the male line.

Chucking the stereotypes

You won't find a stereotype of women in the Bible. You come across mothers (Chapter 19) and daughters (Chapter 20), wives (Chapter 18) and widows (Chapter 21), queens (Chapter 12), matriarchs (Chapter 9), and the poor and destitute. Other stories discuss harlots (Chapter 10), witches and soothsayers (Chapter 16), prophetesses (Chapter 15), a Judge (Chapter 10), and a military leader (Deborah in Chapter 10). Brave and courageous biblical women are forced to contend with cowardly and unscrupulous ladies. Some are shy; others are outspoken. Some are known for their beauty, wisdom, and grace; others for their fidelity, loyalty, and courage. Biblical women aren't cookie-cutter characters — not a Stepford wife in the bunch.

Yes, most of the women of the Bible are wives and mothers, just as most men are husbands and fathers. The males are identified primarily through their occupation (Joseph the Carpenter, for example), whereas most women are identified by their relationship to someone else (mother of Jesus, Peter's mother-in-law, sister of Moses, and so on). You still see that type of identification today to some degree, such as references to the First Lady of the United States. But you also see this in the reverse, such as in the case of Sir Denis, the late husband of former British Prime Minister Margaret Thatcher.

Despite these identifying characteristics, scripture doesn't imply that mere relationships to others (sister, wife, and widow) made these women great or holy. Instead, their faith in God made many of them important. What these women did or did not do and what they said or did not say is the bottom line, even though some are nameless and merely referred to by titles such as Lot's wife, Jairus's daughter, or the widow of Zarephath. Being faithful to God, doing the right thing, and showing courage in times of adversity are the actions that make the nameless and the named women in the Bible truly remarkable and worthy of attention.

Like their male counterparts, the heroines of the Bible aren't perfect any more than the villainesses are totally corrupt. People such as Naomi (Chapter 11) have some really hard knocks in life, yet they remain faithful despite their weaknesses. The good ones made mistakes just like the men, but they never stopped trying to do better, and they never gave up on God or on each other.

Understanding their circumstances

The sacred scriptures offer a glimpse into how women were treated in Old Testament and New Testament times in the Jewish and Christian traditions. The Bible also portrays the tension between the religion and culture and the effects that tradition, custom, and society had upon women. Women weren't the only group treated unfairly in the Bible; the poor, the foreigner, the unlearned, and those conquered by the predominant power at the time were often treated as less than human, as well as less than equal.

Understanding the culture and beliefs of the times is critical to understanding the women of the Bible. Human failure caused the inequality of those days. How do you know this? Consider Abraham (see Chapter 9 for the full story). He treats his wife Sarah disrespectfully by passing her off as his sister rather than as his wife just to protect his own skin. But God intervenes and protects her by getting her out of the sticky situation her husband got her in.

These women had normal human origins and lived ordinary lives. But when their faith was tested, they overcame enormous obstacles by their own human nature endowed by God's grace.

Many of them suffered, but they continued to keep their faith. For example, Elizabeth had no trouble believing that she would become pregnant, even when her husband, Zechariah, doubted the Angel Gabriel (for more on Elizabeth, see Chapter 13). Although she was eventually rewarded with a child, Zechariah's lack of faith was punished when he was struck speechless until the babe was born.

Widows, such as the one of Zarephath (Chapter 21), who was about to starve to death but was miraculously saved, are mentioned in this book. You also have the story of the wise woman of Tekoa (Chapter 19) from whom King David seeks advice. Unlike the witch of Endor (Chapter 16), whom King Saul consults, the woman of Tekoa gets her wisdom not from nefarious occult knowledge but simply because she is a good woman known for her insights that are believed to have come from God.

These and other women exhibit great strength of character and, most important, rock-solid fidelity to God. During a troubled time, had Jochebed not believed, she would never have placed her infant son Moses in the Nile River (see Chapter 10). And the early Christian church owes a debt of gratitude to the kindness, generosity, and assistance of women such as Phoebe, Priscilla, and Dorcas (Chapter 14).

Translating the Stories in Terms of Today

This book includes the theological and religious contributions some women made despite the injustices and inequalities they faced. While their culture and society treated them as second-class citizens at best and domestic servants at worst, the spiritual reality was that these women were just as holy and as important in the eyes of God as many of their male counterparts who receive praise today.

Knowing more about the women of the Bible is good not just for women but also for men, because both genders are made in the image and likeness of God. Despite the patriarchal structure in which they lived, women of strong faith still emerged and were used by God to continue the *covenant* (the sacred and permanent oath between the Lord and his Chosen People). Women readers can be empowered by the examples set by the women of the Bible, and everyone can perhaps better understand how women impacted salvation history.

Accepting our flaws — by reading about theirs

Unlike the old movie Westerns in which the good guy always wore a white hat and the bad guy wore a black hat, the heroes and heroines of the Bible are more complicated, mysterious, imperfect, and unpredictable, which makes them far more realistic. The women of the Bible are not unduly sanctified or vilified within its pages. They, too, struggled with good and evil, vice and virtue, sin and grace.

The Bible is essentially a book of nonfiction. The people portrayed aren't figments of the authors' imaginations; rather, they're real people who had to overcome real weaknesses and shortcomings. Those who persevered and never gave up the struggle are honored as saintly, holy persons, while those who gave up trying to be better — or ultimately succumbed to evil influences — are remembered as villains.

Although no Bible character is sinless, many of them repented and remained faithful. Perfection wasn't the way the Bible personified fidelity. Rather, true biblical faith meant never quitting no matter how many times one fell. The women of the Bible who realized this were as crucial to the story of faith as their male contemporaries.

Of course, individuals in the Bible were flawed to different degrees. There were good examples and bad examples in both genders, and you can take something away from the stories of all these people. Notorious women, such as Delilah (Chapter 16), Salome (Chapter 17), and Lot's wife (Chapter 15), show that the female gender can harbor just as much evil as their dastardly male counterparts.

Other women of the Bible fall somewhere in the middle — they weren't as evil as the Wicked Witch of the West or as holy and virtuous as Mother Teresa of Calcutta. These women weren't by any means spiritually mediocre; rather, they started out a little lukewarm or tepid and later on caught fire with love and zeal for God. Think about Mary Magdalene (see Chapter 7) or Bathsheba (see Chapter 16) or even Rahab (Chapter 10), who definitely was a woman of the evening and ran a house of ill repute only to later give sanctuary to Joshua's spies and thus allow a victory for the Hebrews over the city of Jericho. These women prove that despite a bad or slow start, God can use anyone who is willing to accomplish his will if they but trust and take a chance.

Recognizing the heroines —
and drawing inspiration

Superheroes are purely fictional, so you don't find any of them in the Bible. What you will find, however, are heroes and heroines. A superhero may have special powers, abilities, or equipment, but the heroes and heroines you read about in the Bible do the best they can with mere mortal characteristics. They're ordinary people who do extraordinary things under extraordinary circumstances. The holy women in the Bible are true heroines who can serve as inspiration for all human beings, male or female.

Today, both sexes can benefit from knowing more about the impact made by many biblical women, such as the prophetess Huldah (Chapter 15), the Judge Deborah (Chapter 10), and Queen Esther (Chapter 8). Powerful, influential, and faithful, these women preserved the faith when many of their male compatriots abandoned God's will for paganism. Martha and Mary, the sisters of Lazarus, were close friends of Jesus, and he often visited their home during a time when most Jewish men kept a safe social distance from women. Their platonic friendship was just as real and as important to Jesus as his relationships with his male disciples and friends.

When Jesus was arrested, condemned, and crucified, most of his apostles and disciples abandoned him. With the exception of John, all the big, manly men, such as Peter, James, Thomas, and Matthew, fled. The only other family members and friends who remained at the foot of the cross on Calvary as Jesus suffered were the faithful women in his life. The Virgin Mary (see Chapter 6), Mary Magdalene (see Chapter 7), and Mary, the wife of Clopas (see Chapter 13), are listed by name in the Gospels. Eleven other male apostles and more than 70 disciples were conspicuously absent.

Although secular history may not recognize many of these women, their presence in the Bible is a sign that they had something to do with salvation history — good or bad.

In most cases, their stories demonstrate the resilience and reliability of womanhood. And because they're merely human, their courage, sacrifices, commitment, wisdom, trust, and faith are characteristics to which everyone can truly aspire.

Chapter 2

Bible Basics: Delving into History, Context, and Translation

*Y*ou probably know, in general, how a car works. But unless you're a mechanic, deciphering a car manual can still be a rather puzzling experience. The same goes for the Bible. Although most of you may have a general understanding of the Bible's history and significance, a more in-depth understanding of its background can enhance your comprehension of the stories within.

Before you examine the notable and the notorious women of the Bible, you need to understand what the Bible is and what it isn't, and how it came to be in the first place.

This chapter covers some of the background and history of the Bible and specifically describes how to interpret the roles of women in scripture. Not everyone agrees on which version or translation of the Bible to use, nor is there a universal consensus on what every word and phrase in scripture means. Here we show some viable and reasonable ways to understand the mysterious passages of the Bible. Our aim is to explore what both the sacred author (God) and the human author (the person who wrote a specific book of the Bible) may have originally intended. And we promise it'll be much more interesting than a car manual.

The History of the Bible

The Bible tells us many things about God and humankind, especially in regard to salvation history — the story of how the human race was created, how it fell (into sin), and how it was redeemed. Despite the historical information contained in it, the Bible wasn't written as a history book or as a science book. In fact, comparing it to any other book is almost impossible, because people of faith firmly believe it is the direct Word of God, written by human beings who were inspired by the Holy Spirit. It is a book about and for faith.

Although the Bible can be found almost everywhere today, it's actually quite an amazing feat that the stories of thousands of years ago — when methods of recording were primitive at best — are still preserved today. Comparatively, seemingly old documents such as the Declaration of Independence and the U.S. Constitution are in their infancy.

This section offers a brief history of the Bible: who wrote it, who compiled it, and how it went from a book for the wealthy to a book for the masses. Knowing the Bible's background can deepen your understanding of the stories about its many fascinating women. Before getting an accurate picture of who these women are and what significance their lives hold, it is important to know about the text where the stories of these women are contained. If you thought the information was from an encyclopedia, you would have different expectations and interpretations of what you would read than if you thought you were reading a poem, a play, or a novel, right? Likewise, knowing what kind of book (and books that are contained in it) and what types of literature comprise the Bible can help you better appreciate what you read when looking at the various women in the Bible.

Where the Bible got its name

Ironically, the word *Bible* does not appear anywhere *in* the Bible. The English word *bible* comes from the Latin *biblia*, which is the plural for "books" and based on the Greek word *byblos* (meaning "book"). Before books were written on paper — as we know them today — they were recorded on parchment fashioned from the fiber of papyrus stems. The papyrus center of ancient times — the Amazon.com of its day — was a town called Gubla in what is now present-day Lebanon. Because of all the books created there, the Greeks renamed this town Byblos.

In AD 400, St. Jerome translated the Hebrew and Greek papyrus parchments, which contained the Old and New Testaments, into the Latin language. He was the first person to compile a one-volume edition of all the sacred scriptures. He called his work the Holy Bible *(sacra biblia)* after the Greek usage of the word, because this was to be *the* book of all books.

Preserving the Word: The authors

Lots of different people wrote the books that make up the Bible. From shepherds, farmers, kings, and priests to poets, scribes, prophets, and fishermen (and more), the Bible features the work of many, many people. Each of these writers had different intentions when they wrote, but believers say the authors all wrote from inspiration provided by God himself. Here we discuss both — their intentions and their inspiration.

The authors' intentions

No one took notes when God created the world, and no reporter from the *Jerusalem Daily Times* was covering Jesus' Sermon on the Mount. The sacred authors didn't write as things were happening like people do today. First, people spoke about what happened in the past and told the stories to each other verbally (in what's called the *oral tradition*). At some point, the authors decided to put these oral stories into writing to preserve them.

Every book in the Bible, from Genesis, Exodus, and Leviticus to the Gospels, Epistles, and Book of Revelation (and everything in between), had a human author who had a personal reason and purpose in writing. Often, the author was seeking to encourage his fellow believers in a time of persecution, captivity, or exile, or he was trying to give his readers realistic hope that God would deliver them someday from their suffering.

Matthew wrote as a Jew for a Jewish audience of his contemporaries. He wanted to help them see that Jesus was the fulfillment of the prophecies of old that promised a Messiah. When you read the Gospel of Matthew, you'll find many quotations from the Old Testament and lots of sermons from Jesus explaining that he is the one who was to come. A Jew considering the possibility of accepting Christ would be interested in hearing or reading Matthew's Gospel.

At the same time, a Roman wouldn't know or care about the ancient scriptures that promised a Redeemer. A Roman valued deeds more than words, so Mark wrote for the Roman audience to introduce them to this man of supernatural miracles who could expel demons, cure the sick, and raise the dead. Mark's Gospel is not only the shortest in composition and length, but it is also the most loaded with action — because that's what Roman's wanted. In Mark's writings, Jesus is on the move: healing the sick and exorcizing demons.

The authors' inspiration

Believers have come to understand that the writers of the books of the Bible were "inspired." By *inspiration,* we mean the authors were guided supernaturally — and yet their own memories, imaginations, perspectives, and personal tastes also remained in the texts.

These believers say that God is the ultimate author of the Bible, but that he used numerous individual human authors to accomplish the task. These writers were not possessed zombies who involuntarily wrote things down, however. They retained their same vocabulary and figures of speech, as well as their own likes and dislikes. And these different authors used a variety of forms of literature to write in. (Prose, poetry, narrative, dialogue, allegory, metaphor, hymns, apocalyptic, and more were used; see the later section "Putting the Bible's References to Women in Perspective" for more on this topic.)

Divine inspiration subtly influenced these authors without tampering with their free will. Each author made decisions as to what words to use to describe what he personally thought would be relevant to his audience.

For example, when you read about the Virgin Mary (see Chapter 6) in Luke's Gospel, he alone talks about the Angel Gabriel announcing the future birth of Jesus to his mother. The other three Gospels (Matthew, Mark, and John) don't mention this encounter. Either they didn't know about it and therefore couldn't write about it, or they simply chose not to mention it.

Some scholars believe the biblical authors had no idea that they were being inspired, because not one of the authors ever mentions "inspiration" in the text. Had any of them truly believed that God inspired them, it stands to reason that they would have said so to give their words more credibility. Because not one single author of the Bible has even remotely intimated being influenced by any divine motivation, many scripture experts surmise that inspiration is so subtle that it happens unknowingly to the sacred author.

From separate books to one Bible

With its numerous human authors from different places and times (refer to the earlier section "Preserving the Word: The authors"), the Bible took centuries — 14 to be exact — to write. It was even written in different languages, with different literary styles. That's why you find poetry, prose, monologue, dialogue, allegory, figures of speech, hyperbole, parables, genealogies, and more in the Bible. Because the Bible is a collection of so many authors and literary formats, it can't easily be categorized into one of today's popular book genres.

Think of the Bible in terms of your cable network or satellite company: one source offering a variety of content in diverse styles to different audiences. Like today's cable TV, some books of the Bible are more historical, some more literary or poetic, some mystical, and some practical. The Bible's many authors had different messages and diverse audiences.

The biblical authors had no idea that they were contributing to a larger work — Matthew, Mark, Luke, and John didn't have team meetings where they sat down and divvied up the writing assignments. When Paul, for example, wrote his letters to the various local churches at Corinth, Ephesus, Thessalonica, or Rome, he didn't plan for these letters to be part of the New Testament.

But while the individual author may have had a smaller and more defined audience in mind when he wrote his book, the Jewish and Christian believers were convinced that these particular books were of benefit to the entire faith community, regardless of the original time and place of composition.

Today's Bible is not one book but a collection of books. Because of its many authors and contributors, it's more of a one-volume encyclopedia or an anthology of stories than a single narrative. How many books went into the collection depends on which version of the Bible you're talking about: Protestant, Orthodox, Catholic, or Jewish.

The most ancient example of combining books of scripture in one set is the first five books of the Bible, which the Jewish people call the Torah or the Law (called by Greek-speaking Jews the *Pentateuch,* for five books): Genesis, Exodus, Leviticus, Numbers, and Deuteronomy.

Eventually, the entire Hebrew Bible (which Christians call their Old Testament) was assembled, and later, after the Christians wrote their stuff, those writings were also collected.

It's Greek (and Hebrew) to me

Each book of the Bible was originally written in Hebrew or Greek. Most of the Old Testament books (called the Hebrew Bible), or at least 39 of them, were initially written by their human authors in the Hebrew language. The seven other books that Roman Catholics and Eastern Orthodox call *deuterocanonical* (Protestants call them the *Apocrypha*) were originally written in Greek. All these books combined were simultaneously translated into Greek from 250–180 BC.

The Greek translation created between 250 and 180 BC is called the *Septuagint* from the Latin word for "seventy," because tradition has it that 70 scholars took 70 years to translate all the Hebrew books into Greek. See the following section, "Calling all canons," for more on the history of the Septuagint.

Under Kings Saul, David, and Solomon, there was one Kingdom of Israel (1020–922 BC). During this time the first 39 Hebrew books were written. After that, the empire was divided when Sol's boys fought with each other, creating the northern kingdom of Israel and the southern kingdom of Judah. The north lasted until 721 BC, when the Assyrians conquered it, and Judah fell in 586 BC to the Babylonians.

The Babylonians feared that the Hebrew people would one day reorganize and reconquer their homeland, so they exiled two-thirds to three-fourths of the Jewish people into foreign lands. Those Jews gradually forgot their Hebrew language and learned the local tongue.

By 250 BC, the majority of Jews no longer lived in the former Kingdom of Israel and thus no longer read or spoke Hebrew. The minority left behind, in what was then called Palestine, were the faithful few who still could read, write, and speak Hebrew. Their exiled compatriots learned the *lingua franca* of the time — Greek — starting with the time of Alexander the Great (336–323 BC). The seven deuterocanonical books were composed during this biblical time, also known as the *Diaspora* and the *Babylonian Exile,* when Jews were dispersed to other countries. For this reason, they were written in Greek. Translating the Hebrew scriptures into Greek made sense because the majority of Jews in exile knew Greek, while only the small minority left in the Holy Land still used Hebrew and its dialect, Aramaic.

Now it's one book — in Latin

In AD 382, the Christian Pope Damasus I commissioned St. Jerome to compile the various books of sacred scripture into one single volume. After 18 painstaking years of translation, he finally completed his task of incorporating the Greek and Hebrew books of the Old Testament and the Greek books of the New Testament into one single Latin book. (Latin was at that time the official language of the Roman Empire.)

Jerome's translation was called the *Vulgate* from the Latin for "common speech." The Vulgate was the first complete translation and single version of the Bible containing both Old and New Testaments.

The first Bible printed on press was the Gutenberg Bible, in AD 1450. It was the Latin Vulgate, compiled by St. Jerome in AD 400.

Calling all canons

No sacred author and no inspired text included a list of the "official" books that belong in the Bible. Establishing an official list or *canon* of books (from the Greek word *kanon,* which was a reed used for measuring water depth) isn't based on the Bible itself; in other words, there is no internal evidence from the Bible to determine which books ought to be in it. Because the Bible doesn't say what belongs or doesn't belong (there was no such thing as a table of contents back then), believers had to rely on religious authorities to decide. Councils of rabbis (for the Jews) and of bishops (for early Christians) were convened and determined a canon, or an official list. Books on that list (now called *canonical*) got in the Bible. Books not on the list got left out of the Bible.

The earliest official list of scripture (which *could* be considered a canon, because someone bothered to put together a list) goes back to 250 BC. King Ptolemy II of Philadelphus of Egypt (287–247 B.C.) constructed a library renowned for its exquisite collections of books in many languages. Being sympathetic to the Jews, King Ptolemy II ordered a complete translation of the ancient Hebrew into Greek because 75 percent of the Jewish people then could read and write only in Greek, the national tongue, due to the exile and captivity following the fall of the kingdoms of Israel and Judah. He wanted a copy of this translation to go into his library as the crowning jewel, so to speak.

Seventy scholars allegedly took seventy years (250–180 BC) to translate the 39 Old Testament books from Hebrew into Greek, and then they included the 7 deuterocanonical books (or the Apocrypha) originally written in Greek by exiled Jews. Because it took 70 scholars 70 years, the name *Septuagint* (Latin for "seventy") was given to this first one-volume collection of all the Old Testament writings. Because it was done in the town of Alexandria, Egypt, the list of books in the Septuagint is called the Alexandrian Canon. Had it not been for King Ptolemy and his library, there would have been no instigation nor funding at that time for such a project to collect all the Old Testament writings into one volume and into one language.

Here are the official lists (canons) of the Bible:

- ✔ Old Testament
    - **Alexandrian or Greek Canon (Septuagint):** 250 BC; contains 46 books (39 books, plus 7 deuterocanonical, or Apocrypha)
    - **Palestinian or Hebrew Canon:** AD 90–100; contains 39 books
- ✔ New Testament
    - **Council of Laodicea:** AD 363; determined the canon to be 27 books
    - **Third Council of Carthage:** AD 397; determined the canon to be 27 books

The language (translation) of your Bible is not what determines whether it has 39 books in the Old Testament or 46. The version is what matters. Some Protestant Bibles don't include the Apocrypha; others do and say so on the cover and in the table of contents. In Protestant Bibles, the 7 other books (the Apocrypha) normally come after the 39 Old Testament ones, but before the 27 New Testament ones. Catholic and Eastern Orthodox Bibles have all 46 Old Testament books integrated, as found in the Greek Septuagint version of 250 BC, followed by the 27 New Testament ones.

Clarifying the versions

Christians use the term *Old Testament* to refer to what Jews call their Hebrew Bible. Christian Bibles have both the Old Testament and New Testament. While every Christian Bible has the same 27 books in the New Testament, different versions have more or fewer books in the Old Testament section. The Hebrew Bible and the Protestant Old Testament use the same Palestinian Canon (AD 100), while the Catholic and Eastern Orthodox Old Testaments use the Alexandrian Canon (250 BC).

Just to keep things easy, the Palestinian Canon, Hebrew Bible, and Protestant Old Testament have all the same books, while the Alexandrian Canon, Septuagint Bible, and Catholic/Orthodox Old Testaments have the same as the others plus seven more books. Those extra books are called the Apocrypha (meaning "other writings") in Protestant Bibles, while Catholic and Orthodox Bibles refer to them as the Deuterocanon (meaning "second canon" or "official list"). The names of the seven books are Tobit, Judith (discussed in Chapter 8), Wisdom, Ecclesiasticus (or Sirach), Baruch, and I and II Maccabees. The Orthodox Bible also includes III and IV Maccabees and I Esdras.

Another fly in the ointment is the different use of the word Apocrypha. Protestant, Catholic, and Orthodox Bibles refer to the New Testament Apocrypha (which, for them, means "hidden writings" versus the "other writings" definition mentioned earlier for the Apocrypha for the *Old* Testament). This Apocrypha stands for all the books rejected and not considered inspired text, such as the Gospel of Peter, the Gospel of Thomas, and the Gospel of Mary Magdalene.

Books that were rejected and not considered inspired text and therefore not included in any Old Testament are called Apocrypha by Catholics and Eastern Orthodox and called *Pseudepigrapha* (meaning "false writings") by Protestants. These discarded books include the Apocalypse of Adam, the Assumption of Moses, the Book of Enoch, the Book of Jubilees, and so on.

Sound confusing? It's not. We promise. Here's a breakdown just to make sure you have it straight:

Palestinian Canon, Hebrew Bible, and Protestant Old Testament have all the same books.

The Alexandrian Canon, Septuagint Bible, and Catholic/Orthodox Old Testaments have the same books as the Palestinian Canon, the Hebrew Bible, and the Protestant Old Testament, *plus* seven more books.

These extra seven books of the Old Testament are called the Apocrypha (meaning "other writings") in Protestant Bibles, while Catholic and Orthodox Bibles refer to these seven extra books as the Deuterocanon (meaning "second canon" or "official list").

The New Testament also has an Apocrypha. That Testament's Apocrypha, however, stands for the books that have been rejected and are not considered inspired text. Protestant, Catholic, and Orthodox Bibles refer to these rejected books in the New Testament as Apocrypha (the literal definition of *this* Apocrypha means "hidden writings").

The Protestants call these rejected writings of the New Testament by another name: Pseudepigrapha, which means "false writings."

All in all, the various versions of the Bible include the following books:

- ✔ Jewish: 46 books in previous Alexandrian Canon (Greek Septuagint, 250 BC) and 39 books in current Palestinian Canon (Hebrew Bible, AD 100)

- ✔ Protestant: 66 books (39 from the Old Testament and 27 from the New Testament)

- ✔ Catholic: 73 books (46 from the Old Testament and 27 from the New Testament)

- ✔ Orthodox: 76 books (49 from Old Testament and 27 from the New Testament)

Table 2-1 lists the books of the current Jewish Bible and Catholic, Orthodox, and Protestant Old Testaments.

Table 2-1	Books of the Bible		
Jewish	*Catholic*	*Orthodox*	*Protestant*
Genesis	Genesis	Genesis	Genesis
Exodus	Exodus	Exodus	Exodus
Leviticus	Leviticus	Leviticus	Leviticus

(continued)

Table 2-1 *(continued)*

Jewish	*Catholic*	*Orthodox*	*Protestant*
Numbers	Numbers	Numbers	Numbers
Deuteronomy	Deuteronomy	Deuteronomy	Deuteronomy
Joshua	Joshua	Joshua	Joshua
Judges	Judges	Judges	Judges
Ruth	Ruth	Ruth	Ruth
Samuel	1 & 2 Samuel	1 & 2 Samuel (1 & 2 Kings)	1 & 2 Samuel
Kings	1 & 2 Kings	1 & 2 Kings (3 & 4 Kings)	1 & 2 Kings
Isaiah	1 & 2 Chronicles	1 & 2 Chronicles	1 & 2 Chronicles
Jeremiah	Ezra	Ezra	Ezra
Ezekiel	Nehemiah	Nehemiah	Nehemiah
Hosea	Tobit	Tobit	Esther
Joel	Judith	Judith	Job
Amos	Esther	Esther	Psalms
Obadiah	1 & 2 Maccabees	1 & 2 Maccabees 3 & 4 Maccabees	Proverbs
Jonah	Job	Job	Ecclesiastes
Micah	Psalms	Psalms Psalm 151	Song of Songs
Nahum	Proverbs	Proverbs	Isaiah
Habakkuk	Ecclesiastes	Ecclesiastes	Jeremiah
Zephaniah	Song of Songs	Song of Songs	Lamentations
Haggai	Wisdom	Wisdom	Ezekiel
Zechariah	Ecclesiasticus (Sirach)	Ecclesiasticus (Sirach)	Daniel
Malachi	Isaiah	Isaiah	Hosea

Jewish	Catholic	Orthodox	Protestant
Psalms	Jeremiah	Jeremiah	Joel
Job	Lamentations	Lamentations	Amos
Proverbs	Baruch	Baruch	Obadiah
Song of Songs	Ezekiel	Ezekiel	Jonah
Lamentations	Daniel	Daniel	Micah
Ecclesiastes	Hosea	Hosea	Nahum
Esther	Joel	Joel	Habakkuk
Daniel	Amos	Amos	Zephaniah
Ezra	Obadiah	Obadiah	Haggai
Nehemiah	Jonah	Jonah	Zechariah
Chronicles	Micah	Micah	Malachi
	Nahum	Nahum	
	Habakkuk	Habakkuk	
	Zephaniah	Zephaniah	
	Haggai	Haggai	
	Zechariah	Zechariah	
	Malachi	Malachi	
		1 Esdras	
36	46	49	39

Here are the books of the New Testament in Protestant, Catholic, and Orthodox Bibles:

Matthew	Romans
Mark	1 and 2 Corinthians
Luke	Galatians
John	Ephesians
Acts	Philippians

Colossians	Hebrews
1 and 2 Thessalonians	James
1 and 2 Timothy	1 and 2 Peter
Titus	1,2, and 3 John
Philemon	Jude
	Revelation (Apocalypse)

Return of the native languages

Over time, there was a push to translate the Bible into the languages that believers actually spoke. Although the church and academia continued to use Latin and Greek exclusively to maintain the accuracy and integrity of the Bible (other languages didn't yet have strict rules of grammar, syntax, and vocabulary), Christians still desired translations of the Bible in their native tongues. Table 2-2 offers a quick rundown of the early translations.

Table 2-2	Early Biblical Translations	
Year	**Language**	**Translator**
AD 400	Latin (first complete Christian Bible with Old and New Testaments in one volume)	St. Jerome
c. 995	Anglo-Saxon	Venerable Bede
1384	Modern English	John Wycliff
1455	Latin (Gutenberg Bible — first Bible printed from press with movable type)	St. Jerome
1522	German	Martin Luther
1525	English	William Tyndale
1537	English (Matthew's Bible)	John (Matthew) Rogers
1539	English (Coverdale Bible)	Miles Coverdale
1560	English (Geneva Bible)	Exiled English Protestants in Geneva during reign of Mary I
1568	English (The Bishops' Bible)	Several bishops at request of Elizabeth I

Year	Language	Translator
1609	English (Douay-Rheims). First Catholic Bible in English	Exiled Catholics in France during reign of Elizabeth I and James I
1611	English (King James Version, also called the Authorized Version)	47 scholars working under auspices of James I of England

Spreading the Word: Priests, window panes, and printing presses

Modern women and men are used to having their own personal Bible or family Bible at home to read when they feel like it. But humankind didn't always have such free access to the Bible.

Before Gutenberg invented the printing press in AD 1450, books were hand-written, hand-copied, and thus very expensive (equal to one year's wages!). As a result, most people didn't have access to the Bible as printed text. After the fall of the Roman Empire in AD 476, only the clergy and nobility could read and write; most peasants were illiterate until the end of the early Middle Ages and beginning of the high Middle Ages. University trained students, however, were fluent in Latin, and many also knew Greek.

So most common folk would hear the Bible read in Latin in Church, and then the priest preaching the sermon would give a paraphrased translation in the people's native tongue. They also learned about its stories through visual means; the great stained glass windows in the Gothic cathedrals of Europe weren't mere decoration. They also served a practical purpose: telling biblical stories.

But finally, the printing press came along. No longer outrageously expensive, books — including the Bible (or perhaps we should say, *especially* the Bible) — were available to regular folks. Couple this with the fact that the Bible had been translated into the then-current vernacular (English and German), which many were able to read and write by AD 1450, and for the first time, ordinary people could read the words for themselves.

Translating Ancient Languages: Interpreters Needed!

Just as the Greek-speaking Jews of the third century BC needed a Greek translation of the Hebrew Bible, so, too, English-speaking people today need a Bible translated into their own language. Strictly speaking, *translation* refers to the actual conversion of one language (words and phrases) into another. This section looks at the kinds and styles of translating used by Bible scholars. We look at the direct (literal) word-for-word translation method as well as the conceptual (idea-for-idea) method.

Choosing a translation

Since the Reformation in 1517, numerous translations (371, in fact) of the Bible have been made, and billions of copies have been distributed all over the world. To choose a translation that works best for you, keep in mind that there are three different styles of translation:

- ✔ *Formal correspondence,* which translates the Bible word for word from the ancient languages to the modern ones

- ✔ *Dynamic equivalence,* which is a looser translation that seeks to keep the intended original meaning but uses modern idioms (concepts), a thought-for-thought translation

- ✔ *Biblical paraphrase,* which uses contemporary jargon and vocabulary to get the main point across

The one you choose depends on your preference.

Trying to discover what the human author (albeit inspired by God) intended to say depends on getting to the literal sense of what was actually written. There is a difference between literal translation (the formal correspondence translation) and a literal interpretation (the dynamic equivalence and biblical paraphrase translations). In the first case, you seek to know the precise word(s) used by the original author. In the second case, you make a judgment and use your own words. This is why getting a version of the Bible that works for you is very important.

Depending on your religious affiliation, theological perspective, and personal taste, choose the type of translation that conforms to your needs.

Formal correspondence

In a formal correspondence translation, the Bible is translated word for word from the ancient languages into the modern. This style of translation is more faithful to the literal text of the original. Here are examples of formal correspondence translations from John 1:14:

And the Word was made flesh, and dwelt among us.

—King James Version

And the Word became flesh and dwelt among us.

—Revised Standard Version

And the Word became flesh, and did tabernacle among us.

—Young Literal Translation

In the three preceding passages, most of the words are exactly alike and the differences between "dwelt" and "tabernacle" are minor because both words appear in the same Greek-English dictionary. Obviously, the translator makes a choice when he or she opts for one possible translated word over another — when multiple ones are available in the dictionary. The literal meaning, however, remains intact. A dynamic equivalence translation, on the other hand, does more than just give alternative words ("dwelt" or "tabernacle"); it also gives alternative idioms or concepts ("become flesh" or "become human"). Formal correspondence tries to keep the original sequence of noun, verb, adjective, and adverb, whereas dynamic equivalence attempts to use similar thoughts that were intended.

For example, if you translate the phrase *"heureth_ en gastri echousa"* literally word for word from Greek into English, you get "she was found having in the belly." An idiomatic (thought-for-thought) translation is "she was found pregnant" or "she was found to be with child" (Matthew 1:18). Similarly, the English phrase "pulling my leg" can be translated literally, but someone who speaks Italian, German, or French may think someone was tugging your limb when you were really trying to say someone was playing a joke on you and never even physically touched your leg.

If you use a formal correspondence type of translation, remember the context of the biblical text you read (see "Considering the larger framework: Reading within context" later in this chapter). When the word *man* is used in these word-for-word versions, it can mean humankind, or it can mean the male gender. Because most of you probably don't speak Hebrew or Greek and therefore can't go back to the original and see exactly which Hebrew or Greek word was used, rely on the context to determine the accurate reading.

Dynamic equivalence

A dynamic equivalence translation is looser, seeking the same meaning but using different words and using thought for thought rather than word for word. This type of translation is more faithful to the intended meaning of the text, which is why it is sometimes called an *idiomatic translation*. Here are some examples from John 1:14:

> *The Word became a human and lived among us.*
>
> —New Century Version

> *The Word became flesh and made his dwelling among us.*
>
> —New International Version

> *The Word became flesh, he lived among us.*
>
> —Jerusalem Bible

One disadvantage of a dynamic equivalence translation is that you're reading someone else's interpretation of what the original text meant, as opposed to the actual words of the author. Although these versions are often easier to read and understand, they aren't a word-for-word translation from the original.

Biblical paraphrase

Biblical paraphrase translations use contemporary jargon and vocabulary to get the main point across, as in John 1:14:

> *The Word became flesh and blood, and moved into the neighborhood.*
>
> —The Message

> *So the Word became human and lived here on earth among us.*
>
> —New Living Translation

> *The Word became a human being and, full of grace and truth, lived among us.*
>
> —Good News Bible

A biblical paraphrase translation is often easier to read and understand than the formal correspondence translation, but bear in mind that, like the dynamic equivalence translation, it is someone else's interpretation of the original text.

Tinkering with typology

In early Christianity, wise scholars called the doctors and fathers of the Church loved to find, recognize, and elaborate on connections between the Old Testament (Hebrew Scriptures) and the New Testament (Christian Scriptures). Whenever they made parallels between the Old and the New, sort of connecting the dots, as we would say today, it was called *typology*. *Types* are real people, places, or things from the past that point to, predict, or promise something in the future. When these parallels are found, the connection is made.

When Jesus reminded his audience about Jonah being in the belly of the whale for three days (Matthew 12:40), he connected that passage with an event about to happen in their near future — his resurrection three days after his death. Here he used a typological interpretation of the biblical passage. By using this language, he shows how something in the Old Testament can point toward a future realization in the New Testament.

Putting the Bible's References to Women in Perspective

The women described in the Bible play an integral part of the work's meaning. These women aren't mentioned accidentally or peripherally. Each one had a positive or negative impact on salvation history and/or on the evangelization of the world. Good or bad, the women discussed in the Bible are more than statistics and data. They're active players in the drama between good and evil and in the dynamic interaction of the divine and the human. More than window dressing, some of the women of the Bible are cast as leading ladies and others as best supporting actresses.

But problems do arise regarding the discussion and interpretation of how women are written about in the Bible. The social, cultural, and political lenses that people use color their vision of the world around them — this goes for the writers of the books of the Bible as well as the people reading the Bible today. As St. Augustine once remarked about alleged contradictions or apparent mistakes in the Bible, one of three things has happened: The translation is faulty, the copied manuscript has mistakes, or the reader is misinterpreting the text.

Different times, different cultures

The women written about in the Bible are described in the cultural, social, and historical context of the author who wrote each book. Therefore, when you approach the Bible, don't read it as if the authors are from your own era or century, let alone from your own culture. First, remember that you're living two, three, or more thousand years *after* the text was written. Second, these works were produced by men who lived in *patriarchal* (male-dominated) societies.

Ancient cultures, especially nomadic ones in the desert, were extremely male-oriented and male-dominated. Lineage was determined by the man and his sons. Women were given in marriage and became part of their husband's family. In this society, at least one son guaranteed the continuation of the lineage. Daughters, on the other hand, were sold into marriage and thus could potentially provide a handsome income for dear old dad in terms of the dowry he received.

Unlike the family counterparts in non-Hebrew families, in which the father of the bride paid a dowry to get his daughter married, the Hebrew tradition recorded in the Bible shows the opposite. The groom paid a bridal dowry to his future father-in-law in order to have the daughter become his wife.

Although patriarchal cultures were and are not fair to women — wives, mothers, and daughters are not treated equally — the Bible merely reports the facts as they occurred when written thousands of years ago. Here are some of those facts:

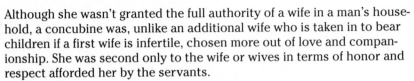

- The Law of Moses didn't allow a wife to divorce her husband but guaranteed that a husband could divorce his wife.

- Some of the patriarchs had more than one wife or concubine, but each woman could have only one mate.

  Although she wasn't granted the full authority of a wife in a man's household, a concubine was, unlike an additional wife who is taken in to bear children if a first wife is infertile, chosen more out of love and companionship. She was second only to the wife or wives in terms of honor and respect afforded her by the servants.

- A woman couldn't inherit any land or money from her father or husband unless she had no sons and no other male heirs.

Of course, you can find some exceptions to the general rule. The Bible tells of the power, influence, and significance of women who held important positions, such as Judge (Deborah; see Chapter 10), prophetess (Miriam; Chapter 10), queen (Esther; Chapter 8), and matriarch (Sarah; Chapter 9), despite this patriarchal society. Other examples include Lydia (Chapter 14), who is mentioned in the New Testament Acts of the Apostles as a wealthy merchant. Phoebe and Priscilla (both in Chapter 14) were vital helpers to Paul, as he says in his epistle (letter) to the Romans. And Mary Magdalene (Chapter 7) was the first person to see Jesus after he had risen on Easter, and she's the one he charged with the important task of telling Peter and the others he had risen from the dead. You can find out more about the roles of women in the Bible in Chapter 3.

The mistreatment of women by some individual men or by a male-dominated culture is a sad fact of history, and it appears in the Bible, but only insofar as the authors used contemporary experiences, perspectives, and language to describe what actually took place or to make things comprehensible to their intended audience. That the Bible mentions and describes instances of discrimination doesn't mean that it endorses, condones, or encourages discrimination.

Here's an analogy: A history book that describes pre–Civil War United States inevitably mentions slavery because that horrible evil existed at the time. You can't infer, however, that the historian-author is a racist just for accurately reporting the existence of heinous bigotry and prejudice from the time period. Likewise, when the scriptures speak of the social stigma a barren woman endured as a wife or widow, it is simply reporting historical fact. It isn't a biblical recommendation to mistreat women with fertility problems.

Translation trouble: Making gender distinctions

Some misreading of the Bible springs from the challenges of translating the original from the Hebrew or Greek into Latin and from Latin into English. One word in particular that gives translators fits is the word *man*.

The biblical languages have one word for a male human being and another word for the human race. Consider these examples:

- ✔ Greek uses the word *aner* to mean human male and *anthropos* to mean humankind.

- ✔ Latin uses *vir* for male and *homo* for humankind.

- ✔ Hebrew uses *ish* for a male person of the human race and *adam* for humankind.

   Even Old English made distinctions, using *werman* to designate a male human being and using *man* to refer to all human beings. Eventually the term *man* came to mean male human being, too. And things stayed that way in the English language until fairly recently, when *humankind* came into vogue.

Yet most modern English Bibles use *man* to mean both the male gender and the entire human race. For that reason, when you read the Bible, be sure to always examine the context for clues that can lead you to an accurate reading. And remember, when *man* means "humankind," the text is referring to ladies and gents together, not just males.

Consider this passage from Genesis 1:27 in the World English Bible: "God created man in his own image. In God's image he created him; male and female he created them."

In this instance, *man* means "mankind" (or humankind). The contextual clues that let you know this are the plural pronoun (them) and the last sentence, which specifically refers to both male and female. In other words, this passage says that both men and women are made in the image and likeness of God. The interpretation? That one is not better than the other, because they both come from the same place.

Theology: The Bible's purpose

The theology contained in the sacred scriptures is its primary message. Teaching that creation has a creator, that this creation is intrinsically good, and that human beings, made in the image and likeness of God, have a supernatural destiny beyond this world are but a few of the religious truths that the Good Book, in its totality, wants to communicate.

The sacred scriptures are often *descriptive* more than they are *prescriptive*. This means that the Bible often describes — and was written — within the social and cultural context of the human author. For example, when most people thought the earth was flat, it wasn't the Bible's purpose to correct their erroneous science. Similarly, the role of women is portrayed within the context of the day.

The issue isn't that the Bible is deficient in defending and teaching the invaluable worth of women; rather, the issue is that many men have not consistently, aggressively, or enthusiastically sought to fully implement all that the book has to say about equality of the sexes.

Ancient prejudices that women weren't intelligent enough to understand or even be taught the theological refinements that rabbinical scholars have pondered over the centuries were based on false information and primitive understanding of human physiology and psychology. These erroneous beliefs didn't come from the Bible itself. The Bible has numerous examples of men being outwitted by women despite their physical strength advantage. It also has examples of men doing some really stupid things, while the gals surpass them spiritually and mentally.

Considering the larger framework: Reading within context

Although the Bible was written a book at a time by various authors over many centuries, the individual parts aren't meant to be read in isolation. In order to understand the Bible's meaning, you have to read things in context — that is, within the larger framework of the book as a whole. Every sentence should be taken in the context of a paragraph, which should be taken in context with a chapter, which is in context to an entire book. All these books of the Bible are connected together to form one organic whole — Old Testament and New Testament.

Pay attention, because this is probably the best advice we can give you for understanding and correctly interpreting the Bible: Never take a text out of context, lest you get a *pretext* (a fictitious reason or false conclusion). This concept definitely applies to the evaluation and interpretation of women's earthly roles, according to the Bible. Yes, the literal text is absolutely essential, but the text doesn't exist in a vacuum.

An example of the problems you can encounter if you read passages out of context concerns Paul's letter to the Ephesians:

> *Wives, be subject [hypotassomenoi] to your husbands, as you are to the Lord. For the husband is the head of the wife just as Christ is the head of the church, the body of which he is the Savior. Just as the church is subject to Christ, so also wives ought to be, in everything, to their husbands.*

> *—Ephesians 5:22–24*

Once again, understanding biblical context is crucial. Some people have misinterpreted this passage and used it as a chance to intimidate their wives or as a way to rationalize abusive behavior. When taken out of context, the text becomes a pretext for prejudice and discrimination.

But a closer reading reveals that this isn't what Paul intended. He used the Greek word *hupotasso,* which is a military term meaning "to cooperate fully." He uses the exact same word in Ephesians 5:21, when he says, "Be subject *[hypotassomenoi]* to one another out of reverence for Christ" — an injunction to all Christians of both genders.

Before you jump on the Bible-is-sexist bandwagon, however, keep in mind that Paul goes on to say to the husbands:

> *Husbands, love your wives, just as Christ loved the church and gave himself up for her, in order to make her holy by cleansing her with the washing of water by the word, so as to present the church to himself in splendor, without a spot or wrinkle or anything of the kind — yes, so that she may be holy*

and without blemish. In the same way, husbands should love their wives as they do their own bodies. He who loves his wife loves himself.

—Ephesians 5:25–28

So here's what you have: Paul says in Ephesians 5:21 that all Christians should submit to one another and not just wives to their husbands. The sense of the term *hupotasso* is the same throughout Ephesians 5:21–33: loving cooperation in service to one another. That is how Christ expressed his love for his bride, the Church, and Paul says that is how husbands should act toward their wives and vice versa. Because Jesus never bossed anyone around, it's an inaccurate interpretation to infer that Paul is giving guys carte blanche to be the king of their castles while they lock up the wife in some dungeon.

You can find out more about Christian and Jewish viewpoints on women in Chapter 3.

Chapter 3

Discerning the Roles of Women

This chapter looks at the religious, social, and cultural viewpoints on women during the time of the Bible and today, examining both the Jewish and Christian outlooks. While some people may claim the distinction between how women *should* be treated and how they actually *are* (and have been) treated is merely one of theoretical versus the practical, because of human free will and the weakness of a fallen human nature, what faith and religion often asked (if not demanded) was not always rapidly nor thoroughly implemented. Nevertheless, the Bible both *teaches* the intended goal of justice and equality among men and women in most areas of human life, while at the same time scripture accurately *reports* the unfortunate actual historical record, which shows that the intended goal wasn't always sought, let alone achieved.

With certain exceptions, leadership roles in religion were not open to women, either in the Temple or synagogue or in the Christian church. Yet women played a vital role in the life of faith for both Judaism and Christianity, and they continue to do so.

This chapter takes a look at what the Bible says about women, as well as how Jewish and, later, Christian religions incorporated these ideas in relationship to their female worshipers.

Studying the Contrasts: Biblical Viewpoints on Women

The Bible is primarily a religious book about the covenant between the creator and creation, between God and humankind. But it's important to remember that the people described in the Bible and the human authors who wrote the Bible (even though inspired, according to Christian and Jewish tradition, by the Holy Spirit; see Chapter 2) were born, grew up, lived, and died within a specific culture and society. Often, those cultures and societies weren't determined, controlled, or sometimes even influenced by the Judeo-Christian faith and religion by itself, so contrasts inevitably arise. In other words, the Bible teaches in Genesis that all men and all women are made in the image and likeness of God — but secular, political, economic, and cultural practice rarely reflected that truth, as revealed in biblical history.

Women as spiritual equals

The Bible teaches that women are equal to men at the supernatural level — the level of grace:

✔ Women have spiritual equality to men; they have the same kind of immortal soul and the same possible eternal destiny.

✔ Like men, women are made in the image and likeness of God.

✔ Also like men, women are called to live lives of holiness.

✔ Human nature is the same for women as it is for men (body and soul, intellect and will), yet there are some real differences, physiological and psychological, between the sexes. These differences distinguish and complement each other.

Although women have suffered from inequality socially, economically, and culturally, it is unfair and erroneous to use the Bible to justify such inequalities merely because you can read in scripture of instances where inequality was practiced. God didn't inspire injustice, and the Bible doesn't condone it. Just because the book reports sins, crimes, and injustices doesn't mean that it endorses or approves of those evils. The Bible has many stories of notable women like Deborah, who was a Judge in Israel in the twelfth century BC, the first female political and military leader of her people. In addition, women were afforded equal respect in the Ten Commandments when God instructed us to "Honor your father and your mother" (Exodus 20:12). Nevertheless, keep in mind that other women in the Bible were treated shamefully or as property because of the weaknesses of humankind in general and because of the specific weaknesses of the men who lived during that time.

Morality, free will, and Fido

Morality is gender blind because moral acts, which can be either good or bad, are possible only when free will is invoked. Only deliberate and voluntary actions can be qualified as moral acts. For that reason, your kitty, your pooch, and your laptop computer can't ever sin, because they lack free will. The first two work on instinct, the other by program. Men and women, however, can freely choose to act or not to act.

According to Hebrew history as outlined in the Bible, harmony existed among the Hebrews as long as they stayed united with God by keeping the *covenant* (the sacred oath between God and the Hebrew people). When the people were unfaithful to their promise, sin occurred and brought disunity and division. False prophets arose, and authentic ones were ignored, killed, or chased away. When *idolatry* (idol worship), the epitome of religious infidelity, raised its ugly head, the kingdom itself was divided into north and south, and both were eventually wiped off the world map. Jews and Christians believe that the current divisions among nations and even among the Christian churches are signs of this division and that much work has to be done by both genders to repair the schism.

Because of the importance of the first and last points (women are spiritually equal to men and human nature is the same for both genders), the following sections offer a more in-depth discussion. To find out about the Jewish and Christian positions on the roles and spirituality of women, head to the sections "Jewish Perspective on Women" and "Christian Perspective on Women."

Good versus evil: A gender-blind concept

When Moses received the Ten Commandments (the Law) from God on Mount Sinai, he didn't come back with two versions, one for men and one for women. The Law applied to all men and women.

The significance of a single set of laws is the idea that evil has no claim on either gender. Throughout biblical salvation history, women and men alike have been individually good or individually bad. Each person had to make his or her own personal choice: Do I do good or do I do evil?

You see good women and bad women in the Bible, just as there are good men and bad men. Jezebel (bad) and Esther (good) are as much a part of the Bible as are Herod (bad) and John the Baptist (good).

Jewish Perspective on Women

The Hebrew religion is heavily based on and determined by the Law — that is, the covenant between God and the Jewish people (also called the *Chosen*

People). This covenant was first established with Abraham and then literally written in stone with Moses. The Law of God as found in the Hebrew scriptures (what Christians call their Old Testament) teaches that women have equal dignity in terms of their spiritual nature and that both men and women are created in the image and likeness of God.

Judaism in the pre-Christian era treated women as equal but separate (different but complementary) when it came to religious matters. Socially, economically, and politically, however, the treatment of women as second-class citizens and sometimes as property was as evident in Jewish culture as it would be in Christian.

Conflicting realities — political versus spiritual

Hebrews during the time of the Old Testament saw no problem in two conflicting realities. On the one hand, the Hebrew Bible and Jewish religion itself taught the intrinsic equality of women and men in respect to metaphysical composition (rational intellect and free will) or spiritual nature (body and soul). On the other hand, women were treated as political, social, and economic inferiors. Although discrimination based on skin color wasn't evident, people from other nations who spoke other languages and had other customs were often treated the same way as Hebrew women when it came to social, political, or economic matters. You can see this conflict in other aspects of Jewish life and faith.

- ✔ The practice and teaching of the Hebrew religion was primarily done by the mothers. Until a boy reached the age of religious maturity (bar mitzvah), he spent most of his day like his sisters — with mom. At home, the woman taught the children the stories of the Hebrew Bible — stories about Abraham and Isaac, Noah and the Ark, and David and Goliath. Yet, despite women's role in the religious education of their children, temple and synagogue prayer and worship segregated the women from the men. In addition, only men could become rabbis or priests (until reformed, reconstructionist, and liberal Judaism allowed female clergy).

- ✔ Unmarried Old Testament women were considered the property of and subject to the authority of their fathers, and married women were the property of and subject to the authority of their husbands. Yet, if a wife or daughter were killed, the act wasn't considered theft of property, as would be in the case of a slave in Greek or Roman culture. At the same time, Jewish women weren't seen as possessions or objects, and wives couldn't be casually divorced or discarded for petty reasons.

✔ Hebrew slavery was actually more a kind of indentured servitude. For example, people sold themselves into service to pay off a debt, or citizens were put into domestic service when a nation lost a war and sued for peace (conquering nations often demanded a percentage of the population that surrendered to be handed over as slaves as terms of the peace treaty). Yet Exodus 21:7 says that if a man sells his daughter as a servant, she shall not automatically become free after seven years, as her male counterparts would. Daughters were often sold into slavery, not so much as domestic servants but as concubines or secondary wives for their masters or the sons of their masters. As concubines or secondary wives, they couldn't be resold to foreigners and had to be treated like daughters (Exodus 21:9).

Comparing Hebrew women to women from other cultures

Although many aspects of Hebrew society weren't fair or equal, Hebrew custom before the time of Christ was much more favorable to women socially, politically, and economically than alternative contemporary cultures. The ancient Assyrians and Babylonians, for example, treated their own women more as commodities and personal possessions. Women were frequently forced into pagan temple prostitution against their wishes, and aside from their conjugal privileges, there was little or no socializing between the two genders.

The ancient Greeks and Romans were a little better in protecting some rights of women in law. While not equal in law, women could initiate lawsuits, petition for divorce, and seek to protect their limited rights. They couldn't vote or hold public office, but Greek and Roman law, culture, and custom tended not to treat women as property but as unequal co-workers for the family and the state.

The Etruscans, who were later conquered and absorbed into Roman society, gave the greatest latitude to women in terms of commerce, politics, and society. In fact, the Etruscan women were known for their stamina and competitiveness with their male counterparts, a fact that classical Romans regarded as another example of Etruscan decadence and licentiousness (in contrast to Roman stoicism).

Cultures and societies that were still very tribal, and in which the family clan was the keystone to the entire structure, placed the highest priority on marriage and procreation because these institutions established blood ties rather than merely political affiliations. Women were obviously indispensable in these societies, yet their personal gifts, talents, and accomplishments were often eclipsed until the tribe and the clan were eventually replaced by the nation and especially the kingdom. When the tribes and clans were assimilated into the larger unified nation, the family as a unit (and the importance of women as pillars of the family) gradually declined and was replaced by a different creature, the nation family or clan. The king became the father of a single national tribe or clan, which previously had been several autonomous or semiautonomous tribes or clans. Women weren't as highly regarded when the family itself became nothing more than a cog in the larger machinery that comprised the nation.

Honoring the female

Judaism is unique in that its custom and practice dictate that the mother determines the religion of the children. So children born to a Jewish mother married to a Christian father are considered Jewish.

Judaism is also unique because of its practice of an exclusively female holiday — Rosh Chodesh — on the first day of each month. Women are exempt from working on this day in gratitude for the fact that no woman participated in the idolatrous worship of the golden calf (Exodus 32) while Moses was at Mount Sinai receiving the Law (Ten Commandments) from the Lord. Apparently, only men committed this sin when Aaron, the brother of Moses, was persuaded to melt the gold taken from Egypt and fashion a god for the people to worship. Rabbinic tradition teaches that the women refused not only to worship the false god but also to melt down their jewelry to make the idol. This is but one example where you can see the value placed upon women and their spirituality in Hebrew society.

Although the primary role of most Hebrew women was wife, mother, and caretaker of the household, Judaism also had a few female prophets (like Huldah; see Chapter 15), a Judge (Deborah, discussed in Chapter 10), and a few monarchs (like Queen Esther, introduced in Chapter 8).

Christian Perspective on Women

Because Jesus of Nazareth was a Jew; his mother, Mary, was a Jew; and his 12 apostles were all Jews, it's no surprise that much of the Hebrew perspective on the role of women influenced the early Christian church. While Christianity was much more enlightened in many ways than most religions of the time, Christian treatment of women changed noticeably when the early Christian church grew away from its Jewish roots due to converting more and more Greeks and Romans to its faith. (Judaism at the time of Jesus wasn't missionary or evangelical — that is, it didn't actively or aggressively seek out new converts. If someone wanted to embrace the Hebrew faith, he was warmly welcomed and embraced. Christianity, on the other hand, actively pursued new members.) The next sections explain how the early Christian church viewed women and then trace the changes in the church's views over time.

Women as key players

Although women in the New Testament are still not treated as complete political and economic equals, they're much more involved in life than they are in the Old Testament. In the Old Testament, women's identification and partici-pation are often based in whole or in part on their roles as wife, mother, or daughter. Old Testament women didn't interact with men outside the home, especially in religious contexts, as much as Christian women of the New Testament. Although some Old Testament women broke the mold and stood out, like Deborah (see Chapter 10), the overwhelming majority of women at that time associated with other women and the men associated with other men. The New Testament shows the gradual integration of the two sexes in religious, cultural, and social life. Consider these examples from the Gospels:

- ✔ Two sisters, Martha and Mary, are dear friends of Jesus, along with their brother, Lazarus. These sisters are very vocal and very active, whereas no dialogue is described between Lazarus and Christ.

- ✔ In the Gospel of Luke, Luke begins his narrative from the viewpoint of the Virgin Mary (Jesus' mother). Scholars believe that she was his primary source for material; he didn't have as much access to original information as the other Gospel writers (because he wasn't one of the 12 apostles who traveled with Jesus). Luke writes of dialogue between Mary and the Angel Gabriel, as well as a conversation Mary had with her cousin Elizabeth. In fact, because Luke reports more about more interaction between Jesus and females than any other Gospel writer, his book often gets the nick-name "the Gospel of Women."

- ✔ In John's account of the Gospel, Jesus speaks with Samaritan women, such as the woman at the well in John 4:1–42. He visits the home of Martha and Mary frequently enough that they're familiar and comfort-able with him.

- ✔ All four Gospels attest to the fact that more women disciples were with Jesus as he was crucified and died, while most (11 out of 12) of his male apostles had abandoned him. All four Gospels show it was the women, like Mary Magdalene, who first discovered the empty tomb on Easter morning, before any of the apostles had heard about it — and even then, only from the women who had gone there before them.

- ✔ Jesus heals and speaks with women and men, children and adults, Jews and Gentiles alike. That women listened to his teaching and followed him as he preached, just as the men did, shows a spiritual equality, even though no women were selected for formal leadership roles in the infant church. What they lacked in authority to govern, these women sur-passed with their teaching, witness, example, and courage.

- ✔ The phrase "certain women" appears in the Acts of the Apostles to describe the female disciples who were present when the Holy Spirit descended upon the 12 apostles at Pentecost (50 days after Jesus' resurrection and 10 days after his ascension to heaven). In those days, Jewish men worshiped and prayed separately from the Jewish women (except at home, of course). The fact that women were present with the apostles and male disciples is therefore noteworthy.

Spiritually equal, subordinate role

Christian women, like their male counterparts, were initially Jewish converts (Jesus and his 12 apostles were all Jews, and early Christianity was not first seen as a separate religion). For almost half a century, Christians were mostly Jewish, which meant they observed both the Hebrew traditions and religion as well as professed their faith in Jesus and gathered with fellow Christians. It wasn't until the destruction of the Temple of Jerusalem by the Romans in AD 70 that Judaism and Christianity parted ways and separated from one another. Until then, Christianity was treated as a branch of Judaism, just like the branches called Pharisees and Sadducees.

The Jewish roots of Christianity continued to influence and affect the new religion even after it became independent and as it gradually became more and more Gentile in composition through Greek and Roman converts. Women in ancient Christianity were encouraged to teach the faith and to practice it, especially by doing charitable works like feeding the hungry, clothing the naked, sheltering the homeless, visiting the sick, comforting the sorrowful, and so on. Wealthy women of privilege often donated their money generously and provided the use of their estate for holding Christian gatherings as well as for helping the poor and needy.

Although women weren't invited into the formal realms of church leadership, they nevertheless provided a service to the faith community. They were indispensable in maintaining Christianity in the home, which was often called the *domestic church* by many spiritual writers over the ages. Teaching children the faith was but one aspect. Just as Jewish women upheld various prayer rituals in the home for certain holidays, so, too, Christian women ensured that the faith was promoted not just on Sunday (the day Christians finally chose as their day of worship, as opposed to the Saturday Sabbath of the Jews or Fridays for Muslims) but throughout the week.

Pharisees and Sadducees

Pharisees were lay theologians and scholars of the Law of Moses who tended to be more liberal in their interpretation of the scriptures, respecting the rabbinical commentaries on the Hebrew Bible.

Sadducees were Temple priests and clergy who tended to be more conservative and fundamentalist in their interpretation of the Hebrew Bible.

Pharisees, for example, believed in life after death and in the resurrection of the body, whereas the Sadducees did not believe the body and soul ever reunited after death.

The Christian view is similar to the Jewish view that a division and separation of responsibilities should not and does not imply a hierarchy of importance. Though men and women in Jewish and Christian religion have some distinct and different duties unique to their gender, neither faith tradition would regard one as being superior to the other. Motherhood and fatherhood are seen as equally important obligations. Adultery is equally sinful for either the cheating husband or wife. Today, modern human beings are accustomed to gender integration, whereas in biblical times, men and women rarely worked or socialized together, let alone worshiped and prayed as a unified group.

When ancient Jews and Christians delineated the responsibility of the wife and mother to take care of the home while the husband and father went to work, these roles weren't seen as attempts to make women subordinate to men. Socially and culturally, women didn't have the opportunities they have today. Family was the primary value, so spending time feeding, caring for, teaching, and loving the children was considered a holy vocation for Jews and Christians. Christians even saw the family as the domestic church or faithful assembly, so that when groups of families gathered together, the local parish was viewed as a large family of faith.

Spiritually, Christianity tried to balance the limitations of contemporary culture and society with the revealed theological truths of religion, like men and women being equal in the eyes of God in terms of grace and salvation. Even when church leadership was restricted to certain ordained men, it was done with the perspective that differentiation of tasks, duties, responsibilities, and obligations is part of the natural world. Different doesn't have to mean better or superior, however.

Societies or cultures may create distinctions and differentiations, but individuals choose whether to regard and treat everyone as equal in dignity, respect, and honor or to sinfully decide to demean, intimidate, patronize, or discriminate against their neighbor. Christianity sees the value in different roles but doesn't see any difference in the spiritual value of each and every single person. Holiness and sanctity may be expressed in different forms and through different roles, duties, obligations, and responsibilities, but the bottom line is not what you do as much as how well you do it.

Empires fall, and Christendom begins

As their role and interaction with the domestic church (the home), local church (the parish), and regional church (the diocese) grew over time, Christian women became more involved in spiritual and even ecclesiastical matters. When the Roman Empire finally crumbled in AD 476 and the Barbarian invasions ravished Europe, men and women turned to the monastic life, fleeing the decaying cities and finding refuge in the countryside. There, away from the urban mayhem, women and men — under separate roofs, of course — consecrated to a life of poverty, chastity, and obedience could live together in harmony of faith and purpose.

All good things must end

There were no major divisions among Christianity until AD 1054, when the Orthodox and Catholic churches parted company. Until then, for a thousand years there had been one Christian church, with the bishop of Rome (also known as the pope) as patriarch of the West and the other bishops of Jerusalem, Antioch, Alexandria, and finally Constantinople as fellow patriarchs of the East. The schism between the (Greek) Orthodox and the (Roman) Catholics later subdivided into the Russian and Greek Orthodox churches in the East (AD 1448) and the Catholic and the Protestant churches in the West (since the Reformation in AD 1517). Before the schism of the eleventh century, the terms "Catholic" and "Christian" were often used synonymously by believers in both the East and the West because "catholic"' merely meant "universal" (from the Greek word *katholikos*).

The monasteries of religious women (called *nuns*) paralleled that of their male contemporaries (called *monks*). The women who held an office of authority and leadership over the other nuns was often called the *abbess* (as the male head monk was called the *abbot*). St. Thecla (first century A.D.), St. Macrina (fourth century A.D.), St. Scholastica (sixth century A.D.; twin sister of St. Benedict), and other women like them not only established monasteries for women throughout Western Europe but also established orders to care for the sick (precursors of modern-day hospitals), teach the youth, and help the poor (forerunners of modern day charities like the Red Cross). They wielded power and influence, because the monasteries often owned property on which the nuns grew crops and raised livestock to subsist upon.

The New Testament impetus to preach the Gospel wherever possible (called the *missionary* role of the Church) involved men and women and therefore laid the groundwork for women to get more involved in the life of the church. However, in ancient Christianity, a differentiation of duties, tasks, and responsibilities existed between men and women, husbands and wives, mothers and fathers. Rather than subordination of women to men, this differentiation was seen as a division of labor: The men typically worked outside the home, while the women at that time took care of the home and children.

Evolving Equality

Since biblical times, some famous women of history paved the way for greater appreciation, recognition, and acceptance of the equality of the female gender: Nefertiti and Cleopatra of Egypt, Helen of Troy, Empress Theodora (Byzantium), Eleanor of Aquitaine (England and France), Isabella of

Spain, Catherine de Medici (Italy and France), Mary Tudor (England), Elizabeth I (England), Catherine the Great (Russia), Empress Maria Theresa (Austria), and Queen Victoria (England) are just some of the many women who wielded power as well as influence in a world predominantly run by the male gender. Women like Queen Elizabeth I, Empress Catherine the Great, and Empress Maria Theresa had an enormous impact on the shape and development of Europe. They had long, powerful reigns and were able to surpass their male contemporaries many times over.

Like the women of the Bible, the women of history show that gender doesn't determine the path one chooses to take — good or evil — any more than does the color of one's eyes or hair. While marriage and family are still the building blocks of society, be it church or state, the restriction of women to being only wives and mothers has gradually dissolved over time in Western civilization.

Changing times, unchanging word of God

Bible text itself hasn't changed since it was first written, even though it has been translated into numerous languages. Biblical interpretations and applications, however, have changed from person to person, from religion to religion, and from age to age. The Bible was written by men who lived in specific times and places and who were affected by the cultural and social outlooks of the time as much as they were by their own personal faith. Even though considered divinely inspired by believers, the Bible wasn't made in a vacuum, nor is it read in one, either.

Women's roles today

Golda Meir (Israel's third prime minister), Indira Gandhi (former prime minister of India), Margaret Thatcher (the United Kingdom's first female prime minister), U.S. Supreme Court Justice Sandra Day O'Connor, former U.S. Ambassador to the United Nations Jeane Kirkpatrick, and former Secretary of State Madeleine Albright are just a few of the powerful and influential women the modern world has known. Doctors, lawyers, professors, astronauts, CEOs, mayors, governors, elected officials, generals, and admirals are all not only possible posts for women, but are currently filled by many outstanding women.

Women today can still be wives and mothers, but they can also be blue-collar or white-collar workers, run for elected offices, serve in the military, and so on. None of these careers require them to surrender their femininity or their giftedness as members of the female gender. Different but complementary to their male counterparts, women continue to be a necessary and integral component to the economic, social, political, academic, and spiritual dimensions of human living.

The challenge of believers through the centuries is the task of identifying and isolating the cultural and social conventions that established the ways women were to be viewed and treated from the spiritual and theological teachings the Bible is meant to convey and uphold regarding the dignity and value of every woman — whether she was in the Bible or not, whether she is reading it or not.

Modern Christian and Jewish women

In recent years, some Christian denominations have allowed and encouraged women to participate as deacons, elders, ministers, pastors, and even bishops. These groups maintain that the exclusion of women from church leadership and ministry at the time of Christ, the apostles, and the early Church was cultural and not theological. They share ordained ministry equally among men and women and believe that they are faithful to the spirit of the New Testament.

At the same time, some conservative evangelical, fundamentalist, Catholic, and Eastern Orthodox churches still retain an exclusively male ministry and church authority. They don't consider the exclusion of women in church leadership positions as a matter of injustice and inequality because they see this arrangement as a divine decision, not a human one, and therefore not subject to cultural or historical reinterpretation. Many of these branches of Christianity esteem the value of sacred tradition on the same par as sacred scripture and feel they are also being faithful to the New Testament.

Like Christianity, present-day Judaism is divided on the same issue. Some branches of Judaism, like the orthodox and conservative, have only male rabbis, whereas some reformed, liberal, and reconstructionist branches have female rabbis.

In both religions, however, leadership alone won't get you into heaven. The church office or job a person has isn't the crucial factor to salvation; what matters is how well one does his or her job of doing God's will. The criteria for being "made in the image and likeness of God" (Genesis 1:26–27) has nothing to do with gender or ecclesiastical function. The Bible shows that it's not who you are, but how you live — either in harmony with the will of God or contrary to it — that matters.

Chapter 4

Judges, Prophetesses, and One Smart Lady

In This Chapter

▶ Getting to know the Bible's female Judge

▶ Finding out about the role of prophetesses

▶ Wising up to Lady Wisdom

*T*he only female Judge of the Old Testament (Deborah), the few prophetesses mentioned in the Bible (Miriam, Anna, Deborah, and Huldah), and Lady Wisdom are discussed in terms of their duties and their everlasting meaning in this chapter. (You can read more specific details about Miriam and Deborah in Chapter 10 and about Huldah in Chapter 15.) These women stand out, second only to the matriarchs in terms of importance, for their unique role in salvation history as recorded in sacred scripture.

Except for Lady Wisdom, these women were real, flesh-and-blood females. We include Wisdom because the Bible describes "wisdom" in feminine terminology, as if she were an actual woman. Because both wisdom and womanhood are honored, this book of the Bible (the Book of Wisdom) deserves discussion as well.

Judge Judy She's Not: Deborah

Judges were political, military, charismatic leaders who ruled the Israelite nation before the time of the Kings (Saul, David, Solomon, and on), but after the period of the Exodus from Egypt when Moses and then Joshua led the Chosen People. The Book of Judges mentions the 12 Judges who ruled over Israel before the establishment of the monarchy: Samson, Gideon, Othniel, Ehud, Shamgar, Barak, Tola, Jair, Ibzan, Elon, Abdon, and Deborah — the only gal in the bunch.

The Hebrew word *shaphat* is what has been translated as *judge* in English (*krites* in Greek) and means a national charismatic leader or a local magistrate. When the Bible uses the word, though, it is almost always as the leader of the nation rather than a Judge Judy or Judge Ito whom you would see in court today.

These leaders were also known as "deliverers" because they helped lead the people in time of turmoil and chaos. After Moses and Joshua were gone, the 12 tribes argued and often fought with one another. When the people prayed to God for help, he raised up these eleven men and one woman as his Judges to govern the people. Unlike today, when local judges run for election or the president nominates a judge to the Supreme Court contingent on the approval of Congress, the Judges of the Bible were picked by God and not by popular or legislative vote.

Deborah is not only a charismatic leader (as you can see in Chapter 10) but also a military leader who joins her general in battle, just like Joan of Arc did for France in the fifteenth century AD. Although women leaders were uncommon in patriarchal societies and cultures, history still shows examples of intelligent, courageous, influential, and powerful women leading and ruling their people (like Cleopatra of Egypt, Empress Maria Theresa of Austria-Hungary, and Queen Victoria of England). Deborah is unique, however, in that she was a religious as well as political leader. She wasn't elected by the people, nor did she inherit her position. God chose her as he did the other 11 Judges. Deborah brought her intelligence, wit, courage, and faith into her leadership at a time when most of her secular and male contemporaries used brute force, fear, and intimidation as their methods of governing.

On Behalf of the Lord: Prophetesses

A prophet (male) or prophetess (female) was not a psychic, fortuneteller, soothsayer, spiritualist, or someone who read tea leaves, gazed into crystal balls, or read tarot cards. Biblical prophecy was first and foremost a teaching job. A *prophetess* was a woman, like Miriam (Chapter 10) or Anna, who spoke to the people on behalf of the Lord. She was a spokesperson or ambassador of sorts. Ninety-nine percent of the time, prophecy was limited to a message from God about current affairs, and only 1 percent of the time did it involve the future (as found in the Book of Daniel or in the Book of Revelation/Apocalypse).

When a prophet like Samuel or a prophetess like Huldah (see Chapter 15) spoke, they usually warned the people about impending doom and dire consequences if the people didn't heed the word of the Lord and repent from their evil ways (which usually involved some form of idolatry or pagan worship).

Living in obscurity: Anna

Of the four women (Anna, Deborah, Miriam, and Huldah) named as prophetesses in the Bible, Anna is the most obscure. Her name appears once (Luke 2:36), whereas the other two are mentioned at greater length. (Deborah is discussed in Judges 4 and 5, and Huldah is mentioned in 2 Kings 22:14–20 and in 2 Chronicles 34:22–28). Ironically, Anna's words aren't recorded in scripture, as are Deborah's and Huldah's, but she is named nevertheless.

A widow for most of her life, Anna is described as the daughter of Phanuel of the tribe of Asher. She lived during the end of the first century BC and the beginning of the first century AD. The Bible says she spent all day in the temple of Jerusalem worshiping God by fasting and praying, waiting for the coming of the Messiah (Luke 2:37). After the prophet Simeon greets Mary, Joseph, and the baby Jesus (Luke 2:25–35), Anna appears and praises God and speaks to the people about the destiny of this child. Her old age (probably around 104) represents the long wait for the coming of the Savior, according to many New Testament scripture scholars.

Prophets and prophetesses usually weren't well liked or received. Often, if the message was unpleasant, the people hated the messenger rather than the message — and sometimes they'd even kill the messenger. Jesus himself said that no prophet is without honor except in his own native place (Luke 4:24). Some prophets, such as Jeremiah, were imprisoned (Jeremiah 37:15–21), and others, such as Zechariah, were stoned to death (2 Chronicles 24:20–22).

Miriam, the sister of Moses and Aaron, is the first and one of the most important prophetesses of the Bible. She leads the people by her singing and charismatic personality as they flee the slavery of Egypt. Deborah, Huldah, and Anna are other prophetesses we examine in this book as well (see the nearby sidebar for more details on Anna). God blessed each woman with a strong character, a keen insight, and sound intuition, and most of all, they were instructed to pass along his message to the people on his behalf.

Like their male counterparts (the prophets), the prophetesses did not primarily predict the future or prophesy about things yet to happen. Instead, they spoke on behalf of God to the people about things that were happening at that time. Prophecy was mostly a communication between the Lord and his people through the mediation of the prophet or prophetess.

The prophetesses, though very few in number, are significant simply because of their mere existence. The Bible doesn't explain why more weren't used or why there were only these four women, but like the male prophets, a prophetess was chosen and appointed by God — you didn't apply for the job on your own. The people or the leaders didn't select the prophets. Each woman who was named a prophetess showed profound faith, not just by her existence but also by what she said or did. Their fidelity often helped encourage the people during times of adversity or uncertainty or on the verge of epic events.

You Can Learn a Lot from Lady Wisdom

The Book of Wisdom (sometimes called the Wisdom of Solomon) doesn't mention any women by name. (You can find the Book of Wisdom in the Apocrypha of Protestant Bibles or in the Deuterocanon of Catholic and Eastern Orthodox Bibles.) What it does do, however, is refer to Wisdom, in concept, as a feminine entity. For this reason we include it as a theoretical "woman" of the Bible. Biblical wisdom isn't what you know, or even whom you know — rather, it's how you think, how you speak, how you act, and how you live. Wisdom means making correct judgments and good choices. It's an art that anyone can practice. However, if you don't practice it regularly, the quest for wisdom can fall as flat as a musician hitting the wrong notes.

In the Book of Wisdom, the concept of wisdom is personified as a woman, often called *Lady Wisdom,* which is an attempt to humanize and personalize a sublime idea.

In the Christian sense, wisdom isn't the same as truth or knowledge. Wisdom isn't just intellectual insight or book learning, either. Wisdom is the ability to make good judgments. A wise person doesn't have to be the most intelligent or the most accurate but does have to be someone who knows what to do with the knowledge he or she has, where to find more, and how to apply it. The author of the Book of Wisdom (purported to be King Solomon, but in reality not; see the later section "Getting historical perspective") underscores the connection of wisdom with righteousness. The smart and not-so-smart can each sin in their own way. The fool, however, disregards the dangers of evil, whereas the wise person avoids danger by staying away from sin and evil.

The personification of Wisdom

The Bible, of course, is a collection of different books, by different authors, in different places and times, with different narrative formats. Besides the historical narrative of straight storytelling, the Bible also includes various literary devices, including the following:

- ✔ **Personification:** Attributing personal qualities and characteristics to abstract ideas or inanimate objects
- ✔ **Allegory:** Using symbolic fictional figures to represent abstract concepts
- ✔ **Metaphor:** Using an implied comparison between objects or events to indicate an analogous relationship
- ✔ **Typology:** Using the Christian doctrine that says that events and people in the Old Testament prefigure the events, particularly the coming of Christ, in the New Testament

The Book of Wisdom uses personification. In this case, wisdom is spoken of as a woman, even beyond using simple feminine grammatical endings. The Hebrew word *chakmah,* like its Greek (*sophia*) and Latin (*sapientia*) equivalents, is a noun with feminine gender. Even outside the Book of Wisdom, this device is employed — Proverbs 1–9 not only uses the word wisdom but also speaks of wisdom as if it's a she.

Hey, good lookin'! Picturing Wisdom

Scripture teaches that "wisdom will not enter a deceitful soul" (Wisdom 1:4), that "wisdom is a kindly spirit" (Wisdom 1:6), and "those who despise wisdom and instruction are miserable" (Wisdom 3:11). In Wisdom 6:12 and afterwards you can see that a definite female persona begins its association with wisdom (like the use of the feminine pronoun "she"). Following are some key quotations from the Book of Wisdom. Note how the descriptions attribute personal qualities to an abstract idea:

- ✔ "Wisdom is radiant and unfading, and she is easily discerned by those who love her, and is found by those who seek her" (Wisdom 6:12).

- ✔ "The beginning of wisdom is the most sincere desire for instruction, and concern for instruction is love of her" (Wisdom 6:17).

- ✔ "I will tell you what wisdom is and how she came to be, and I will hide no secrets from you, but I will trace her course from the beginning of creation, and make knowledge of her clear, and I will not pass by the truth" (Wisdom 6:22).

- ✔ "For wisdom is more mobile than any motion; because of her pureness she pervades and penetrates all things" (Wisdom 7:24).

- ✔ "With you is wisdom, she who knows your works and was present when you made the world; she understands what is pleasing in your sight and what is right according to your commandments" (Wisdom 9:9).

- ✔ "Wisdom rescued from troubles those who served her" (Wisdom 10:9).

Wisdom is called the "fashioner of all things" (Wisdom 7:22). She has a spirit that is intelligent, holy, unique, subtle, mobile, clear, unpolluted, distinct, invulnerable, loving the good, keen, irresistible, humane, steadfast, sure, and free from anxiety (Wisdom 7:22–23). She is easily found and quickly recognized. She swiftly goes to anyone who earnestly seeks her. It's worth every effort to pursue her because she gladly meets all who come to her. (See Wisdom 6:12–16.)

> *For she is a breath of the power of God . . . she is a reflection of eternal light, a spotless mirror of the working of God, and an image of his goodness.*
>
> —Wisdom 7:25–26

For all these reasons, God loves nothing more than a person who seeks wisdom.

Why the alluring image?

Wisdom is presented as more than an abstract concept like justice. By personifying wisdom as a woman, the abstract idea becomes more immediate and attainable. And the description, beautiful and poetic as it is, makes Lady Wisdom someone you want to know and know well. As described, wisdom becomes someone whose company you enjoy and look forward to. She is approachable to anyone and everyone. The goodness of your heart and purity of your spirit — not your I.Q. — is what attracts wisdom. The desire and resolve to do what is right and just in the eyes of God are the first steps toward wisdom that anyone and everyone can take, if they so choose.

Deciphering biblical intentions

Wisdom is portrayed as a lady — a woman of social status, refinement, charm, and wit. But why? Some Bible scholars believe that the feminine is used because in ancient Old Testament times many women weren't taught to read and write as were their male counterparts. Knowledge, especially gained through reading, was described in masculine terms, whereas wisdom, which wasn't derived from book knowledge but from experience and from communication with God, was described in feminine terms because women had access to wisdom even if many of them were illiterate. Other scholars propose that the "lady" terminology is a literary device to depict wisdom as an honorable, noble, beautiful, elegant, and cultured object in itself while using a personification technique to give some intimacy to wisdom as well. But the Bible never actually explains why wisdom is portrayed as a lady, just that it does.

Although a few contemporary authors have proposed some controversial theories, like the idea that Lady Wisdom is the feminine side of God, most accredited scripture scholars offer a deeper reason why wisdom is referred to as a feminine concept. God is a pure spirit, unlike human beings, who are body and soul. Our sexuality and gender are a part of who we are because they're important components of our physical makeup. God, however, is neither male nor female, neither masculine nor feminine (Galatians 3:28). Wisdom can't be the feminine side of God. Neither is wisdom a goddess to parallel God the Father, as believe some philosophies. If not a deity, then who is wisdom? Here are some ideas that scholars have proposed:

> ✔ Wisdom as described in the Book of Solomon is a *type* of lady suitable to become the bride of an equally honorable, virtuous, intelligent, and respected groom. (*Type* refers to someone or something in the Old Testament that prefigures someone or something in the New Testament.)

Who's the lucky guy? Christ. Wisdom was intended to be the image of the future bride of Christ — the Christian church. The image of Christ as groom and of the church as his bride is first used by Paul and later by many of the fathers and doctors of the church. In this scenario, wisdom is united to Christ but distinct and separate from him. Wisdom is considered created by God and endowed with the highest authority and respect.

✔ The Gnostic sect of the ancient church did in fact deify wisdom to the level of a goddess, or at least a demigod. For Gnostics, salvation was secret knowledge (*gnosis* in Greek), which only the few and elite could possess. *Logos* (Greek for "word" and often used in reference to Christ as the Word of God) and sophia (Greek for "wisdom") were seen as complementary powers that only the learned could appreciate.

✔ Wisdom is a *type* (biblical prefigure) of the Holy Spirit, which is revealed only in the New Testament. The Holy Spirit gives the gift of wisdom, knowledge, and understanding to the apostles at Pentecost.

✔ Lady Wisdom is a *type* (biblical prefigure) of the Virgin Mary, who becomes intimately connected to the *Logos,* the Word, often used to identify Christ: "And the Word became flesh and dwelt among us" (John 1:14).

Christ is given the name *Logos,* which denotes a knowledge of truth: "I am the way, and the truth, and the life" (John 14:6). Wisdom *(sophia)* is a little different, however, because it's considered the bride of the Word made flesh, or Jesus Christ.

Bride and bridegroom is an image used heavily in the Bible, not just at a realistic level, as in the case of Adam and Eve, but also in the typological sense. For example, the relationship between God and the Hebrews — the "Chosen People" — is described as a spousal union. Even when the people become unfaithful by experimenting with idolatry, the covenant is not dissolved, and the union is intact. Later, when Paul uses the same image, both bride and groom are portrayed as faithful partners in this covenant of love. Similarly, the Word and Wisdom are faithful partners — the ultimate biblical bride and groom.

Getting historical perspective

The Book of Wisdom (or the Wisdom of Solomon) isn't found in the Hebrew Bible (AD 100), but it is part of the Greek Septuagint (250 BC) and is part of the Christian Old Testament known as the Deuterocanon or Apocrypha (head back to Chapter 2 for more on these books). The Septuagint is the Greek translation of the Old Testament done in Alexandria, Egypt, in the third century BC for the Greek-speaking Jews in exile. The 39 books of the Old Testament originally written in Hebrew were translated into Greek and included the 7 Greek books of the Old Testament Apocrypha (considered the Deuterocanon by Eastern Orthodox and Catholic Christians).

Because the book was originally written in Greek, even though for a Hebrew audience (albeit one in captivity and exile), it was rejected by the Jewish Council in AD 100, and that council's list of approved "official" books of the Bible is what Martin Luther and the Protestant Reformers used as the guide for their Old Testament. Eastern Orthodox and Catholic Christians, however, use the older Greek Canon (sometimes called the Alexandrian Canon) established in 250 BC when the Septuagint was formulated.

The Book of Wisdom was written at a time when 75 percent of the Jews were in exile, and most of them were embracing Greek philosophy, culture, language, and so on. Written in Greek, probably by an Alexandrian Jew, the Book of Wisdom was intended to remind the Hebrews that despite the sophisticated philosophical wisdom of the Gentiles, the Jewish religion, as revealed by God, possessed an even more profound wisdom.

Although many people thought that King Solomon was the author of the Book of Wisdom, because he was considered the wisest man ever to have lived on earth, someone else actually wrote it. Solomon lived in the tenth century BC, and the Book of Wisdom dates to the first or second century BC. The anonymous author uses the literary device of writing in the tradition and perspective of a well-known person (like Solomon), a technique that was very common in those days. Ancient authors weren't trying to deceive readers, nor were they plagiarists or impersonators. Instead, they used famous names and well-known styles to catch people's attention. They were essentially saying, "This is how Solomon would have written it."

Part II
The Big Six: The Most Famous Women of the Bible

The 5th Wave   By Rich Tennant

@RICHTENNANT

"When the minister said the sermon was going to be about Esther, Martha, and Naomi, I thought we were going to hear about an Olympic swimmer, a homemaker, and one of the Judds."

In this part . . .

The chapters in this part discuss six of the most well-known women of the Bible, what they said and did, and the impact they had on salvation history as a whole or the part they played in it. You meet the three most famous women of the Bible: Eve, the first woman; Mary of Nazareth, the mother of Jesus Christ; and Mary Magdalene, an often controversial figure who was the first person to see the Risen Lord. We also include here a discussion of the only three women of the Bible who each have an entire book named after them: Ruth, Judith, and Esther.

Chapter 5

And Then There Was Woman: Eve

*E*ve is sometimes given a bad rap as a temptress to Adam. She is, according to the Bible, the first woman, the first wife, and the first mother of the human race. Eve isn't the first to sin, however. She shares that dishonor equally with her husband, Adam. That's why the act of disobedience these two commit is called *the sin of Adam and Eve* (what Christians call *original sin*). She was tempted by the serpent and then, in turn, she tempted Adam. Eve could have said no, and Adam could have too.

Before you look at Eve's mistake, you need to see her place in creation, not just chronologically but, more important, her spiritual place in salvation history. Eve is created by God and in the image and likeness of God. She has the same free will and rational intellect as her mate, Adam, the first man. They are united into one flesh before they break God's law. Her importance to the human race is partially her sin but also the good she still possesses even after the fall.

Paul claims in one of his New Testament epistles that death entered the human race through one man, Adam, but that eternal life also came through one man, Jesus Christ (1 Corinthians 15:22). Eve is therefore not blamed with bringing death to the human race — Adam gets that dishonor.

This chapter starts with the beginning of the Bible, the Book of Genesis and the creation of the first woman, Eve. It looks at the two different stories of creation and examines their impact on the dignity of women. Adam calls his wife "Eve" which means "life-giving" or "mother of all the living." We examine her role as first woman, first wife, fellow human being, and fellow sinner here.

Examining the Two Stories of Creation

When you open the Bible and read the first book, Genesis, you notice that the first two chapters tell a similar story — but with subtle differences. Why two versions of the same tale? Some scholars attribute the two different stories to having two entirely different authors, each with his own audience and purpose. Other Bible experts explain that whether it was one, two, or several authors, the difference is not so much in who wrote, but why. In other words, the two versions provide two perspectives on the same story, telling a different meaning and message about the same event.

The Bible wasn't written as a history book or science report — but neither was it written as a fictional novel. It is a book of faith that tells the Jewish-Christian story of salvation — why God made people, how God and the human race interacted over history, and how people should respond to his word as it appears in the Bible. The Bible is a book of books, written by numerous authors over many centuries, from different places, and for different audiences. To find out more about the Bible's history, go to Chapter 2 of this book.

Interpreting Genesis 1

Chapter 1 of Genesis represents the beginning of the story of salvation history. Although myths and fairy tales often open with something like "Once upon a time" or "Long ago, in a galaxy far, far and away," the Bible opens with "In the beginning." The book aims to connect to the actual beginning of creation, when something (the universe) was made out of nothing (the void). This chapter has a sequence of events that document the order of creation; you can think of it, in other words, as God's flowchart.

First, God said, "Let there be light" (Genesis 1:3), and there was light. Interestingly, here's how scientists, like astrophysicists, describe the Big Bang (the cataclysmic event that created the universe): At the moment of the Big Bang, an enormous amount of energy was released, when all primordial matter was condensed into one tiny speck. The colossal gravity and energy and mass that emanated from this explosion followed the gigantic flash of light that this major event caused.

After creating light on the first day, Genesis says God then made sky on the second day; the earth and its vegetation on the third day; the moon and the stars on the fourth day; and the animals on the fifth day (Genesis 1:6–25).

On the sixth day, God created humankind. This is how the first chapter of Genesis explains it: "So God created humankind in his image, in the image of God he created them; male and female he created them" (Genesis 1:27). He then tells them to be fruitful and multiply. God then rests on the seventh day.

So in Genesis 1, God creates inanimate matter first, and then plant life, and then animal life, and finally humankind (*adam* in Hebrew), both male and female (*zakar* and *naqebah* in Hebrew). No names are mentioned at this point. But what's interesting to note is that the Bible makes clear that male and female are partners in this equation. Both make up humankind, and both are made in the image and likeness of God, unlike the rest of creation. No inequality exists between the maleness and femaleness in human nature (whether you call it *humankind* or *mankind*) from this perspective.

Understanding Genesis 2

Genesis 2 offers a different sequence of events. In this chapter, God creates man first by taking dust from the earth and breathing (*nephesh* in Hebrew) into it. Then God creates all the plants and other things of the world. At one point, God says, "It is not good that the man should be alone" (Genesis 2:18), and so he creates animals to keep man company, and man names all the animals.

But no matter how cute Whiskers is or how loyal Fido may be, no animal or pet is a suitable partner and mate for man. So Genesis says God puts Adam into a deep sleep and then he takes a rib from the man and fashions a woman from it. The Hebrew word for *woman* is *ishshah*, which is close to *ish*, the Hebrew word for "man." (A nonbiblical, rabbinic tradition is that Eve was created from the 13th rib on Adam's right side and from the flesh of his heart.)

Putting the chapters together

So which sequence of events and which story of creation are you supposed to believe? You don't have to make a choice. These chapters aren't meant to be compared as if they were two newspapers covering the same event.

Instead, you can glean knowledge from both chapters:

- ✔ Genesis 1 teaches that all human beings, male and female, are made in the image and likeness of God.
- ✔ Genesis 2 teaches that only in the union of their complementary differences can man and woman find happiness and fulfillment. True companionship exists only between two humans.

When reading the Bible, never take a text (or passage) out of context; otherwise, you end up with a pretext (see Chapter 2 for more info on reading in context). Scripture must be interpreted by the literal text but always in context with the rest of the Bible. You can't accurately interpret Genesis 1 without the context of Genesis 2, and you can't properly understand Genesis without the other books, like Exodus, Leviticus, Numbers, and Deuteronomy. For Christians, the Old and New Testaments give each their full context.

Becoming one from two: The origin of marriage

In Genesis 2, Adam utters his oft-quoted line about Eve: "This is bone of my bones and flesh of my flesh" (Genesis 2:23).

The following line, Genesis 2:24, is later quoted by Jesus in the New Testament (Mark 10:7–8) when someone asks him about divorce. "Therefore a man leaves his father and his mother and clings to his wife, and they become one flesh." The word he uses, "cling" or "cleave" in English, is translated from the Hebrew word *dabaq,* which means to unite together, tightly and permanently.

After these passages, the woman (Eve, although she's not yet named at this point) is referred to as the man's wife, even though no wedding ceremony takes place (hard to get a caterer at the last minute, you know). Adam and Eve are, therefore, not just the first human man and woman; they're also the first husband and wife. Genesis 1 and 2 both affirm that woman is a partner with man, and it is implied that they're equal in the eyes of God in terms of dignity and spiritual importance. Only after they both sin does inequality enter the equation as a consequence of sin (foretold in Genesis 3:16).

Oops, I Probably Shouldn't Have Done That

Soon after God creates Eve and she and her husband Adam begin their domestic life, they get into some trouble, which is documented in Genesis 3. Their first act of disobedience to God was the first sin committed by the human race, and it is therefore known as *original sin* or *the sin of Adam and Eve.* According to the Bible, because they were the original parents of humanity, their sin is handed on or transmitted to each and every subsequent descendant — in their case, the rest of humankind.

The tale

Alas, nothing good lasts forever, and the story behind original sin takes place in the Garden of Eden, soon after man and woman were created. The following sections take you through the highlights.

"The devil made me do it!"

Eve is alone until the serpent enters the picture. The Bible describes the serpent as the most crafty or cunning of all the animals. (The Hebrew word *nachash* can be translated as "serpent" or "snake." Some Bibles and Bible commentaries use the word "snake" rather than "serpent" but the two mean the same thing.)

A dialogue develops between Eve and the serpent. Although it may be tempting to pick apart the story of a talking serpent — stupid pet tricks are perhaps better left to late-night talk shows — neither the author nor Eve concerns themselves with this detail. The point of the Bible story is that someone or something other than Eve and Adam — a nonhuman — is the catalyst for the original sin.

Biblical scholars point out that the Hebrews were very familiar with the pagan fertility idolatry practiced by the Canaanites — their nemesis — much of which involved worship of a serpent or snake god. Hearing that a serpent was a part of the Fall would make perfect sense to a Hebrew. In addition, some theologians speculate that the devil, a fallen angel, took the form of a serpent or used a snake as a puppet tool to communicate his insidious temptation.

The serpent asks Eve if God said that she and her husband could eat of any tree in the garden. She replies that God said they could eat the fruit of any tree — except the one in the middle. If they touch it or eat from it, they'll die.

The serpent then tells Eve that she won't die if she eats from the tree, but that her eyes will be opened and she and Adam will become Godlike, knowing good and evil. Eve sees that the tree does indeed have food on it that is pleasing to the eye, and the potential to have divine wisdom and knowledge entices her to eat from it.

Although most people think that the forbidden fruit was an apple, the Bible never once uses the word *apple*. The tree of knowledge is not described as an apple tree, nor is the fruit ever referred to as an apple. Christian artists depicted Eve biting into an apple or Eve handing a half-eaten apple to her husband, Adam. All it took was one artist to choose a fruit, and from then on, subsequent artists followed suit.

Share and share alike

Eve eats the forbidden fruit and gives some to Adam. He also eats the fruit, thereby disobeying the command of God himself. Sure enough, after they consume the food from the tree of knowledge, "the eyes of both were opened, and they knew they were naked" (Genesis 3:7), so they sewed fig leaves together and made loincloths for themselves.

God questions for a reason

Many folks ask the logical question, if God knows everything; then why does he ask the questions "Where are you?" and "Who told you that you were naked?" You must remember that the members of the first audience of the Book of Genesis were Hebrews. The Jewish rabbis taught by asking questions. They already knew the answers, but by asking the questions and then working with the answers of their pupils and students, the religious teachers taught more effectively. (This approach is also called *the Socratic method of learning*.) So when God asks, it isn't because he is ignorant; rather, he wants to engage the person being questioned to figure out the answer for himself.

Didn't Adam and Eve know they were naked before they ate the forbidden fruit? No. How would they know they were naked unless they saw another human being with clothes?

Genesis says that God couldn't find Adam and Eve at first because they were hiding. The Lord calls out to Adam, "Where are you?" Adam steps forward and admits that he and his wife hid because they were naked. The Hebrew word used is *eyrom,* which can mean unclothed (naked) or also unprotected. Adam and Eve are both unclothed and unprotected (not counting the loincloths) because, before this time, God had protected them, but now they're on their own.

The blame game and passing the buck then ensues, as told in Genesis 3:8–13. God asks, "Who told you that you were naked?" It's obvious that Adam and Eve have eaten of the forbidden fruit and thus disobeyed God. The man points the finger at his wife. "The woman gave it to me." When God then questions Eve, she blames the snake: "The serpent tricked me into doing it."

Time out for both of you!

When Adam and Eve admit what they did, God punishes them, along with the serpent who tempted Eve in the first place, and the day of reckoning thus begins:

- ✔ God punishes Eve by telling her that she'll bear children in pain (no one had invented the labor epidural yet). Giving birth and raising children won't be easy, and her relationship with her husband will be disrupted at times. The point? Sin causes division, not just between God and the sinner but also between human beings.

✔ God punishes Adam by making him toil and labor for his food. He also tells Adam that he will die and his body will decay and decompose and turn back into dust (Genesis 3:19). "You are dust, and to dust you shall return" are the ominous words.

✔ God also punishes the serpent (who is Satan, or the devil) with a promise: He says that one day an offspring of the woman will conquer the serpent once and for all:

The LORD *God said to the serpent: "Because you have done this, cursed are you among all animals and among all wild creatures; upon your belly you shall go, and dust you shall eat all the days of your life. I will put enmity between you and the woman, and between your offspring and hers; he will strike your head, and you will strike his heel."*

—Genesis 3:14–15

Eve's offspring who will crush the head of the serpent is considered by Christians to be Jesus. Catholic religious art (especially statues) often depicts the Virgin Mary standing on the head of a serpent. This image represents that Mary is the new Eve, whose offspring, Jesus, is the new Adam (see Chapter 6 for more about Mary). Mel Gibson's film *The Passion of the Christ* also alludes to this promise when he has Jesus, during his agony before the crucifixion, stomp on a snake — the devil — that slithers toward him (an event that is not found in the Bible). The idea here is that the promise that was made involving the first Eve took form in the offspring of the second Eve — Mary, whose offspring, Jesus, would destroy the power of evil when he died on the cross to save humankind.

Understanding original sin

Just as genetics pass on physical traits like eye and hair color from parent to child, original sin is the spiritual inheritance passed on to children from their parents, and ultimately from Adam and Eve themselves. According to Christian and Jewish theology, *original sin* is a spiritual disease of the human soul, a disease that is passed on to future generations as much as physical characteristics or physiological defects.

The phrase *the Fall* is used by Jewish and Christian theologians to describe the consequence of original sin. Prior to their disobedience, Adam and Eve were created and endowed by God with spiritual integrity and sanctifying grace. After they sinned, they lost that integrity and grace, hence the idea of fallen human nature or wounded nature. In other words, they fell from the spiritual level of being in communion with God to the level of being in sin. In turn, sin divides and causes further division.

"The Diaries of Adam and Eve"

For an amusing and nonbiblical interpretation of what Adam and Eve could have written if they had a diary or journal of their own, check out *The Diaries of Adam and Eve* by Mark Twain. Toward the end of the nineteenth century, he wrote several entries for Adam's diary and then composed one for Eve. The entries humorously describe the trials and tribulations of being the first man and woman on earth: naming all of creation, talking to snakes, and so on. The entries have been compiled into a single book. You can read the ingenious and funny speculation that Mark Twain uses to describe the lives of humankind's first parents.

The point of the story of original sin is not to pick apart the details, but to understand the message. Had Adam and Eve remained obedient, God would have revealed to them what was good and what was evil. But they wanted to know for themselves. Because of their transgression, human beings would have to learn the hard way, discovering good and evil for themselves, instead of being told and believing in what God says. Men and women would have to struggle to discern morally correct behavior.

Bible scholars use this analogy to clarify the lesson: Think of a curvy roadway. Without a speed limit sign to tell you how fast you should go, you have no way of knowing how fast you can drive before your speed becomes dangerous. Without a road sign, you must determine the correct speed on your own and, as a result, you're at greater risk of getting into a nasty accident. Before Adam and Eve sinned, God would have functioned as that road sign. Instead, pride caused the first man and woman to drive recklessly, ignoring every traffic code in the book. So they, and in turn humankind, now have to figure things out by using their conscience and their reason, which are not perfect and certainly not infallible.

Mother of All

Despite original sin, which causes the fall of humankind and allows death to enter the human equation, life nevertheless continues in the form of future generations, and Eve is the matriarch of all humankind.

In Genesis 3:20, Eve is first called Eve: "The man named his wife Eve, because she was the mother of all living." The Hebrew word *Chavvah,* which is the proper name for Eve, comes from the word *chay,* which means "the living."

Lilith

According to the Bible, Eve is the first woman and the wife of Adam and the mother of all the living. But according to some arcane nonscriptural writings, Eve is actually Adam's second wife. His first wife was a woman named Lilith. She was created from the dust of the earth — not from one of his ribs, as was Eve. She also allegedly refused his sexual advances and left him. Although the lore about Lilith is still popular with some New Age authors, no evidence exists to corroborate her story in either the Bible or in sacred tradition.

Kabalistic (ancient esoteric Hebrew mysticism) folklore doesn't portray Lilith in a very good light. She is sometimes identified as the mother of his demonic offspring (also part of the legend or folklore but never part of Christian or Jewish doctrine). And she doesn't get much good press in other cultures, either. Case in point: Lilith was the name of a Sumerian demoness who plagued pregnant women.

Experiencing tragedy

The beginning of Genesis 4 reveals that Eve gives birth to two children — Cain and Abel. Nothing is said of their childhood, and the boys eventually grow up and get jobs: Abel as a shepherd and Cain as a farmer. Unfortunately, sibling rivalry raises its ugly head and leads to a heinous tragedy.

One day, each man offers a sacrifice to God. Abel contributes the best of his herd, but Cain offers only the rotten produce he himself wouldn't eat. Abel gave the best he had; Cain gave the worst. When the smoke from their respective sacrifices emanates from the fire, Abel's goes straight up to heaven (a sign of God's approval), and the smoke from Cain's offering blows into his face (guess what that means).

Envy fills Cain's heart. He becomes so angry and hateful he actually kills his brother Abel. God punishes Cain by making him an outcast. He places a mark on Cain so that no one will take revenge by killing him, and he can never again see his mom and dad. (Genesis 4:1–16 details the events leading up to and including the murder of Cain.)

Thus, the first act of murder takes place very early in human history. And Eve becomes the first mother to grieve the death of a child; even worse, she must live with the knowledge that her other son is a murderer. She must not only bury Abel but also must say goodbye forever to her only other son, Cain. Eve endures this nightmare the best she can.

Giving birth again

Though she loses two sons, Eve is at least comforted in her third child, Seth. Fittingly, his name translates from the Hebrew word meaning "compensation."

The Bible says that when Adam was 130 years old, he became the father of Seth, and that he and Eve also had other sons and daughters until his death at the age of 930 (now that's an old man). The Bible doesn't say anything, however, about Eve's age when she died, or whether she lived as long as her husband.

Appearing in the New Testament

Only two more references to Eve are made in the Bible. Those references appear in the New Testament: 2 Corinthians 11:3 ("But I am afraid that as the serpent deceived Eve by its cunning, your thoughts will be led astray from a sincere and pure devotion to Christ") and 1 Timothy 2:13–14 ("For Adam was formed first, then Eve; and Adam was not deceived, but the woman was deceived and became a transgressor"). The first one uses Eve as an example of being duped by false teaching, and the second is using her submission to Adam's authority as a reason why the apostle Paul says the husband is head of the family.

In the nonbiblical (and mostly Gnostic) books the *Apocalypse of Adam,* the *Life of Adam and Eve,* and the *Testament of Adam,* you can find stories about the missing years between the birth of Seth and the death of Eve. However, no Jewish or Christian community considers these books to be inspired or factual.

The Three Faces of Eve

So what does Eve represent to humankind in general, and what does she represent to women in particular? The following sections take a look at these questions. Eve was made in the image and likeness of God just as much as her husband, Adam. She committed sin but apparently learned from her mistake because the Bible doesn't mention any further sins or punishments. Finally, Eve was created to be a partner for man and vice versa. We will look more closely at these three realities of Eve.

Woman as likeness of God

Because the Bible says that God created humankind "male and female" (Genesis 1:26) and that both were made "in the image of God" (Genesis 1:27), woman is as much an integral expression and reflection of God as is man. God, being a pure spirit, is neither male nor female, but human nature is both. Divinity has no gender, but humanity does. Only when male and female are together is the full expression of God reflected here on earth.

In addition, humankind and God are represented within the larger symbolic sense of marriage. The entire human race — both male and female — represents the bride, and God is the ever faithful and loving groom. The metaphoric use of marriage is intended to make all human beings feel they are in an intimate and personal relationship with God. Humans are not simply creatures and God the creator.

Eve as believer

After her decision to eat the forbidden fruit, Eve learns her lesson, and she emerges from the Garden of Eden a little bit wiser, along with her husband, Adam. She experiences the pain of giving birth to her children, the joys of raising those children, and the sorrows of burying one of them killed by his own brother. Eve is an example to believers in that she is truly a repentant sinner. After the Garden incident, the Bible doesn't mention any other incident where she disobeyed the Lord. Like someone recovering from alcohol or drug abuse, Eve is a recovering sinner striving to stay on the straight and narrow.

A message for women

Eve isn't only the first woman on earth; she's also the only one of God's creations who can be a suitable partner for Adam. Genesis 2:20 uses the Hebrew word *ezer,* which can be translated as "partner" or "companion." The Greek word *Boethos* is used in the Septuagint version of the Old Testament, and one of its meanings is "helper." Nowhere is Eve described as being a servant or slave to Adam. She is his partner, and because she is made in the image and likeness and God, just like her husband, Eve deserves the same respect and honor. Her value as a woman is that, with man, they together reflect the image and likeness of God. Neither gender alone can do that.

As wife, Eve epitomizes the biblical teaching that in marriage, two become one flesh. Not someone who merely agrees to a contract, Eve is a person who enters a *covenant* (sacred oath) with her husband, Adam, and their covenant symbolizes the covenant between God and all humankind. (For more on the complementary roles of Adam and Eve, see Chapter 3.)

Chapter 6

A Famous Mom: Mary, the Mother of Jesus

In This Chapter

▶ Recounting the events of Mary's life

▶ Examining her relationship with her son

▶ Understanding Mary's relevance in biblical history

▶ Reviewing Mary's connection to women today

According to Christian belief, God became man and lived among humans for 33 years. Now, God didn't just pretend to be human, nor did he merely use a human body (like some sci-fi movie where aliens take on human form). Christians believe that divinity and humanity were united in one person known as Jesus of Nazareth. As God, he existed from all eternity, but as man, he was born in time and space like you. The God-Man Jesus Christ had a real, flesh-and-blood human mother who conceived him in her womb and nine months later gave birth to him. That woman was Mary.

Other than Jesus himself, Mary is one of the most important persons in the New Testament. The number of references to her in the Gospels alone merits attention, as well as her dynamic interaction with her son, Jesus.

Motherhood is but one dimension of Mary's role in the Bible. She is also a *disciple* (a student and follower of Christ) and powerful symbol of the new Christian church. This chapter examines the various roles that Mary plays in Christian theology. We also look at the parallels that some Christian religions draw between Mary and Eve. (For the lowdown on Eve, go to Chapter 5.)

The Life and Times of Mary

No other woman of the Bible has captured imaginations or captivated millions as much as Mary of Nazareth, the mother of Jesus. And neither has a biblical woman been the center of as much controversy as Mary. Her name in Hebrew is Miriam, but because the Gospels were written in Greek, she is known by her Hellenized name, Mary. Loved by many, she is also confusing to some and even problematic to others (see the nearby sidebar "Beliefs about Mary vary" for the scoop).

The earliest references to Mary are made in Luke's Gospel. Luke wasn't one of the original 12 apostles. He was a Gentile (that is, a non-Jew) before he accepted Christ, and he didn't witness many of the events of Christ's life as had the other Gospel writers who were apostles (like Matthew and John). Yet Luke's book contains more details than any other Gospel regarding the miraculous Virgin Birth. Many scholars suspect Luke interviewed an excellent source — the mother of Jesus herself — to get his information. After all, who else would know and remember with such vivid details the events leading up to and including the birth of the Savior?

Her early life

The Bible is silent about the birth and background of Mary. She first appears in scripture (Matthew 1 and Luke 1) as a young maiden engaged to a man named Joseph, who was from the tribe of Judah and of the lineage of King David (back when there *was* a Kingdom of Israel). Nonbiblical sources like the Apocryphal Protoevangelium of James give the names Joachim and Anne for Mary's parents (who would be Jesus' maternal grandparents, of course). This text was written around AD 120 and attributed to James the Less or the Just, but most likely written by one of his pupils — this short document offers some peripheral information on the infancy of Jesus and on his mother as well. However, nothing is said in the officially accepted texts (those books that all Christian religions consider to be inspired) of sacred scripture about Mary's past before the *Annunciation* — the day when the Angel Gabriel announced that she would become the mother of the Messiah.

Receiving the good news: You're gonna' have a baby!

According to the Gospel of Luke, when Mary is a young woman, the Angel Gabriel visits Mary in Nazareth, a city of Galilee. Luke describes Mary as a virgin (*parthenos* in Greek), and Gabriel greets her with these words: "Hail, full of grace, the Lord is with you!" (Douay-Rheims Bible).

Beliefs about Mary vary

That Jesus had a real human mother has never been disputed among Christians. Catholic, Protestant, and Eastern Orthodox all believe in the *Incarnation* (the doctrine that God became man, from the Latin word *carne* meaning "flesh," as found in John 1:14: "and the Word became flesh") and in the Virgin Birth (that Mary, the mother of Jesus, conceived him by the power of the Holy Spirit and without the assistance of any human father). Everything else about this woman is somewhat controversial. Eastern Orthodox and Catholic Christians believe that Mary remained a virgin before, during, and after the birth of Jesus (called perpetual virginity), whereas many Protestant Christians believe that she had other children with her husband, Joseph, before or after the miraculous Virgin Birth of Jesus.

The Catholic and Orthodox churches also believe that after her time on earth was finished, Mary was taken up body and soul (called *the Assumption*) into heaven by her son, Jesus, who had already died, resurrected, and ascended many years beforehand. Protestant churches believe that she died a normal death and awaits the resurrection of the body at the end of time with all the rest of humanity.

A Catholic dogma known as *the Immaculate Conception* maintains that Mary was given a special grace from God that preserved her from original sin at the very moment of her conception in the womb of her mother, Anne (so as to be able to give Jesus an untainted human nature). All Christians do not share this belief; the same is true of belief in the Assumption and perpetual virginity.

Mary's role and importance after giving birth to Jesus are a matter of theological debate among various denominations. Some claim that one side gives her too much attention and emphasis (which a few go so far as to call idolatry), while others claim that she is casually and disrespectfully dismissed as nothing more than a baby maker.

The angel's phrase "full of grace" is *kecharitomene* in Greek from the root word *charis* (grace). Mary is full of grace because, as Gabriel says, "the Lord is with [her]" *(kyrios meta sou).* No one has ever said this to Mary before, nor has anyone in the entire Bible been addressed in such a fashion. Because of this special greeting, you already know that something's up.

The Latin Vulgate Bible reads *"Ave Maria, gratia plena, Dominus tecum,"* which is the first phrase of the prayer known as the Hail Mary or Ave Maria. Much of the text of this oft-spoken prayer is taken right from the Gospel. The phrase of the Angel Gabriel (Luke 1:28) is joined with one from Elizabeth (Luke 1:42) to form: "Hail, Mary, full of grace, the Lord is with you. Blessed are you among women, and blessed is the fruit of your womb, Jesus."

The words startle Mary, so the angel tells her not to be afraid, for she has found favor with God. Gabriel goes on to say:

> *And now, you will conceive in your womb and bear a son, and you will name him Jesus. He will be great, and will be called the Son of the Most High, and the Lord God will give to him the throne of his ancestor David. He will reign over the house of Jacob forever, and of his kingdom there will be no end.*

—Luke 1:31–33

Stop the presses: Mary wonders if she heard correctly. Conceive and bear a child? She asks Gabriel how this can happen. Although she's officially engaged to Joseph the Carpenter, they don't live together yet as husband and wife. Some translations, such as the Douay-Rheims Bible, say that Mary said, "How can this be since I know not man?" while others, such as the New Oxford Annotated Bible, render it "since I am a virgin?"

No problem, implies the angel. He tells Mary that the Holy Spirit (God) will come upon her and the power of the Most High (God again) will "over-shadow" her. (Although the meaning of the word "overshadow" remains mysterious, Christian theologians explain it in terms of Mary becoming pregnant solely by divine intervention and without any human father.)

The doctrine of Christianity is based on the Holy Trinity (one God, three divine persons: Father, Son, and Holy Spirit). This concept is new to religion at the point in time in which Mary lived.

Gabriel then reveals that Elizabeth, Mary's 80-year-old cousin whom every-one thought was barren, is six months pregnant, "for nothing will be impossi-ble with God" (Luke 1:37). Despite what was probably wonder, confusion, and awe about all this news, Mary nevertheless gives her consent: "Here am I, the servant of the Lord; let it be with me according to your word" (Luke 1: 38).

Visiting Elizabeth

As soon as Gabriel goes back to heaven, Mary goes "with haste" (*meta spoudes* in Greek; *cum festinatione* in Latin) to the hill country to see her preg-nant cousin, Elizabeth. In the first chapter of his Gospel, Luke tells of Elizabeth's conception. Her husband, Zechariah, it seems, had been visited by the Angel Gabriel, who told him that she would give birth to a son, John the Baptist.

Mary's fiat

"Fiat mihi secundum verbum tuum" (Latin) or *"genoito moi kata to rēma sou"* (Greek). Mary speaks these words, which literally translate to "let it be done unto me according to your word," when Gabriel approaches her with the news of Jesus' coming. Her acquiescence is often termed *Mary's fiat.* Not to be confused with the Italian car, *fiat* is also a Latin word for "let it be."

It is a formal and polite way of saying yes, and an affirmation of God's will. Those who see Mary as the new Eve see her submission to God's will as a stark contrast to Eve's disobedience: Mary said yes, and Eve said no. See the later section "As the new Eve" for a more in-depth comparison of Mary and Eve.

While implying on the one hand that Mary goes quickly, the phrase "with haste" also denotes a spiritual attentiveness to one's duty and responsibilities. Even though Mary has just learned she is pregnant herself, she quickly and diligently goes to Elizabeth, because she is an older woman who probably needs help. The 100-mile journey from Nazareth to Juttah, where Elizabeth and Zechariah probably lived, took Mary a few days.

The meeting of these two expectant mothers, also cousins, is called the Visitation. In Luke 1:42, Elizabeth greets Mary with these words: "Blessed are you among women, and blessed is the fruit of your womb!" She continues her greeting with "And why has this happened to me, that the mother of my Lord comes to me?" (Luke 1:43). Elizabeth makes this bold proclamation of faith because the very moment she heard Mary enter the house, the unborn baby in her womb leapt for joy. John the Baptist, only six months in the womb, already assumes the role of prophet and heralds the arrival of Christ — only a few days conceived in his mother's womb. The meeting of these four — Mary with Jesus and Elizabeth with John — is what makes this a "pregnant" moment.

The phrase "the mother of my Lord" is important, too. Not only does the unborn John recognize the presence of the unborn Christ, but Elizabeth also discerns that something special is happening. The word "Lord" in English is the translation of the Greek word *Kyrios,* which in Hebrew is *Adonai.* Only God was addressed as *Adonai* by Jews. The Old Testament often uses the phrase "the Lord God" or just "LORD." When Elizabeth addresses Mary as the "mother of my Lord," she is affirming that the unborn child within Mary is of divine origin. (Read more about Elizabeth in Chapter 13.)

When Elizabeth gives birth to John three months later, Mary, now in her third month of pregnancy, goes back home. Her state of impending motherhood will soon be evident to anyone who sees her.

Reacting to the news: Joseph

In Matthew's Gospel, Joseph is the last one to find out about Mary's pregnancy. At the time, he and Mary were engaged, probably by arrangement through their parents, as was the custom back then. Even though the wedding contract had been signed, they weren't yet fully husband and wife because Joseph hadn't taken Mary into his home and they hadn't consummated the marriage. So when he learns his fiancée is with child, he knows he isn't the father.

Joseph is a just man. Without recriminations and accusations, he decides to divorce Mary quietly and get on with his life. Matthew 1:19 says that Joseph could have exposed Mary (but was unwilling to do so) to public shame as an unwed mother of sorts, because even though they were legally united on paper, they were not yet united spiritually. He and Mary were *betrothed* (engaged) but not married by the rabbi. If he drew attention to her situation, someone might erroneously conclude that Mary had cheated on Joseph. So Joseph plans a discreet and gentlemanly way out — until, that is, he goes to sleep and has a dream. In his dream, an angel tells Joseph not be afraid to take Mary into his home as his wife, because she has conceived by the power of the Holy Spirit (Matthew 1:20–23). Joseph complies.

Giving birth to Jesus

Every Christmas Eve around the world, children re-enact Luke 2:1–7 just before Christian worship services or Mass. In this passage, the Roman Emperor, Caesar Augustus, orders a census that requires all the people to register in their native hometowns. For this reason, Joseph has to take his very pregnant wife all the way from Nazareth to Bethlehem (about 90 miles) to comply with the order. Late in her pregnancy, Mary can't travel easily, but when Caesar commands, people listen.

When Joseph and Mary arrive in Bethlehem, the city of King David of old, there is literally no room at the inn; the town is packed with people who have also returned because of the census. So there they are: Mary is about to give birth, and Joseph can't find them a decent place to stay the night. Finally, someone offers the use of a stable where the animals were protected from the elements. While the stable is certainly no four-star hotel (not even a one-star), it nevertheless provides much-needed shelter and privacy. There, Mary gives birth to a son, whom they name Jesus (Luke 2:7, 21).

Did the Virgin Mary stay a virgin forever?

Eastern Orthodox and Catholic Christians staunchly believe in the perpetual virginity of Mary — that is, that she had no sexual relations with any man before, during, or after the birth of Christ, and that he was her only child. Many Protestant Christians, however, believe that Joseph and Mary had children of their own who would be considered today the half brothers and half sisters of Jesus, but back then would simply be known as his brothers and sisters. There are a couple of reasons for the disparity of beliefs.

First is the interpretation of the term *firstborn*. The Bible says Mary gave birth to her "firstborn" son (Luke 2:7). Some people maintain that the word *firstborn* implies that Mary had other children after Jesus was born. In Greek, the word is *prototokos,* in Hebrew it's *bekor,* and in Latin it's *primogenito.*

However, this term was always given to the first son born, even if no other sons were born afterward. *Firstborn* in this context is a title of honor, privilege, and responsibility. It doesn't imply or declare that there was a second, third, or fourth son born. Because no one back then planned their families, it was presumed that a couple would have as many children as God would bless them with. If only one child was born, that was by God's design and not the explicit wish of mom and dad. You wouldn't know at the time of the first child's birth whether or not you were going to have more children. So even if only one boy was born, he was called the firstborn, because he inherited the birthright from his father.

Thus, the argument that Luke's usage of *firstborn* implies that Mary had other children isn't strong. However, there is also no unequivocal proof that she *didn't* have other children afterward. What

the Gospels do explicitly teach is that Mary gave birth to Jesus without the biological cooperation of a human father. That's why it's called the Virgin Birth. Nothing is said in favor of or against the possibility that she had any future children.

Second is the ambiguity of the phrases "his mother and his brothers" (Matthew 12:46–47 and Luke 8:19–20) or "your mother and your brothers and sisters" (Mark 3:32), which are found in the Gospels when Jesus meets up with his relatives on a few occasions. Whether you think Jesus had siblings or not depends on how you translate and interpret the Greek word *adelphos* (remember that the New Testament was originally written in Greek; see Chapter 2 for more details on the original writings).

Ancient Hebrew and Greek didn't have separate words for specific relatives like uncle, aunt, niece, or nephew. Instead, ancient languages used an inclusive word such as *ach* (Hebrew) or *adelphos* (Greek) to indicate a familial bond. And *adelphos* can mean "brother" in the singular form and "brothers and sisters" when in the plural *(adelphoi),* but it can also mean "relative" or "kinsman." The most obvious example of the use of *adelphos* meaning "kinsman" is in the Old Testament. Genesis 14 talks about Abram and his "brother" Lot. But Lot isn't the biological brother of Abraham; he's a nephew. Genesis 11:27 explains that Lot was the son of Haran, who was the brother of Abraham.

Using a broader interpretation for *adelphoi* to include cousins and other relatives, as well as brothers and sisters, doesn't end the debate, but it gives a viable alternative interpretation to the brothers and sisters of Jesus mentioned in scripture.

Receiving visitors — kings and shepherds

After the birth of Jesus, Mary has some visitors. First to come are the shepherds, who were told by angels "to you is born this day in the city of David a Savior, who is the Messiah, the Lord" (Luke 2:11). The next guests are the Magi (also known as the three Wise Men or the Three Kings), who came from the East after having been guided by a star (Matthew 2:1–12). These visitors arrived to give homage to the child. Luke 2:19 says that Mary pondered (*symballousa* in Greek) all these things in her heart, meaning that she meditated and thought about the visitors and what they told her and often wondered what they meant.

Although the Bible doesn't mention their names, Christian tradition has it that the Three Kings were Casper, King of Tarsus; Melchior, King of Arabia; and Balthazar, King of Ethiopia, who brought, respectively, gifts of gold, frankincense, and myrrh.

Escaping King Herod

After the Magi come to pay their respects to Jesus, King Herod gets wind of it and feels threatened. He seeks to destroy the child, whom he sees as a potential rival. Like Pharaoh centuries before, Herod orders the massacre of all male infants 2 years of age and under. Jesus, Mary, and Joseph flee into Egypt to escape the bloodbath of King Herod (Matthew 2:16–18).

When Herod is dead, Mary, Joseph, and baby Jesus can return. They don't go back to Bethlehem, however, because Herod's son Archelaus now rules Judea. Instead, they settle in Nazareth, where Jesus grows up. He is hence sometimes called "the Nazarene" or "Jesus of Nazareth." (See Matthew 2:19–23 for the account of these events in Mary's life.)

Hearing a prophecy

Mary and Joseph were devout Jews and followed the laws and customs of the Hebrew religion. So eight days after his birth, Jesus was circumcised according to the Law of Moses, and 40 days after giving birth, Mary went to the Temple of Jerusalem to present her firstborn son and to receive the ritual purification required of all mothers (Luke 2:21–24). While in the Temple, two elderly people who had been patiently waiting for the arrival of this child greet Joseph and Mary.

Son of Joseph

Although Joseph isn't the biological father of Jesus, he becomes the legal father as well as guardian to Jesus as the legal husband of Mary. That's why even the Bible often refers to Jesus as the "son of Joseph" (John 1:45 and 6:42).

They didn't use terms such as stepfather or foster father like we do today. Yet because the scriptures also affirm that Mary had her son by the power of the Holy Spirit, Joseph would have failed any modern paternity blood test.

Simeon is one of them. He says to Mary, "This child is destined for the falling and the rising of many in Israel, and to be a sign that will be opposed so that the inner thoughts of many will be revealed — and a sword will pierce your own soul too" (Luke 2:34–35). Bible scholars consider the last phrase, about a sword piercing her soul, to be a prophecy of the pain Mary will experience when she witnesses Jesus' death, some 33 years later.

The second person to greet Mary at the Temple is Anna, the prophetess, daughter of Phanuel of the tribe of Asher. Her words to Mary aren't recorded in scripture, but the Bible says that as a 104-year-old widow, Anna spent most of her time in the Temple fasting and praying in anticipation of the arrival of the Savior, Jesus (Luke 2:36–38).

Trying times with a preteen

The period in Jesus' life between birth and the age of 30, when he begins his public ministry, is often called the "hidden years." Luke does record one story that occurs when Jesus is around 12 years old. The Bible jumps from Jesus' presentation in the Temple as an infant to a dozen years later when he and Mary and Joseph are in Jerusalem for Passover.

As told in Luke 2:41–52, after the Passover religious festival, Jesus stays behind in the Temple while Mary and Joseph head back to Nazareth. Each one thinks that Jesus is with the other — an assumption that is easy to understand if you consider that the men and women were separated in the Temple and often traveled in segregated groups. Until Jesus is bar mitzvahed, he spent most of his time with his mother; after that rite of passage, he spent more time with Joseph and the other adult men. So because they didn't travel as a family unit and because each thought Jesus was with the other, neither Mary nor Joseph initially panicked when he wasn't with them when they left.

But then, of course, the mistake is realized, and Mary experiences a mother's worst nightmare. She and Joseph search for their missing son for three days. Just as it would be today, a missing adolescent is no light matter. She must have worried herself sick wondering if he were alive or dead, hurt or injured, or even sold into slavery. Mary and Joseph finally find Jesus in the Temple, conversing with the scholars and teachers. When asked the typical questions that mothers pose to their children in situations like these — "Where in the world have you been?!" and "Don't you know your father and I have been looking all over for you?!" — Jesus merely replies "Did you not know I must be in my Father's house?" (Luke 2:49).

What do you say to an answer like that? The Bible simply states that they didn't understand what he said. Luke 2:51 does says that Mary kept (*dietērei* in Greek) all these things (what her son said to her) in her heart, just like she did when Jesus was born and the shepherds and the Magi visited him. But after they were all reunited, Jesus went with Mary and Joseph to Nazareth and was obedient to them and grew in wisdom and age (Luke 2:50–52). We know nothing of the years he spent growing up, except that he must have learned some carpentry skills from Joseph. Jesus is not only called the carpenter's son (Matthew 13:55), but he's also a carpenter himself (Mark 6:3).

Supporting Jesus' mission

The next time Mary appears, she is at a wedding feast (John 2:1–11). Because Joseph is no longer mentioned, it's presumed that he died sometime during those so-called hidden years, when Jesus was between the ages of 12 and 30. John says that Mary had been invited to a wedding in Cana, a little village in Galilee near Capernaum. Jesus and his disciples were also invited.

At one point, the wedding reception runs out of wine. Mary notices the fact and informs Jesus that they have no more wine. His response to her is very interesting and has been interpreted in different ways, depending on what translation and version of the Bible are being examined.

The original Greek text of Jesus' response to his mother reads "*gynai, ti emoi kai soi,*" which literally means "woman, what to me and to you." (Greek often implies a verb instead of stating it explicitly.) Here is how some different Bibles translate this phrase (John 2:4):

- ✔ "Woman, what does this have to do with me" (English Standard Version).

- ✔ "You must not tell me what to do" (Good News Translation).

- ✔ "How does that concern us, woman" (International Standard Version).

- ✔ "Dear woman, why do you involve me" (New International Version).

- ✔ "Woman, what do you want from me" (New Jerusalem Bible).

✔ "Woman, what have I to do with thee" (King James Version).

✔ "What to thee and to me, woman" (Young's Literal Translation).

Some of these translations sound like a sharp rebuke from Jesus. Yet the literal translation is much more benign, especially when taken in context of the very next verse in which Mary says to the servants "Do whatever he tells you" (John 2:5). Following this response, Jesus performs his first public miracle, changing water into wine.

This context — that Jesus actually responds to Mary's request rather than ignoring it — tends to encourage a softer interpretation of John 2:4. It's more likely that Jesus said to his mother something like, "What affects me, affects you, and vice versa." If the fact that the groom was going to be embarrassed when they ran out of wine bothered Mary; then it would bother Jesus as well. Others speculate that Jesus may have meant that after he performs this miracle, the quiet life he and his mother have enjoyed up to now will be over. Word about the miracle does, in fact, spread, and Jesus is asked to do more miracles, mostly healings and exorcisms. His quiet life ceases, and so does hers, because he won't be staying home anymore.

Mary's biological connection to Jesus is no small matter, but her emotional bond is no less real, because Christians firmly believe he had a true human nature as well as a divine one. Because Christians hold that Jesus is both God and man, human and divine, his human emotions (like when he wept at the grave of his friend Lazarus, John 11:35) must be equally real and authentic. So Mary and Jesus did love each other, as mothers and sons do.

Witnessing Jesus' death

Mary is conspicuously present at the Crucifixion of her son, Jesus. The "brothers" or "brethren" of the Lord, whether you believe them to be siblings or other relatives, are noticeably absent. The Bible says in John 19:25 that the following people are with Jesus as he dies: his mother, Mary; his mother's sister (Mary, the wife of Clopas); and Mary Magdalene, whom we examine in Chapter 7. Verse 26 mentions the presence of only one of the 12 apostles, "the disciple whom Jesus loved." This was an affectionate term for John, the Gospel writer and the brother of James.

Affirming his mother

Alongside the one apostle (John) who attended Jesus' crucifixion, Mary says nothing while she helplessly watches her son suffer for three hours before he finally dies. Just before his last breath, however, Jesus speaks to Mary: "Woman," he says, "Here is your son" (John 19:26). Then he speaks to John: "Here is your mother" (John 19:27).

One heck of a barkeep

After Jesus transforms six stone water jars into wine, each containing 20 to 30 gallons, the headwaiter remarks how good the wine tastes. He comments in John 2:9–10 that usually people serve the good (and expensive) wine first, followed by the cheaper and lesser vintage wine after the guests have been drinking awhile. He is amazed, however, that the best wine was saved for last. The water turned into wine by Jesus was the best wine anyone ever drank.

The act of entrusting Mary to John the Beloved is both practical (if there are no siblings to care for her) and spiritual. Because they are present at the crucifixion while the rest fled, these two will have to continue their discipleship and thus preserve the infant church until the coming of the Holy Spirit at Pentecost (Acts 2:1–4).

Jesus uses the same word for "woman" as he did at the wedding feast of Cana: *gyne* in Greek or *ishshah* in Hebrew. Many scholars believe the use of "woman" was intended as a compliment, rather than an insult, to his mother, affirming Mary's role as disciple as well as mother. Genesis 3:15 — when God curses the serpent and says that he will put enmity "between you [the serpent] and the woman" — uses that same word. This language affirms that Mary is the true human mother of Jesus, a faithful daughter of God the Father, and, because of the Virgin Birth, a spouse of the Holy Spirit. Despite her elevated status, she is still a human being, so she has no divine prerogatives or attributes.

Grieving for her son

When Jesus finally dies and is taken down from the cross, his body is placed in Mary's arms. This heart-wrenching scene is poignantly portrayed in the *Pietà* (from the Italian word for *pity* or *sorrow*), a marble sculpture by Michelangelo (AD 1499). Whether you believe Mary had other children or that Jesus was her only son, no doubt she felt the pain that only a mother can know at the death of a child.

Despite Jesus' divine nature, he was also her son, her flesh and blood. She bore him in her womb for nine months, gave birth to him, nursed him, and fed, clothed, and educated him. Mary loved and cared for Jesus like any normal mom. Perhaps, while she mournfully held his body in her arms, she remembered Simeon's prophecy spoken to her 33 years earlier: "A sword will pierce your own soul too" (Luke 2:35).

Examining further references

Although no other obvious references to Mary appear in the New Testament, some Christian scripture scholars see her indirectly or *typologically* (symbolically; see Chapter 2) in the last book of the Bible, the Apocalypse or Book of Revelation. Chapter 12 begins with "A great portent appeared in heaven, a woman clothed with the sun, with the moon under her feet, and on her head a crown of twelve stars. She was pregnant and was crying out in birth pangs, in the agony of giving birth."

Just as the possibility of Jesus' siblings is still being debated, so is the preceding passage. Some Christians (Catholic and Orthodox) see this sign as a symbol of Mary because her son was "destined to rule all the nations." Protestant Christians say that the woman is the kingdom or nation of Israel, or perhaps she is the Christian church. The 12 stars seem to represent the 12 tribes of Israel or the 12 apostles. The sun and moon could be Jacob and Rachel, and thus the woman would be the nation of Israel, formed from the 12 tribes that originated from the 12 sons of this couple. Alternatively, the sun could symbolize the Son of God (Jesus, who calls himself the *Light of the World*) and the moon his mother, Mary. A moon gives off no light on its own; instead, it reflects the light of the sun, as Mary reflects not herself but the light of her son. Interestingly, this same image of a woman clothed with the sun, with the moon under her feet and wearing a crown of 12 stars and obviously with child, is depicted in the 1531 image of Our Lady of Guadalupe, Mexico.

Serving the early Church

The last explicit reference to Mary, the mother of Jesus, is in the Acts of the Apostles. She is in the upper room with the apostles on the day of Pentecost (50 days after Jesus' resurrection on Easter Sunday). "All these were constantly devoting themselves to prayer, together with certain women, including Mary the mother of Jesus, as well as his brothers" (Acts 1:14). This same upper room is where Jesus had his Last Supper with the 12 apostles on what some refer to as Holy Thursday, the day before his death (the day called Good Friday).

The Latin word for church is *ecclesia,* which is from the Greek word *ekklesia.* Unlike the English word *church* that often refers to a building or house of worship, *ekklesia* refers more to the people in the building — that is, the faithful who are gathered together to praise God. Acts 1:14 shows that Mary was present at those first gatherings in the upper room to pray, and in that room was the early Church, or *ekklesia.*

The Importance of Mary

Mary's role in the Christian faith is both instrumental (she was the real and true human mother of Jesus the Savior) and educational (she shows how to be a disciple of the Lord). She is a woman, a wife, a mother, and a disciple. As a woman, she shares in being made in the image and likeness of God (see Chapter 3), and she possesses the strength, courage, and faithfulness of the woman in the Bible who preceded her.

As the mother of Jesus, Mary embodies these traditional characteristics:

- ✔ **Humility:** Mary's humility is exemplified when she accepts the will of God after the Angel Gabriel tells her she is to be the mother of the Messiah. Her submission is not a surrender of her personal dignity, however. She freely allows God's will to replace her own will and thus becomes a humble servant of the Lord.

- ✔ **Obedience:** Mary obeys the Word of God, but her submission isn't a surrender of her personal dignity. She isn't an unwilling slave but a willing and faithful servant of the Lord who does what she is asked to do.

- ✔ **Service:** Mary serves the Word made Flesh by caring for and loving Jesus, from the time he was a baby who nursed at her breasts to the time his lifeless adult body lay in her sorrowful arms the day he died. She is a servant in good times and in bad, in joy and in sorrow.

Mary's role isn't incidental or peripheral; it's always contingent and secondary to the unique and singular work of her son, the Redeemer and Savior, Jesus Christ. She shows that a woman can play an important part in salvation history as did Sarah, Rebekah, Rachel, Deborah, Miriam, Esther, Judith, Ruth, and so on.

As a pillar of faith

Most of all, Mary demonstrates the ability to trust the Lord even when she didn't understand what was going on or how things were going to happen later on. Reverend Benedict Groeschel, CFR (a spiritual writer), has often said that Mary had a lot of unanswered questions like any human being. Why did she have to give birth in a stable rather than a clean hotel? Why did she have to take the baby and flee into Egypt? Why couldn't something happen to Herod to prevent such a journey? Why would an old man tell her that a sword will pierce her heart, or why did Jesus go missing for three days when he was only 12 years old? Mary "pondered in her heart" all these unanswered questions but never found the answers.

Mary's claim to fame wasn't that she had insider information, as if God had whispered the secrets of the universe into her ears; rather, it was that she had the courage and strength to trust enough to live with those unanswered questions.

As a disciple of Christ

Mary relates to Jesus in both his human and divine natures. She is his mother in terms of his humanity, and she is his obedient servant and discile in terms of his divinity. She loves him as her son, and she loves him as God. Her love for him, in fact, is just as powerful as his love for her. The best description of Mary is that she was faithful to the Word, especially the Word made Flesh (Jesus).

Trusting completely and totally in God and especially in Jesus Christ, Mary epitomizes what it means to be a disciple. Her words to the servants at the wedding feast in Cana are succinct and profound: "Do whatever he tells you" (John 2:5). Her existence isn't limited nor is it totally defined by her role as wife to Joseph, as daughter to Joachim and Anne, or even as mother to Jesus. She is first and foremost a child of God — like the rest of us. She is human with a heart and soul made of flesh and blood. She is no goddess or superhero from another planet.

As a symbol of the church

The early Church always saw itself not as a neutral, abstract institution or organization, but as a living and mystical body of believers. The assembly, or *ekklesia* as it was called in Greek, cannot exist separate from its founder, Jesus Christ. Like Mary, the church is always in a relationship with Jesus. Mary is his mother in terms of his humanity, and she is a disciple in terms of his divinity. The church, too, is both disciple (one who studies and learns from the teacher) and simultaneously is also the bride of Christ (the beloved spouse whom he is willing to die for). Mary symbolizes the church in that both hear the Word (Mary hears it from Gabriel; the church hears it from the lips of Jesus himself) and both obey the Word. Mary's response to Gabriel's message is "Let it be with me according to your word." The church likewise is expected to do what Jesus commands: "Go therefore and make disciples of all nations, baptizing them in the name of the Father and of the Son and of the Holy Spirit" (Matthew 28:19), "proclaim the good news" (Mark 16:15), and "love one another as I have loved you" (John 15:12).

As the new Eve

In Romans 5:14, Paul says that Adam is a "type," meaning that he *typologically references* or symbolically predicts Christ, the one who was to come. This typology is so strong that Christian scholars often say Jesus is the new or last Adam (1 Corinthians 15:45). If there is a new Adam, it makes sense that there would be a new Eve. This new Eve, according to Eastern Orthodox and Catholic Christians, is Mary, the mother of Jesus.

Typology is a literary device in which something from the past, such a person or an event, predicts something in the future; go to Chapter 2 for a more complete discussion of typology and other literary devices used in the Bible. *Types,* which are real people, places, or things from the past that point to, predict, or promise something in the future, are not identical or clones. Melchizedek, the king of Salem (Genesis 14:18), is considered a type of Christ (Hebrews 7), because both are kings in their own right and both offered a sacrifice of bread and wine. Yet, there were also differences between them. Likewise, Jonah, who dwelt three days in the belly of the fish (Jonah 1:17), was a type of Christ who spent three days in the belly of the earth when he was buried after his death (Matthew 12:40). So, even though the original Adam and Eve were husband and wife, it doesn't make a difference that the new Adam and the new Eve are son and mother rather than spouses. What is symbolized is that the first Adam and first Eve said no to God by disobeying, whereas the new Adam and new Eve said yes by obeying the Lord. Despite a different relationship (mother and son versus husband and wife), Adam and Eve are considered types of Jesus and Mary.

The reason Mary is called the new Eve is because of the comparisons that can be drawn between the women's stories:

- Each woman launches a different Testament (Old and New).

- Each had a choice to make: submit to God's will or not. Although Eve, in Genesis, disobeyed God's request to avoid eating from the tree of knowledge, Mary embraced God's word when told she would be the mother of the savior: "Let it be with me according to your word" (Luke 1:38).

- According to some Christians, the connection between Eve and Mary is most evident in Genesis 3. The passage tells the story of God cursing the serpent for tempting Eve, when he makes this prophecy, "I will put enmity between you and the woman, and between your offspring and hers; he will strike your head, and you will strike his heel" (Genesis 3:15).

  The point of the story is this: Although the serpent was successful in tempting Adam and Eve, humankind's first parents, he will ultimately lose and be conquered. And the offspring who will conquer the serpent is Christ. Although the devil will try to strike at Christ's heel in myriad ways — Judas's betrayal, the disciples' abandonment of Jesus at the Crucifixion, and so on — Jesus, who is Mary's offspring in his human nature, will nevertheless vanquish Satan.

Other Christians do not readily accept nor embrace the connection between Mary and Eve. The connection is subtle to be sure. Depending on your faith tradition, you may appreciate or disregard the typological aspect of Mary as the new Eve, but at least you now know where it came from.

What she represents to Christian women then and now

To Christian women of the past and present, Mary represents the idea of active participation in the life of grace. The universal call to holiness embraces men and women. Sanctity isn't a male or female pursuit; it is a human one for both genders. Mary's journey of faith leads her down a path of uncertainty, sorrow, and joy; it leads to more questions than answers, but it ultimately ends in eternal happiness. She is no spectator; she is an active participant. She has a conversation with the Angel Gabriel, whereas her cousin Zechariah argues with him. She accepts, consents to, and practices the Word of God as revealed to her, instead of just passively listening. Mary "goes in haste" to serve her elderly cousin Elizabeth for her last three months of pregnancy. She intercedes for her friends at their wedding when an embarrassing moment occurs (they ran out of wine).

Mary shows that God chooses and uses women to accomplish his will and to fulfill his plan as much as he uses men. Divine Grace filled Mary, and that same grace is available to all men and women who seek God. Her greatest virtue is her ability to say yes when she doesn't know all the consequences and circumstances that response will bring. She does know that no matter what happens, the grace of God will enable her to overcome obstacles and persevere to the end. Mary knows that her son, Jesus, means what he says and keeps his word, so she trusts him completely. The men to whom Jesus entrusted his church don't intimidate her, and she doesn't slip into the shadows — she is present at the coming of the Holy Spirit at Pentecost in the upper room. Mary isn't an apostle, and she doesn't lead a local community, but that doesn't mean she isn't a disciple. Mary is certainly a disciple of Christ.

Chapter 7

Befriending Jesus:
Mary Magdalene

- ▶ Understanding scriptural references
- ▶ Sifting through speculation about her identity
- ▶ Examining alternative theories about her influence and role in early Christianity

Mary Magdalene is one of the most famous — yet most mysterious — women of the Bible, a woman who lived and served in close proximity to Jesus. A contemporary of Christ, Mary Magdalene lived in the early first century AD and was probably around the same age as Jesus.

Some of what we know about Mary Magdalene is stated explicitly in the Bible. Other info is speculation, based on biblical text. This chapter pieces together a picture of Mary Magdalene that relies on biblical accounts and traditional Christian belief. We examine what the Bible says about her enigmatic past, her conversion of faith, her fraternal love of and devotion to Christ, and her impact on Christianity and the Christian church.

Her role in Jesus' life has inspired a great deal of speculation, particularly in the pop culture of recent years. For that reason, this chapter examines the nonbiblical speculation — like the suggestions that perhaps she was more to Jesus than a faithful follower and that she is the matriarch of a line of European royalty.

What the Bible Says about Her

Chronologically, Mary Magdalene first appears in the Gospel of Luke:

The twelve were with him, as well as some women who had been cured of evil spirits and infirmities: Mary, called Magdalene, from whom seven demons had gone out, and Joanna, the wife of Herod's steward Chuza, and Susanna, and many others, who provided for them out of their resources.

—Luke 8:1–3

Theological views on possession

Traditional branches of Judaism, Christianity, and Islam have always believed in supernatural evil and in the existence of demons or evil spirits (that is, *fallen angels* — angels who chose to disobey God and therefore ended up in hell and became demons, as opposed to the angels who remain faithful to God and entered heaven). They believe that demons and the devil exist side by side with human beings in this world. Orthodox Jews, fundamentalist Protestants, Eastern Orthodox, Roman Catholics, and Muslims still maintain that it is *possible* (but not always *probable*) for these evil spirits to tempt and, on very rare occasions, to actually possess a person's body.

More contemporary and modern elements of these religions believe that demonic possession is a medieval relic and that the outward signs that some point to as evidence of possession can be explained by psychology and psychiatry. Even the conservative religious experts agree, however, that before any prayer or ritual to *exorcise,* or cast out, the demon from the person occurs, a thorough physiological and psychological evaluation should take place to first rule out the possibility of a medical or mental phenomenon, and only as a last resort should one conclude that the individual is in the throes of a spiritual and supernatural occurrence.

Those theologians who believe in demonic possession point out that you shouldn't infer that a possessed person is evil or has sinned to deserve this punishment. There is no human fault or cause to discover. Rich and poor, men and women, young and old — demonic attacks are like germs, bacteria, and viruses in that they don't discriminate about whom they afflict. So you shouldn't infer that Mary Magdalene was afflicted due to guilt on her part.

Supporting Jesus and the apostles

From Luke 8:1–3, we know that Mary Magdalene generously supported the material needs of Jesus and the apostles. This role was an important one, particularly during that time period in history. Jesus and his apostles spread their message by traveling from town to town, and they didn't have the luxury of inexpensive motels or cheap fast food. Nor did the carpenter's son or the former fishermen who followed him get a weekly salary for their preaching and teaching. They depended on the kindness of followers and on the hospitality of new believers to stay alive. Mary Magdalene, along with Joanna, Chuza, and Susanna, took care of the guys from their own means.

Where Mary Magdalene got her modest wealth no one can say with certainty. She may have inherited it from her father (if he had no sons; refer to Chapter 3 for details about the lives of women during the time), or she may have been the widow of a man who was well-off. Some speculate that she may have had a lucrative nest egg from a former life as a high-class call girl — a supposition that is hotly contested and considered in greater detail in the section, "What Folks Speculate about Her," later in this chapter. The Bible never explicitly explains how she provided or what she provided, just that she helped Jesus.

Being possessed by demons

Luke's initial passage also says that Mary Magdalene was possessed by demons — seven devils, to be exact, haunted her. Though the Bible never describes when she was delivered from her spiritual bondage, Mark 16:9 specifies that Jesus was the one who exorcised her demons. Why and how she became possessed is never said, but certainly being cured of such a malady would make most people extremely grateful to the person who healed them. This gratitude may be part of the reason why Mary Magdalene became such a devout follower and supporter to Jesus.

Staying with Jesus as he died

Biblical accounts also affirm that Mary Magdalene was one of the women who stayed with Jesus at the foot of the cross the day he was crucified and died (the anniversary of that day is honored as Good Friday by many Christians). Matthew 27:56, Mark 15:40, and John 19:25 explicitly mention Mary Magdalene as being at Calvary, the place where Jesus was crucified, with the Virgin Mary and a few other ladies. John the Apostle is the only man recorded as being there (John 19:26).

Tradition has it that the other men and apostles abandoned Jesus and left him, while the women, like his mother and Mary Magdalene, remained faithful and stayed with him. Magdalene's act of solidarity — while others chose to run and hide to protect themselves — illustrates her fraternal love for Jesus.

Witnessing the Resurrection

Mary Magdalene is present not only at the cross when Jesus dies but also at his burial (Matthew 27:61 and Mark 15:47). Most significant, however, is her role as the first one to discover his empty tomb on Easter morning.

Jesus had just risen from the dead when Mary Magdalene dutifully went to the tomb on Sunday to complete the Jewish burial rituals. (According to Christian tradition, Jesus died on Friday and rose on Sunday. Saturday was the Jewish Sabbath, and no work was allowed on that day, not even burial rituals.)

Matthew 28:1, Mark 16:1, Luke 24:10, and John 20:1 all tell essentially the same story:

Mary Magdalene goes to the tomb where Jesus was buried. When she arrives, she finds the *sepulcher* (a tomb or crypt) empty and fears that someone has stolen the body. She sees two angels in the tomb dressed but no Jesus.

Usually the sight of angels invokes either fear or joy, but Mary Magdalene is so overwhelmed with grief about Jesus' death and now suspected desecration, that their presence has no effect on her. She cries intensely, and when the angels ask her why, she replies, "They have taken away my Lord, and I do not know where they have laid him" (John 20:13).

Turning around, Mary Magdalene sees Jesus standing there, but she doesn't recognize him because he has just risen from the dead. (Christian theologians claim that his glorified, resurrected body was the same body crucified on the cross, but it was also changed in some way.) Thinking that the man before her is the gardener, she asks him where he put Jesus' body so she can retrieve it; she doesn't realize she's talking to Jesus in his resurrected body. Jesus then calls her name, and she finally recognizes who he is. (You can read this account in John 20:14–16.)

Reporting to the apostles

After this awesome and emotional reunion, Jesus sends Mary Magdalene to the apostles to bring the good news. She tells them, "I have seen the Lord" (John 20:18). Because Mary Magdalene was sent by Jesus to bring the message that Christ is risen, she is often metaphorically called the "apostle to the Apostles." Peter, James, John, and the rest first learn of the Resurrection from Mary Magdalene. Although they don't initially believe her, almost dismissing her claim as hysterical grief, Peter and John still go to the empty tomb to see for themselves.

The word *apostle* comes from the Greek *apostolos,* which means "messenger" or "one who is sent."

Mark 16:9 emphasizes that the resurrected Jesus appeared to Mary Magdalene first before anyone else, even before Peter or John — let alone the rest of the 11 apostles (Judas hanged himself, so their number went down from 12). She is also the bearer of the greatest message in Christian theology: that Christ has risen from the dead. She is the one sent by God to deliver that news to the apostles.

This is where the Bible ends its mention of Mary Magdalene. Her name doesn't appear in the rest of the New Testament, either in the Acts of the Apostles or in any of the epistles. She seems to almost disappear, while the apostles begin to build the early church. Where her story in the Bible ends, however, some of the writings that haven't earned a seal of approval attempt to fill in the blanks.

What Folks Speculate about Her

This section looks at the various opinions, theories, and hypotheses about this very mysterious woman of the New Testament. The Bible offers few details about Mary Magdalene's history, her occupation, her activities, and even her actual involvement with the early church. The ambiguity of scripture has encouraged speculation for the past 2,000 years. Some speculation is based on reasonable and logical arguments from what the Bible and history tell us; some is conjecture that has no proof or evidence but that makes interesting reading nonetheless.

One question that has been hotly debated and argued by biblical scripture scholars for centuries is what Mary Magdalene did for a living. Some scholars maintain she was a *harlot* (the biblical name for a prostitute). Others say she was a notorious adulteress. Still others claim that she was merely one of several middle-class women of modest wealth who provided for the material needs of Jesus and his apostles — in other words, a benefactor — and nothing else.

In the next sections, we examine this speculation and the scriptural references that may or may not apply to Mary Magdalene.

The public sinner

Through the ages many people have speculated that Mary Magdalene is the woman featured in the story that begins in Luke 7:37. Because this woman is never named — either as "Mary" or as "Mary Magdalene" — the speculation continues to this day.

Luke's story describes a notorious public sinner — a woman — who comes to Jesus while he is visiting a Pharisee. This unnamed woman washes his feet with her tears, dries them with her hair, and anoints them with costly perfumed oil. The host, who knows of this woman's past, wonders why, if Jesus is really a prophet, he doesn't reject her for what she is — a public sinner. Jesus recognizes this man's thoughts and asks him who is more grateful — a man who owes 500 days' wages and whose debt is dissolved, or the man who owes 50 days' wages and has his debt erased? The Pharisee believes it is the man who owes more money, and he tells Jesus so.

Jesus then turns toward the woman and says that her many sins are forgiven and that she has shown great love.

Though the name of this "public sinner" is never mentioned, tradition says this woman was Mary Magdalene. But why, if the woman is never mentioned by name, would anyone suspect it was Mary Magdalene? For the reasons outlined in the following sections.

Investigating other biblical accounts of the same event

John's Gospel (12:3) relates another account of a woman anointing Jesus' feet with expensive aromatic ointment and drying them with her hair. John identifies this woman as Mary, the sister of Martha and Lazarus. (Matthew 26:6–13 and Mark 14:3–9, tell similar stories about a woman anointing the feet of Jesus from costly perfume in an alabaster jar, but again this woman remains nameless.) Only John identifies the woman as Mary, the sister of Martha, but only Luke classifies the woman as a public sinner. (In addition, Luke 7:37–50, which outlines the story of the public sinner and washing of feet, later mentions Mary Magdalene by name in the very next chapter along with Joanna, Susanna, and Chuza.)

Could more than one woman have anointed the feet of Christ? Possible, but somewhat improbable. The humble act of drying someone's feet with one's own hair and then anointing those same feet with costly oil isn't a common practice. In fact, it's so rare, uncommon, and unusual that all four Gospel writers (Matthew, Mark, Luke, and John) mention it. The mystery of why the woman is nameless in three Gospels and called Mary only in John remains. Washing feet was a humble act in itself, but having a woman touch a man, especially a rabbi, and having her dry his feet with her hair and then anoint them with expensive perfume is so extraordinary that it is improbable (but not impossible) that this happened more than once.

If all the stories involve one particular woman, the next question is, could this other Mary, the sister of Martha, also be the same unidentified public sinner that Luke mentions? If so, the latter Mary had been a very naughty girl, at least at one time. If she were the forgiven sinner, it would explain why she was so attentive and entranced when Jesus came to visit their home, even to the extent of annoying her sister, Martha (Luke 10:38–42). Ahhh, yet another theory to ponder.

Because John's Gospel names the woman who washes the feet of Jesus as being Mary and this act takes place in the home of Martha and Lazarus, one could assume it was Mary the sister of Martha and Lazarus and not another Mary who did it. The nameless woman in Luke's Gospel is identified as a "public sinner." So either there were two women who separately anointed the feet of Jesus in the same unusual and unique way, or the public sinner and Mary the sister of Martha and Lazarus are one and the same.

Giving her a motive for her generosity

Some scholars maintain that if Mary Magdalene is indeed the public sinner who washes Jesus' feet, it supplies a motive for Mary's actions as a generous benefactor. She was simply grateful for what Jesus had done for her. (Of course, she may have also been extremely grateful because he delivered her from the seven devils; see the earlier section "Being possessed by demons.")

If the Mary who washed the feet of Jesus was in fact the sister of Martha and Lazarus and was the public sinner, she would have been grateful for being forgiven as well. Until the time Jesus appeared, no one heard the words "your sins are forgiven" spoken to them. A former public sinner now reformed and forgiven would be very grateful. If this same sinner had been public in her sinning, then there would have been no reason why her brother and sister, if she had them, would know not only of her immoral past but also of her turning over a new leaf.

Obviously, these conflicting accounts present more questions than they answer about exactly who did what. But no matter which Mary was responsible for anointing Jesus' feet (if it was either Mary at all), you can glean from the story that Jesus came to forgive sinners — and that those who are healthy don't need a physician; sick people do (Matthew 9:12).

The adulteress

Mary Magdalene is also frequently given credit as a woman in another well-known story of the New Testament. Again, the woman in the passage is never called by name, and so her identity is cause for speculation.

John 8:3–11 tells of an unnamed woman caught in adultery who is about to be stoned to death. Jesus confronts her potential executioners, saying, "Let anyone among you who is without sin be the first to throw a stone at her." Jesus then begins writing in the dirt in such a way that the men can see what he writes. One by one the potential executioners leave the scene, dropping their rocks and going away.

What Jesus wrote is unknown, but his actions somehow convince the men to give up, even after they'd been so sure of this woman's fate. After they leave, Jesus and the woman are alone. He says to her "Woman, where are they? Has no one condemned you?" She replies, "No one, sir." So Jesus says, "Neither do I condemn you. Go your way, and from now on do not sin again" (John 8:10–11).

Biblical scholars debate both the identity of the woman and the content of Jesus' writings in the dirt. Some experts hypothesize that he wrote the names of other women on the ground, the adulteresses and prostitutes whom some of these very righteous men may have been secretly intimate with. Others think that Jesus may have written other sins in the dirt, like lying, cheating, stealing, and so on, whereby each man saw his own sin identified.

Whatever he doodled in the sand, the result was that the woman's life was spared. More important to Christians, Jesus saved her soul. So the next conclusion that many scholars draw is that this adulteress is the very same woman depicted as Luke's public sinner, the one who would later anoint Jesus' feet and dry them with her hair and who would be very grateful to Jesus. For this reason, these scholars believe that the women in each story are one and the same. Their next conclusion, of course, is that this woman in both cases was Mary Magdalene.

Weighing the interpretations

The problem is that all the evidence pointing to the fact that these stories are about Mary Magdalene is very circumstantial and not incontrovertible. Making the leap that the public sinner, the woman caught in adultery, and the woman who wiped the feet of Jesus are Mary Magdalene is a difficult theory to prove beyond a reasonable doubt. However, disproving it just on grounds that such a notorious sinner couldn't possibly repent and rise to the level of friend and disciple denies the message of the Gospel completely.

Mary Magdalene may not have been the woman featured in any of these stories. But if the woman was Mary, it certainly portrays, in Christian minds, God's great mercy as well as any sinner's potential to repent, be forgiven, and become close to God. The scriptural evidence that the woman who washed the feet of Jesus and identified as Mary in John 12:3 is the same nameless woman who washed the feet of Jesus in Matthew 26:6 and Mark 14:3 and is the same woman as the public sinner in Luke 7:37–38 who washed Jesus' feet is persuasive. Matthew, Mark, and Luke all mention the detail that the ointment was contained in an alabaster jar. The very uncommon, possibly unheard of, practice of a Hebrew woman washing a Hebrew rabbi's feet also lends to the conclusion that this incident happened only once.

Although the circumstantial evidence is good that one woman washed Jesus' feet, anointed them, and dried them with her hair and that the woman's name was Mary, the evidence to support that Mary, the sister of Martha and Lazarus, is also Mary Magdalene is much less solid and self-evident. The implication that Mary the sister of Martha was a repentant, forgiven public sinner doesn't seem unlikely or incredible. The suggestion that she was also the Magdalene is somewhat more tenuous.

Some people believe that it's a violation of Mary's dignity to claim she is the one portrayed as a former prostitute or adulteress. They point out that it is a subtle attempt to denigrate, demean, and diminish the importance of Mary Magdalene by insinuating she was at one time a harlot. But some other Christians insist those folks are missing the point of what Christianity believes Jesus came to do — forgive sins. Luke 15:7 states that there is more joy in heaven over 1 repentant sinner than in 99 righteous who have no need of repentance. Scripture never explicitly identifies Mary Magdalene as the woman caught in adultery (John 8:3), but Christian tradition from ancient to medieval times has associated the public sinner of Luke, the woman caught in adultery of John, and the woman who washed the feet of Jesus in Matthew and Mark as being one and the same woman. This idea was never a doctrine of faith, however, and recent historians and biblical scholars agree that the evidence for Mary Magdalene being all these women is a little unconvincing — but it was believed for some time to be true.

Even the identification of Mary Magdalene as a reformed prostitute is hotly debated today. Remember that the Bible often poses more questions than it provides answers to, in terms of details and the like. During the early days of the church and especially during the Middle Ages, western Christians took for granted that Mary Magdalene was a repentant sinner, and they named many charitable homes for unwed mothers and for recovering prostitutes after her to encourage women who had fallen into sin to believe that anyone was capable of being forgiven and of being given a second chance. Even if Mary Magdalene wasn't the woman caught in adultery or the public sinner who washed Jesus' feet, she is still a woman who was healed of seven demons and who conspicuously was present at the foot of the cross the day Jesus died.

If conclusive evidence is ever discovered disproving Mary Magdalene's lurid past, it won't change the fact that, according to the New Testament, Jesus forgave a woman known as a public sinner and a woman caught in adultery. Even if one of the women or both women turn out not to have been Mary Magdalene, the story's message remains the same, no matter her identity.

Controversial References to Mary

Some controversial references and theories about Mary Magdalene go beyond the theological and scriptural ones of her past and whether or not she was the woman who washed the feet of Jesus. The speculation on her relationship to Jesus is the epicenter of current discussion. Another hot topic is her role in the early Christian Church. We examine both subjects in this section.

What is Gnosticism?

The word *gnosis* means "knowledge," and Gnosticism is the philosophy that salvation comes through secret knowledge that isn't intended for everyone. Gnosticism originated in the early pre-Christian era and continued through the beginnings of Christianity until it died out. Gnosticism was in opposition to the Christian religion because it viewed the material world as evil — matter was bad, but spirit was good. This belief led to forms of self-abuse, masochism, and self-inflicted torture, because Gnostics believed that only pain and suffering, along with secret knowledge, could lead to salvation. The belief that any physical pleasure was sinful and that the material world, especially the human body, was bad led Gnostics to abhor and avoid reproduction and marriage. Not surprisingly, they died out.

Despite recent theories brought on by fictional books such as *The Da Vinci Code* by Dan Brown (Doubleday) and subsequent media speculation, the Bible and Christian tradition do not indicate any kind of a romantic relationship between Jesus and Mary Magdalene. Many Christian believers find this type of speculation offensive, and in the professional opinion of these authors and many other biblical scholars and historians, there is no credible evidence to support it. Each of the many varieties and denominations of Christianity, whether Protestant, Catholic, or Orthodox, officially denounce the idea of any romantic involvement between Jesus and Mary Magdalene, although some Christians may believe in such a theory.

So where does this theory come from? And from where do other theories about Mary Magdalene's actions stem? In the following sections, we examine references to Mary Magdalene from beyond the Bible and sacred tradition.

Apocryphal accounts

Apocryphal writings of the New Testament (ones you won't find in any Bible of any religion or denomination) mention Mary Magdalene. (See Chapter 2 for more on the Apocrypha.) The Apocryphal Gospel of Peter and Apocryphal Epistle of the Apostles say that she went to the burial place of Jesus on the third day to fulfill the Jewish funeral rituals that were not completed because of the Sabbath. But no mention is made here about any deeper relationship between Mary Magdalene and Jesus.

Gnostic accounts

The most controversial accounts of Mary Magdalene's life come from Gnostic writings, like the apocryphal Gospel of Philip and the Pistis Sophia (Greek for "faith wisdom"). (See the sidebar "What is Gnosticism?") These manuscripts depict Mary as a *companion* of Jesus, a term that some folks today interpret in romantic terms. The Gnostic accounts of Mary Magdalene purport her to be the real "Beloved Disciple" and author of the Fourth Gospel (rather than John, the brother of James and the son of Zebedee) and a competitor with Peter for leadership in the early church, among other claims. Still, none of these Gnostic gospels ever refer to Jesus and Mary Magdalene as being husband and wife.

The Gnostic Gospel of Philip says, "The companion of the Savior is Mary Magdalene." This text was written in the second half of the third century, 200 years after Mary Magdalene lived, so it is highly unlikely that the author was an eyewitness to the life and times of Jesus or Mary Magdalene, or even that the author heard first-hand accounts of those times. The Greek word used is *koinonos,* which is translatable in English as companion but can also be rendered as *comrade, associate, partner, friend,* or even *neighbor.* The Greek word doesn't connote anything romantic, sexual, or marital in nature, whereas the English word *companion* is sometimes used in modern times for a significant other — a boyfriend or girlfriend, a sexual partner, or a common-law spouse. Ancient use of the term, however, is so benign and generic that even the Apostle Paul uses the Greek *koinonoi* (plural of *koinonos,* meaning partners or companions) in Hebrews 10:33 to refer to compatriots who shared in his experience of being mistreated in prison for their faith. Had this author wanted to describe Mary Magdalene as the wife of Jesus, he likely would have used the Greek word *gyne* (woman) and not *koinonos* (companion).

The Gnostic Gospel of Mary Magdalene is the epicenter of controversial theories about her and Jesus. This nonbiblical manuscript was discovered in the late nineteenth century and features Mary Magdalene and Peter fighting with each other over an alleged revelation she had from Jesus after his resurrection and ascension. The Gospel of Mary Magdalene has Mary revealing secrets from Jesus, now in heaven, telling the select few that the body is evil while only the soul is good — the essence of Gnostic belief. Christians would say the idea that the body is inherently evil contradicts what the biblical New Testament says — specifically, that because Christians believe Jesus is both divine and human, their doctrine of the union of God and man in a human body shows the intrinsic good of the material as well as the spiritual worlds, rather than a battle between the good spirit and evil body. Even Genesis 1 speaks of the creation of the material world, from the planets to the human body, and says that God saw that it was good.

Later theories

Unproven theories also exist about Mary Magdalene and Jesus producing offspring, either inside or outside wedlock, and these children allegedly became the ancestors of some of the Western European monarchies.

Hypotheses from fiction

One of the suggested hypotheses of some contemporary fiction writers is based on forged documents from the 1960s in France. Pierre Plantard (1920–2000) forged documents that supported his claims that the Merovingian kings were descended from Jesus and Mary Magdalene, that the Priory of Sion (which allegedly guarded the secret of the supposed offspring) was founded by Godfrey of Bouillon, and that Leonardo da Vinci was once Grand Master of the Priory.

Plantard himself claimed to be a descendant of Merovingian blood and thus French royalty. He established a second Priory of Sion in 1956 after the original one (a monastic order), which was founded in 1100 by Crusaders in Jerusalem (which had no connections whatsoever to the military order of the Knights Templar). The first priory was strictly a religious order that resided on Mount Zion until the 1291 Mameluke (Islamic power before the Ottoman Turkish Empire) conquest of the Holy Land after the unsuccessful Ninth Crusade.

Dan Brown's wildly popular work of fiction, *The Da Vinci Code,* capitalized and expanded on some of these notions. Interesting though they may be, no scholarly evidence supports these theories.

Claims that Leonardo da Vinci actually painted Mary Magdalene into the Last Supper as one of the apostles are implausible. Using feminine qualities to symbolize the innocence and softness of youth was a common technique of Renaissance artists. Museum and art curators agree that medieval and Renaissance artists such as da Vinci used this style to distinguish young men from old ones. So depicting John the Beloved Disciple with feminine qualities was just to draw a contrast between him (youthful) and the older, rougher, and more mature (manly) apostles.

Chapter 8

Three Women, Three Books: Ruth, Judith, and Esther

. . . .

In This Chapter

▶ Discovering the meaning of family loyalty with Ruth

▶ Defending the Hebrews with Judith

▶ Following the heroic exploits of Esther

. . . .

*T*hree books of the Bible are named after women: Ruth, Judith, and Esther. Written during the reign of King David (1000–961 BC), the Book of Ruth centers on the life and person of Ruth and her mother-in-law, Naomi. It tells of their devotion and loyalty to each other as well as their endurance during difficult times. The Book of Judith was written in the second century BC, and it tells the story of an independent and determined woman who risks her life to fix a bad situation that her people are in. The Book of Esther, written in the fifth century BC, tells about a woman who became queen and used her power to save her people's lives from the genocide that seemed sure to take place.

These books are part of the historical writings of the Old Testament, and each one is situated in a different period of time. Judith and parts of Esther are found in different places in the Bible depending on what translation and version of the Bible you have. Eastern Orthodox and Catholic Christian Bibles designate these books as *deuterocanonical* (meaning *second canon* or *second authorized list*), whereas Protestant Christian Bibles classify them as *Apocrypha*. In the Bibles in which they're included, these seven books appear at the end of the Old Testament or as an appendix to the Bible as a whole, after Revelation. For more about the difference between versions of the Bible, see Chapter 2.

In this chapter, we discuss all three phenomenal women of faith whose tenderness, patience, courage, strength of character, and perseverance in times of adversity keep the flames of hope burning.

Meeting Ruth

The Book of Ruth is a story about family loyalty. A mother-in-law and her daughter-in-law share joys and sorrows in this brief biblical saga. Ruth, a foreigner, shows as much love and devotion to her mother-in-law, Naomi, as would a full-blooded offspring. Trial and tribulation are on the menu for these two women, but they endure together, and sharing their suffering makes them closer.

The Book of Ruth is unlike many books of the Bible in that most of the text is dialogue. It's divided into four chapters but seven sections:

- In the first section (1:1–6), we read about Naomi's husband's family line dying out.

- The widows return to Naomi's homeland in the second section (1:7–22).

- In the third section (2:1–23), Ruth encounters her father-in-law's kinsman.

- The fourth section (3:1–18) recounts a widow's demand and the kinsman's dilemma.

- A solution to the dilemma is found in the fifth section (4:1–12).

- The family line is restored in the sixth section (4:13–17).

- The seventh section is an appendix (4:18–22), which briefly gives the lineage from Perez, the son of Tamar and Judah, down to Boaz and Ruth, who were the great-grandparents of King David.

The Book of Ruth was written during the reign of King David, but the main characters lived about 200 years earlier, during the turbulent era of tribal conflict in which a group of leaders known as the Judges ruled Israel. This was after the Exodus from Egypt. The 12 tribes of Israel fought with each other under the king's rule (successively, these kings were Saul, David, and Solomon). Family squabbles among clans were the first phase when the originators of the tribes (the sons of Jacob, otherwise known as Israel) were still alive. (*Clans* are merely subdivisions among the tribes representing closer familial relations, whereas the *tribes* were larger and more encompassing classifications.) As each clan grew and expanded, they became less connected and interwoven and almost existed as separate nations even though all were considered Hebrew. When a king was anointed to rule over all the tribes and a monarchy established, a short-lived but unified nation of Israel existed (under three kings: Saul, David, and Solomon). After the death of Solomon, the unified kingdom is divided into two parts, northern kingdom of Israel (capital = Samaria) and southern kingdom of Judah (capital = Jerusalem).

Introducing the main character

Ruth, wife of Mahlon, was the daughter-in-law of Naomi (see Chapter 11), and her relationship with Naomi is the best-known relationship in the Bible. We know nothing of Ruth's background, origin, or family, except that she is a *Moabite,* meaning she's from the country of Moab. Despite that she was looked down on by some Hebrews at the time as a foreigner, the Bible describes her through her character, her loyalty, her strength, and her resolve. Ruth stands out as the epitome of a good daughter-in-law to Naomi. She is completely devoted and loyal to her husband's family, which she makes her own. After Ruth's husband (Mahlon) dies, she stays with her mother-in-law, while Orpah (Naomi's other daughter-in-law, whose husband, Chilion, also dies) leaves. Ruth takes care of her mother-in-law, who, in return, helps her daughter-in-law find a good husband.

Leaving Moab

Ruth is living in Moab when Naomi moves to that country with her husband, Elimelech, and her two sons, Mahlon and Chilion, because of a famine in their homeland of Judah. Elimelech soon dies. Mahlon, Naomi's son, takes Ruth as a wife, and his brother, Chilion, marries a woman named Orpah. But tragedy soon strikes again, and both sons die. Ruth, like her mother-in-law, Naomi, and her sister-in-law, Orpah, is left to fend for herself as a widow. The three decide to head toward Bethlehem for better pastures. (See Ruth 1:1–7 for specifics.)

On the way to the land of Judah, however, Naomi realizes that her two daughters-in-law won't find life easy in Bethlehem because they're foreigners. Even though they married Hebrew men, as foreign widows they won't fare as well as a Hebrew widow. In those days, the only hope for these widows would be to marry other sons of Naomi, which she expects she is too old to have — and even if she could, Ruth and Orpah would have to wait an awfully long time. So, with great kindness, Naomi, weeping, advises them to turn back. You can find this story in Ruth 1:8–14 and see William Blake's artistic vision of the scene in Figure 8-1.

Orpah decides to leave, but Ruth won't abandon Naomi, in spite of the circumstances. Ruth decides that she will tough it out with Naomi no matter what. She believes they will be stronger together than apart. Although Ruth must have been tempted to return to Moab, her own homeland, her love and loyalty to Naomi are stronger. Ruth utters her now famous quote often repeated at weddings and religious ceremonies: "Where you go, I will go . . . your God [is] my God" (Ruth 1:16). When they return to Bethlehem, they are warmly greeted. But they are still husbandless, childless, and poor.

Figure 8-1:
Naomi
entreats
Ruth and
Orpah to
return to
Moab. By
William
Blake
(1757–1827).

Victoria & Albert Museum, London/Art Resource, NY

Trying to escape poverty

To deal with their poverty, Ruth goes to work in the only way she can — collecting the *gleanings* from the fields, the leftover grain that remains after reapers have harvested their crop. Although this work is demeaning and difficult, it enables Ruth to provide for herself and Naomi, who is too old to work herself.

Providentially, Ruth ends up gleaning in a field owned by a relative of Elimelech, Naomi's dead husband. This man's name is Boaz, the son of Rahab of Jericho. (Head to Ruth 2:1–18, where this story is described.) Naomi realizes that Ruth's job situation presents an opportunity. A custom of the day dictated that a relative could marry a childless widow. Their firstborn son would be considered the continuation of the deceased father's line.

Naomi sees this ancient practice as a way to help her daughter-in-law, Ruth. She suggests that Ruth doll herself up in her best outfit and visit Boaz. Ruth does as she's told, and Boaz is impressed by this Moabite woman who shows so much love and loyalty to her mother-in-law — word of the plan had already gone around Judah and ultimately to Boaz himself (Ruth 3:1-3:15). Apparently news traveled fast even before cellphones and e-mail.

Happy endings

Boaz falls in love with Ruth's character. She is an honorable and virtuous woman, and Boaz finds these characteristics most attractive. He proposes marriage to Ruth. Scholars speculate that perhaps Boaz was more likely to marry and help Ruth, a foreigner, because his own mother had been a foreigner — his mother, Rahab (discussed in Chapter 10), had been instrumental in helping Moses, Joshua, and the Hebrews overtake Jericho to secure Israel.

There is one fly in the ointment, however. Although Boaz is a relative to Naomi and Ruth, there is another, unnamed relative who is more closely related to them. Boaz wants to marry Ruth and purchase the property Naomi wants to sell (her dead husband's land before they left for Moab during the famine), but the closer relative has first dibs on buying the place and on any marriage proposals.

Boaz is a shrewd negotiator. He approaches the other kinsman of Naomi and Ruth and asks him in front of witnesses if he intends to buy Naomi's property from her. The mystery man (we never find out who he is) says he does want to exercise his prerogative and purchase the land. Presumably, this relative knew Naomi was a widow whose sons also passed away and that she is well beyond childbearing years. What he probably didn't know, however, was that Naomi had a daughter-in-law, Ruth, who was also a widow and childless. Under levirate custom, a relative was to marry her and if a son were born, he would be the heir to the deceased father's legacy.

Ruth is something the kinsman didn't anticipate. Boaz is counting on him seeing only one way out of his dilemma. On the one hand, if the relative marries Ruth and she has a son, junior inherits the land his stepfather would have purchased from grandma Naomi. On the other hand, if he doesn't marry Ruth and buy the land, he will be violating the law that required the nearest relative to help the widow. When he thought there was just an elderly widow in the bargain (Naomi), he did not mind the thought of marrying her because she would not pose any threat by having an offspring who could claim the property for himself. Now that he knows there is a younger widowed daughter-in-law who is also part of the mix, his appetite disappears.

Boaz hoped this would happen: that the kinsman wouldn't want to buy the land from Naomi and marry Ruth because the firstborn son she would have would be the heir of the deceased first husband under levirate law. So Boaz offers to buy the land and marry Ruth as if offering a gentleman's way out of a difficult duty.

The relative doesn't know that Boaz loves Ruth and wants to marry her, purchase the property from Naomi, and raise their first son as the heir of Mahlon. All he knows is that custom required him to have preference in being the first to consider buying the land and in taking a widow as his own wife. Playing his cards well, Boaz has convinced the man to relinquish his claims to buying the property and to asking Ruth to marry him and instead allow Boaz to take on the "burden" (not knowing that Boaz is in love with Ruth).

After Ruth and Boaz marry, she gives birth to a son, Obed. Obed later becomes the father of Jesse, who in turn has a son named David. This David is the man who slays the giant Goliath and one day becomes King David of Israel, the father of King Solomon and an ancestor of Jesus. You can read this account in Ruth 4:13–17. Ruth isn't mentioned again until her name appears in the lineage of Jesus in the Gospel of Matthew (1:5). Her fame, though, is remembered in sacred art (refer the fresco shown in Figure 8-1), often depicting Ruth with her mother-in-law, Naomi, to whom she was a most devoted daughter-in-law.

Ruth's example

Naomi and Ruth didn't act like victims of circumstance. They didn't blame or curse God for their misfortune. Neither of them allowed tragedy to make them hard of heart, nor did it turn them into cranky old widows. The dynamic duo goes through major hardships — death, famine, and ostracism, to name a few — but their loyalty to one another and, ultimately, to God, ensures that their difficulties are transformed to joy over the course of their lifetimes. Ruth's fidelity to her mother-in-law, and her embracing of her mother-in-law's religion as well, makes Ruth, although born a foreigner, a shining example to converts as well as those born into the faith. Ruth and Naomi's names are still held in high respect to this very day by the faithful who read the Bible.

But Naomi was indeed discouraged at one point (heck, her husband and two sons died suddenly). She was so discouraged that she says, "Call me no longer Naomi [which means "pleasant"], call me Mara [which means "bitter"]" (Ruth 1:20). She was merely speaking about her unpleasant run of bad luck, however. Naomi never allowed the tough times to make her nasty or indifferent; it was just that she simply didn't enjoy the pains and suffering she had to endure. She shows that a person can be faithful and still not enjoy the misfortunes life may bring from time to time. Faithfulness, as Naomi and Ruth demonstrate, is not in taking pleasure in adversity but in bravely persevering.

Getting to Know Judith

Judith is one of the most unique and independent women in the Bible. Her incredible faith in God leads her to save the Hebrew nation. Her bravery is equal to that of any Biblical man. And her lifestyle is more akin to today's norms than those of the patriarchal society in which she lived. She is remembered for bravery, courage, and ingenuity in defeating the enemy, accomplishing what none of her male counterparts had the nerve to attempt.

The book of Judith can be broken into two parts. The first seven chapters of Judith detail the political and military doings of sixth century BC. These chapters supply a backdrop to the climate in which Judith lived. The remaining chapters discuss the role Judith played in saving her people and her nation from a powerful and dangerous enemy.

Judith enters the picture

Chapter 8 in the book of Judith introduces her as the daughter of Merari and the widow of Manasseh. Scripture says she was gorgeous, wealthy, and well-respected. A long genealogy is given, showing her prestigious Hebrew pedigree. Judith is a Jew living in Judea when Nebuchadnezzar ruled the Assyrians. He had asked the neighboring nations to help him in his war with the Medes, but many turned him down, including the Jews of Judea. Nebuchadnezzar wants to teach these nonconsenting Jews a lesson, so he sends his military chief of staff, Holofernes, to take care of them. Holofernes is warned, however, that the Hebrews have a powerful God and the only way to defeat them is to lure them into losing faith.

When the Hebrew people of the nation break God's laws and thus show religious infidelity, punishment results.

Holofernes comes up with a plan to cut off the water supply to the Hebrews. He hopes that after days of thirst and no relief, his adversaries will lose hope and trust in God and surrender (Judith 7:8–14).

Uzziah, the local Jewish religious leader, pleads with the people to wait five days before they abandon all hope and surrender to the Assyrians (Judith 7:30–32). But this offends Judith, who addresses the town elders and rebukes them for giving God a five-day ultimatum. She questions their judgment: How dare they give the Lord five days to rescue them or else threaten him with idolatry (Judith 8:9–17)? Judith reminds them of the many times that God has saved his people, despite their infidelity to him.

Some may question why Judith was the one to speak to the elders in this way, but the Bible doesn't comment on any reasons behind her bold actions. It does indicate that this woman is wealthy, and she probably comes from the upper class, but nothing more is explained about why she possesses some divine insight or intuition that enables her to see clearly what has to be done. No one but Judith saw any alternative to surrendering.

Saving her people

Judith decides to take action in the face of the elders' inaction. She fasts, prays, and wears sackcloth and ashes to do penance for the nation. Then she decides to use her beauty to her advantage. While the Israelites sit back and wait for the fifth day to arrive and then surrender, Judith hatches a brilliant plan to outwit Holofernes and defeat the Assyrian enemy before the Jews are wiped out according to Nebuchadnezzar's vendetta.

Before the fifth day comes, she gussies herself up in her finest linens and silks. Her beautiful body and face and stunning attire are breathtaking. If she can somehow lure Holofernes into a trap before the Israelites lose faith on the fifth day, all is not lost.

Judith leaves town to seek out Holofernes, going under the pretext that she wishes to defect before he attacks and destroys Bethulia. Dazzled by her beauty, he agrees to see her. She explains once again that the only way he'll succeed in his quest is if the Israelites sin against God. She assures Holofernes that, after a few more days with no food or water, the inhabitants will lose faith and slay animals to eat forbidden foods (non-kosher fare), and thus incur the wrath of God. She explains that only then can the commander march in and capture the city. (See Chapter 11 of the Book of Judith for more info.)

Meanwhile, her story is a ruse to spend time with him. Judith gets Holofernes to drink copious amounts of strong wine so that he passes out in his tent. The true reason for her meeting then becomes clear. She takes his own sword, decapitates the feared general, and hands the severed head to her maid who shoves it into her food bag! (Read this account in Judith 13:1–10.) This story gives a whole new meaning to "brown-bagging it."

Judith then slips out of the camp as if to go and pray, and none of the soldiers are the wiser. She returns to Bethulia with the severed head of Holofernes and instructs the town leaders to hoist the head of their enemy on the city wall. Then she tells them to fake an attack against Holofernes' army, knowing that the chain of command will require the officers to inform the supreme commander himself. (Judith 13:10–14:5 describes this story.)

When they discover their leader decapitated, the soldiers realize it was by a woman's hand and that she had escaped under their noses. The rank and file are completely demoralized, and mutiny and defections run rampant. The great army of the king of the earth is in utter disarray and shambles. Bethulia is saved thanks to Judith's wits, beauty, and bravery. Instead of surrendering in despair, she single-handedly saved her country from destruction and ruin.

Not only does Judith save her own people, but she also inspires others to follow the Hebrew way. Achior the Ammonite, the man who had originally warned Holofernes against attacking the Hebrews, is summoned to verify the identity of Judith's prized head. When he sees Holofernes' head, he passes out. He is so amazed and moved by Judith's accomplishment and God's will that he professes the faith and is circumcised a Jew. (You can read this account in Judith 14:6–10.)

Commemorating Judith

Every year on the eighth night of Hanukkah, after lighting the *hanukiah* (eight-candle menorah), *Ashkenasim* (Jews from the West) tell the story of Judith in Yiddish. *Sephardim* (Jews from the East) women traditionally gather on the seventh night to tell the story of Judith and eat cheese, pray, sing, and dance. Women are honored with being exempt from work on that eighth day because it was a woman, Judith, who saved the Jewish nation. The other seven nights of Hanukkah commemorate the victory of Judas Maccabeus and the Maccabees in 165 BC and the rededication of the Temple in Jerusalem.

Remaining independent

Judith is indeed an independent woman for her time. After her heroic acts, she receives many offers but never remarries, despite the fact that she is childless. It is believed that she remains unmarried to honor her dead husband. She is also the only woman of the Bible who has another woman (her maid) in charge of her estate. In fact, before her death, she disposes of her property and releases her servant from her obligations to make her a free woman.

Even though she displays much independent thinking and chutzpah — first for chastising the men who were willing to surrender and then by bravely killing the enemy — she also respects convention and tradition by observing the custom of praying, fasting, and wearing sackcloth before she embarks on her secret mission. She is bold and daring, yet still seeks to serve the Lord. Despite the fact that she flouts patriarchal society, her leadership is accepted and her ruse works because of her obvious faith in God.

Judith lives a long life (105 years), which is seen as a reward for her goodness. (For the particulars of her later years, see Judith 16:21–25.) She is remembered by Jews and Christians alike as a woman of bold and decisive action.

Esther: Becoming a Queen

Esther was a Persian Jew who lived in the fifth century BC during the *Diaspora*, which was the massive exile of three-quarters of the Jews from the Holy Land. During this time, being discreet (if not secretive) about your religion was very prudent, especially if you were Jewish. Anti-Semitism was prevalent wherever significant populations of Jews were present. Esther was born with the Hebrew name Hadassah, but her parents later gave her the name Esther. Despite her Persian name, Esther was a very devout Hebrew woman.

No other woman is mentioned as often in the Bible as Esther. Her name appears 56 times while the name of Sarah (see Chapter 9), herself a pivotal figure, appears only 54 times. Esther, who becomes queen, has a life filled with risk, bravery, and faith in God. Twice she risks death for her people. Esther could have kept quiet to save her own hide, but her faith doesn't allow her to remain safe while her people are threatened.

Esther's courage enables her to save her people from genocide during a time in which they had little or no power. Over the ages, her story has given hope to exiled Jews, encouraging them to practice their faith, even outside their homeland. The book of Esther also gives an explanation for the Jewish spring festival of Purim, which commemorates Esther's brave actions that saved the Jews.

The Book of Esther has eight main sections:

- ✔ The first section contains a prologue and Mordecai's dream.
- ✔ In the second section, Esther replaces Queen Vashti.
- ✔ Haman plots to destroy all the Jews in the third section.
- ✔ Esther and Mordecai pray to God for divine assistance in the fourth section.
- ✔ In the fifth section, God answers Esther and Mordecai's prayers.
- ✔ The tables are turned in the sixth section.
- ✔ In the last section, you find the epilogue.
- ✔ Last is the interpretation of Mordecai's dream.

Vying for the king's hand

During Esther's day, the Persian King Ahasuerus (Xerxes in Greek) ruled the kingdom. During the third year of his reign, the king has a 187-day feast to celebrate his victory over his enemies (those folks knew how to party). He has reason to celebrate: His Persian empire is extremely powerful and wealthy, and his palace is adorned with gold and silver and exquisite marble, not to mention fine Persian rugs.

TECHNICAL STUFF

Finding the Book of Esther

Six sections of the Book of Esther are found only in the Catholic and Orthodox Bibles as part of the Apocrypha, also known as the Deuterocanon (see Chapter 2 for an explanation of the Deuterocanon). These sections were found in the Greek Septuagint version of the Old Testament (250 BC). They're not currently included in Protestant Bibles or in Jewish scripture.

After much wine, the king summons Queen Vashti, his wife, so that he can show off her beauty, but she refuses to come. To refuse a royal summons was a big no-no indeed, and King Ahasuerus wasn't used to rejection. He immediately orders Vashti's removal from the palace and divorces her on the spot. (See Esther 1:10–22 for the story.) King Ahasuerus then seeks to replace her with a new wife. All the eligible virgin maidens of the realm enter a beauty contest, and Esther's Uncle Mordecai encourages her to vie for the king's hand. Esther enters the royal harem for consideration.

While in the harem, Hegai, the *eunuch* in charge (a castrated male; a eunuch was in charge of the harem because his physical condition made him no threat), gives Esther beauty treatments and a special diet so she'll overshadow the other women. After 12 months in the harem, Esther wins the king over. And so the beautiful, intelligent, and engaging Esther is chosen over all the other concubines to be the new queen. However, the king doesn't realize that Esther is Jewish, and she heeds her Uncle Mordecai's advice to hide her Jewish identity because anti-Semitism is still very prevalent (Esther 2:1–20).

Foiling an evil plot

In the meantime, a powerful and influential man in the king's court named Haman, the grand vizier, starts to cause problems. His status in the kingdom requires that ordinary citizens bow before him. One day he encounters Mordecai, Esther's uncle, and Mordecai refuses to bow. Mordecai explains that, as a Jew, he bows to no one but God. Ego bruised, Haman is outraged, and he seeks death not only for Mordecai but also for all Jews in the kingdom.

The evil vizier goes before King Ahasuerus and convinces him that the Jews in his kingdom are traitors and that they need to be eliminated as soon as possible. Haman is given the imperial seal to issue a death warrant for all the Jews. Mordecai is on the top of his list, and Haman has a huge gallows constructed to execute him, as well as the rest of his people. (See Chapter 3 of the Book of Esther, where this plot is detailed.)

Mordecai sends word of the death decree to Queen Esther, who fasts and prays for three days to discern what she should do next. She then uses her sharp intelligence to formulate a plan.

With her Jewish identity still a secret, Esther knows that if she reveals it carelessly, she will also become a victim of the death penalty. She understands that she must approach the king — and soon. Unfortunately, in those days, talking to your husband the king was more complicated than just calling his office. She had to approach him at court, which was fraught with risk — law dictated that only the king could issue a summons, and the queen had no right to appear at court on her own. By doing so, she risks death. Nonetheless, she is so moved by the potential plight of her people that she forges ahead with her plan. (See Chapter 4 of the Book of Esther, where more of this story is told.)

Esther knows that two things can happen when she appears at court. If the king extends his scepter to her upon her arrival, this gesture signifies that he welcomes her presence. If he withholds the scepter, he doesn't want to see the queen, and she faces execution for her show of disrespect.

Fortunately, Esther's gamble pays off. When he sees her, Ahasuerus extends his scepter in welcome. He not only tolerates her presence but also offers her the ultimate public display of affection, saying, "What is your request? It shall be given you, even to the half my kingdom" (Esther 5:3). Esther tells the king that she would like to host a banquet for his majesty and the grand vizier Haman. The king approves of her idea, and the dinner goes forward as planned. At its conclusion, Esther invites Haman over for a second dinner the following night. Haman is gleeful about his repeat invitation, believing he's getting in the good graces of the royal family. On his way home, Haman revels at the sight of the gallows, where his nemesis Mordecai is to be executed. Everything seems to be going his way, or so he thinks.

Exposing the rat

Later that night, the king can't sleep, so he requests that the royal chronicles be read aloud to him. His courtiers recount how a certain Mordecai had actually once saved King Ahasuerus's life by exposing a plot to assassinate him, but Mordecai was never rewarded for his act of loyalty. In fact, it was Haman who had reaped the rewards for saving the king's life, even though Mordecai had exposed the plot. (See Chapter 6 of the Book of Esther.)

The king summons Haman and asks him what kind of reward should be given to someone to whom the king wants to show gratitude for faithful service and loyalty. Thinking to himself, "Whom would the king wish to honor more than me?" (Esther 6:6). Haman gives a most elaborate reply:

For the man whom the king wishes to honor, let royal robes be brought, which the king has worn, and a horse that the king has ridden, with a royal crown on its head. Let the robes and the horse be handed over to one of the king's most noble officials; let him robe the man whom the king wishes to honor, and let him conduct the man on horseback through the open square of the city, proclaiming before him: "Thus shall it be done for the man whom the king wishes to honor."

—Esther 6:7–9

The King then throws Haman a curve ball. He commands that all the rewards Haman just suggested should be given to Mordecai the Jew for his former act of patriotism and loyalty. You can imagine the jaw of the vizier dropping to the floor. His worst enemy, the man he has planned to execute, is now to be given the royal treatment (literally). (Esther 6:6–13 describes these events.)

Because this command comes from the king, Haman must endure the ignoble shame of honoring his enemy. He must lead the horse upon which Mordecai rides. When it's over, Haman returns home with his head held low, and the soldiers whisk him away to the palace for his second dinner with the king and queen.

Confessing and protecting her people

It's time for Esther to spring her trap. While at dinner, King Ahasuerus again asks the queen what he can do for her. She decides to expose her secret, an act that once again puts her at great risk. Esther asks the king to spare the lives of all her people — and her own life, because she too is a Jew. She begs the king's mercy, explaining that neither she nor any of her fellow Jews has ever done anything close to treason against the throne. Her Jewish identity is now out in the open. (See Chapter 7 of the Book of Esther for this part of the story.)

The king responds by asking Esther who it is that's responsible for threatening her life — and the lives of all her people. She replies, "the wicked Haman" (Esther 7:6). The vizier's day then goes from bad to worse. When one of the eunuchs shows the king from his window the gallows where Haman intended to hang Mordecai, the king wreaks justice against Haman. "Hang him on that!" (Esther 7:9) Ahasuerus orders. Haman is then killed by the very instrument he intended to use against Mordecai. (You can find these incidents in Esther 7:1–10.)

But Esther isn't yet content, because the death decree is still in effect. She approaches the king and asks for his intervention. Unfortunately, the custom of the day prevents the king from rescinding an order previously given, but Ahasuerus does what he can. He issues another order allowing every Jew to defend himself, even with force of arms. When the order is implemented, the Jews fight back because they are allowed to keep swords as protection, and they defeat any attempt to exterminate them.

The festival of Purim commemorates when the Jews were allowed to defend themselves thanks to Esther's intervention. She is remembered every year around March 14 and 15, when Jews continue to celebrate Purim.

As further reward for his loyalty, Mordecai replaces Haman as vizier. Queen Esther continues as the beloved wife of King Ahasuerus. Esther could have laid low and kept her Hebrew origins secret to save her own skin, but she intervenes for her people and uses her political position as queen and the romantic connection with her husband, the king, to right an injustice. Queen Esther leaves the Bible stage at this point after the book of Esther ends, but her bravery and her invaluable assistance in saving her people are remembered not only by Jewish ritual but also in Christian art, which often depicts heroes of the Old and New Testaments. For more on Esther, and to see her portrayed in art, head to Chapter 23.

Minority report

Parallels exist between women in a patriarchal culture and the Jews during the Diaspora, as well as other periods in history. For example, in Persian culture at that time, women were basically powerless and vulnerable to the whims of their husbands. The Diaspora Hebrews (Jews) were also powerless and vulnerable as an exiled people as a whole, and they were under the same whims of their conquering rulers (which meant they were forbidden to have weapons, even for defensive reasons). Despite the disadvantages the Jews suffered, Esther, as a strong Jewish woman, helps to save her Jewish people.

Part III

Influencing Lives, Shaping History: Women of Faith and Power

The 5th Wave   By Rich Tennant

SARAH - Upon learning she was pregnant at the age of 90, becomes the Mother of Israel and coins the term, "Oy!", on the same day.

© RICHTENNANT

I'm what...?

In this part . . .

We tell you about the influential women of both the Old Testament (Hebrew Scriptures) and the New Testament of the Bible. You're introduced to matriarchs like Sarah, Rebekah, Rachel, and Leah. We show you how these women were not only biological mothers but also founding mothers of the Hebrew nation. You also meet the women who helped form the nation of Israel, beginning with the Exodus from Egypt with Jochebed (mother of Moses), Miriam (sister of Moses), and Zipporah (wife of Moses). The only woman to rule as Judge of the Hebrew people, Deborah, is included in this part, too. Here we discuss the women who persevere through adversity, trial, and tribulation, as well as the regal women who themselves rule or have great influence as members of the royal family. Finally, you meet the gals of the gospel, those women described in the New Testament books of Matthew, Mark, Luke, and John, and the other women of the infant Christian religion.

Chapter 9

Generating a Dynasty: The Matriarchs

• •

In This Chapter

▶ Joining Sarah on her long path to motherhood

▶ Observing Rebekah change the course of history

▶ Witnessing the stories of Rachel and Leah

▶ Meeting Tamar, whose bloodline produces Jesus Christ

• •

L ike your grandmother or mother, a matriarch is a woman who has a profound influence, directly or indirectly, on her family and subsequent generations. Women given the matriarch title are powerful because they inherited it, they married into it, they earned it, or they fought for it. Matriarchs like Queen Victoria of nineteenth-century England or the Empress Maria Theresa of the eighteenth-century Austrian-Hungarian Empire ruled by their wits and wealth, ensuring a dynasty through their children and grandchildren. The matriarchs mentioned in the Bible wore no crowns and did not sit on thrones, but through their deeds and their offspring they established lineages as powerful as any secular dynasty.

These matriarchs are also credited with cofounding the Judeo-Christian tradition and nurturing the creation of Israel. Sarah, Rebekah, Rachel, and Leah are considered the four matriarchs of the religion of Judaism, and Tamar is matriarch of a bloodline that later produces King David and Jesus Christ.

The bloodline that these matriarchs established would lay the foundation for the Jewish and Christian religions because both religions consider themselves spiritual offspring of Abraham and Sarah. Sarah's son, Isaac, would marry Rebekah, and their son Jacob, who married both Rachel and Leah, would father the 12 sons who later established the 12 tribes of Israel. (Israel is the name that God gave Jacob.)

The 12 tribes of Israel

Sarah's grandson, Jacob, had his name changed by the Lord to Israel, and his 12 sons and their large, influential families literally became the foundation of the 12 tribes of Israel. Each tribe or clan took its name from one of the 12 sons of Jacob, and each tribe occupied a different territory as their numbers grew. Eventually, ten tribes settled into what would later be known as the Northern Kingdom of Israel, while two tribes composed the Southern Kingdom of Judah. The Assyrians conquered the north in the eighth century BC and scattered the ten tribes so far and so well that they are now known as the "Lost Ten Tribes." The Babylonians conquered the south two centuries later.

Although women often achieve historical prominence through their marriages to important men, some biblical women are matriarchs in their own right, and they're known for their personal achievements, rather than those of their husbands. These women experienced the complexities of life still common in the modern world — childlessness, deception, challenging marriages, envy of the "other woman," and hard-to-handle children — but they still managed to remain grounded in their faith to God.

Strong-Willed Sarah: Wife of Abraham

Sarah, whose birth name is Sarai (Hebrew for "my princess"), is more than the wife of the biblical patriarch Abraham (who served as a key figure who connected Judaism, Christianity, and Islam). She's known in her own right for both her actions and words, which helped to influence history. The Bible discusses not only her status but also the pivotal role she played as a mother, wife, and devout believer. As grandmother to Jacob, who later fathered the 12 sons (tribes) of Israel, Sarah is, in fact, considered the ultimate matriarch of the Hebrew nation, the Kingdom of Israel, and Judaism as we know it today.

Traveling with Abraham

Sarah's arranged marriage to Abraham leads her through many cities (see Figure 9-1) — enduring many hardships along the way. The two begin their married lives in the city of Ur of the Chaldees (an ancient city of Mesopotamia located in what is now southern Iraq), but then God sends the entire family to Haran (present-day eastern Syria). (See Genesis 11:27–32 for more information.)

Next on Jerry Springer: Sarah and Abraham

There is continuing debate as to whether Sarah may have actually been related to Abraham. One theory posits that they're both the children of one father, Terah, but they have different mothers. Another theory speculates that Sarah is the niece of Abraham — the sister of Lot and the daughter of Haran, Abraham's brother. Regardless of her parentage, Sarah eventually married Abraham. Many scholars also believe that she probably came from some aristocratic background, based on her name and also on the fact that she and Abraham had an arranged marriage, a practice of the more influential families of the day.

If the speculations about her relationship to Abraham seem unsavory, marrying close relatives was actually not uncommon in ancient times, especially among nomadic peoples. Incest then was defined as marriage between a son and mother, a daughter and father, or a brother and sister who shared the same mother (sometimes called uterine siblings). Marriage between half siblings (by the same father), cousins, nieces and uncles, or aunts and nephews weren't considered incestuous until after the Law of Moses (called the Mosaic Law), which came centuries later.

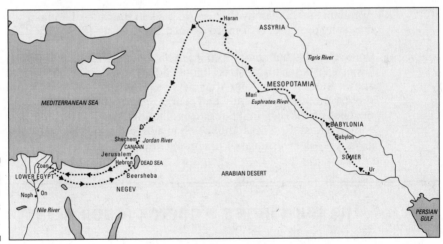

Figure 9-1: Abraham and Sarah's travels.

Sarah and Abraham are later directed by the Lord to move from Haran to the land of Canaan (which later became the Promised Land), but they're instructed to go alone, leaving behind the rest of the clan, except their nephew, Lot, and his immediate family, who come with them. (For the details, see Genesis 12.)

Life wasn't easy on the road, and yet Abraham and Sarah are forced to move again. A famine in Canaan pushes them on toward Egypt. The Bible implies that upon arriving in Egypt, Abraham begins to trust in human ingenuity more than upon Divine Providence. Instead of relying on God to care for his family, Abraham relies on his own wits, using deception when he first meets the ruler of Egypt, Pharaoh. When Pharaoh notices Sarah's stunning beauty, he is taken with her. But instead of admitting that Sarah is his wife, Abraham insinuates that she is his sister. Abraham makes this move to gain favor with Pharaoh; if viewed as a brother rather than a competitor, Abraham gains security and avoids potential rivalry with the ruler.

And indeed the ruse works. Although there may have been some truth to Abraham's claim — Sarah may have been his half sister, too (see the sidebar "Next on Jerry Springer: Sarah and Abraham," earlier in the chapter) — she is first and foremost his wife. Unfortunately for Sarah, Abraham's deceit lands her in Pharaoh's harem, where she is treated like property, while Abraham enjoys the spoils of his deception. Her captivity is seen by many biblical scholars to be a foreshadowing of the Israelite slavery in Egypt centuries later.

The fraud doesn't last long; God punishes Pharaoh for his adultery with Sarah by sending a plague. Pharaoh then figures out that he has taken another man's wife — a practice considered taboo, even for Egyptians at that time. Sarah is returned to Abraham, and the gang is deported from Egypt. Abraham and his family then settle back in the land of Canaan, as God had originally directed. (For more details, see Genesis 12:10–20.)

Ironically, Abraham has yet to learn his lesson. The hoax is repeated in Genesis 20, after the destruction of Sodom and Gomorrah, when Abraham allows another ruler, King Abimelech, to take Sarah as his wife under the pretext that they were only half brother and half sister. Whereas Pharaoh deduces on his own that Sarah is really Abraham's wife (after being besieged with plagues), God tells Abimelech in a dream about her marital status and gives a deadly warning not to commit adultery.

The third time's a charm: A son at last

In the sixteenth century AD, King Henry VIII broke with the Catholic Church and Pope in Rome by making himself supreme head of the church in England. He did this because his wife, Queen Catherine, couldn't produce a male heir (their only surviving child was Mary I). He divorced Catherine and married Anne Boleyn, who gave him only another daughter (Elizabeth I), so he later divorced her, too. He then married Jane Seymour (no, no, not Dr. Quinn, Medicine Woman), who was the mother of Edward VI. That was nearly 3,000 years after Sarah and Abraham, but the influence of the patriarchal society could still be seen. By contrast, Abraham remained a faithful husband to Sarah until she directed him to do otherwise.

This duplicity of Sarah's husband is an attempt on his part to save his life, while God intervenes with plagues, dreams, and threats to preserve this good woman despite her husband's political maneuvering. Sarah is rejoined with Abraham a second time. She remains faithful to both her husband and God and will later become as devoted as her husband, Abraham, to God's covenant. (See the section "Taking a new name," later in this chapter, for more on the covenant.)

Becoming a mother

Sarah is infertile, which creates a precarious situation for herself and her husband. Without sons, upon whom a patriarchal society depends, her family will have no dynasty and no future. Being childless was both dangerous and embarrassing in ancient times because it meant you'd have no one to care for you when you became too old to support yourself — and no one would be around to carry on the family name. Worried about this inevitability, the self-reliant Sarah comes up with a solution. She gives her slave girl, Hagar, (see Chapter 15) over to Abraham so that Sarah can obtain children by her, as described in Genesis 16:1–3.

This action isn't considered an act of bad faith. It is seen as a sacrifice of love: love of husband and love of nation. Sarah is willing to share conjugal rights and allow another woman to have her husband's son. Only after the birth of Ishmael, Hagar's son, does God reveal that Sarah would finally be a mother in the fullest sense and not just by surrogate. Even Paul extols her fidelity to husband, people, and God in his Epistle to the Hebrews: "By faith also Sarah herself, being sterile, received power to conceive, even beyond the age of childbearing years, since she considered the one having promised [God] faithful" (a literal translation of the original Greek; Hebrews 11:11).

Law codes from Nuzi tablets (ancient text from fifteenth century BC Mesopotamia), delineated the custom for a barren wife and described the practice of surrogate motherhood. The child born to the servant was to be considered the child of the wife and therefore regarded as legitimate.

Offering up her slave girl to her husband must have taken great strength of character for Sarah. Yet some people believe that she does this for the love of her husband and of her potential nation because, without a male heir, the lineage ends. Sarah is Abraham's only wife, she is beyond the age of child-bearing, and so the stability of the dynasty is threatened. The paradox is that God had promised Abraham he would be the father of many nations, and yet Sarah is apparently barren. By putting aside her own desire to have a child, Sarah embraces a broader perspective through the custom of the day — surrogate motherhood — to ensure the survival of the Hebrew nation.

Because she was willing to make such a difficult decision — allowing her maid-servant to have a child with Abraham — scholars often consider Sarah to be one of the "founders" of the Hebrew nation, along with her husband. As it turns out, the Jewish people are not traced to Hagar's son, Ishmael, but to Sarah's son, Isaac (whom she finally gave birth to at the age of 90). Despite the fact that it is Sarah's wish, Hagar's carrying Abraham's baby causes animosity between the two women. Sarah accuses Hagar of treating her with contempt, and she blames Abraham for not being more attentive to her needs in preference to his concubine. Abraham responds by giving Sarah permission to mistreat and abuse Hagar, who in turn escapes from her angry mistress. (For more details, see Genesis 16:4–6.)

To rectify the situation, God sends an angel to Hagar to convince her to return as Sarah's servant, as described in Genesis 16:11–12. Hagar does return and gives birth to Ishmael, whose name means "God hears." Ishmael, the son of Abraham and Hagar, will later become the father of the Ishmaelites, the ancestors of modern-day Muslims and believers of Islam.

Taking a new name

Sarai's name is changed to Sarah (and her husband's to Abraham) when, at 99 years old, Abraham makes a *covenant* (a sacred, permanent, and complete bond) with God, in which Abraham agrees to establish the Hebrew nation. (Genesis 17 has all the details.) Name changes are signs of new missions in life, signifying the importance of this covenant and of the new Hebrew nation, which will later become the Kingdom of Israel — and the home to the religion of Judaism.

Sarah's name change is subtle — from Sarai (which means "my princess") to Sarah (meaning simply "princess") — but it's important to note that Sarah is the only woman in the Bible to earn the distinction of having her name changed.

Like her husband's change of name from Abram to Abraham, Sarai's change to Sarah is not as dramatic as her grandson's (Jacob, who became Israel). Nonetheless, a change in name is very rare in scripture, and God is the one who makes the change, so that gives it some extra importance as well.

Soon after, the 90-year-old Sarah gives birth to a child, further underscoring her new mission (Genesis 17:17; 21:1–7).

Sarah has a son, whom she and Abraham name Isaac. But a family feud erupts. Ishmael, the son of the slave girl Hagar, is about 15 years old when Isaac is born, and allegedly mocks his baby brother, Isaac. Sarah orders that Hagar and Ishmael be banished, which causes Abraham great distress because he is very fond of Ishmael. But God assures him that if he gives in to Sarah's request, Ishmael will still become the father of a great nation himself.

Sarah's tenacious protection of son Isaac can also be seen as more than just maternal. Like her husband, she knows that through Isaac, the Hebrew people will become a nation. Sarah perceives Ishmael to be such a rival that she abuses Hagar to the point that she drives the mother and son away, thus leaving Isaac and his inheritance intact. Protective mothers may not always act rationally or logically, but their motivation is clear: love and devotion to their children. In this case, Sarah's motivation is also love and devotion to God's covenant with Abraham.

Succumbing to a broken heart

After becoming a mother for the first and only time at the ripe old age of 90, Sarah lives to the age of 127 years, according to Genesis 23:1. An old rabbinical legend from the Talmud says that she dies of a broken heart. (The Talmud is the collection of ancient extra-biblical rabbinical writings from the third century AD that are considered authoritative by many Jews; the Talmud is equivalent to the Christian Patristics, the writings of the church fathers from the first to fifth centuries AD) Allegedly, Sarah sees Abraham take their son Isaac to Mount Moriah, where God asks that the boy be sacrificed as a sign of complete loyalty.

Thinking that her only child is about to be killed at the hand of his own father, she supposedly dies of a broken heart. An angel stops Abraham, however, before he is about to slay Isaac, but it's too late for Sarah. Her husband and her son return to camp to find her dead. Abraham purchases a cave, where he buries his beloved wife and where he himself will later be interred. (For the details, see Genesis 22.)

Bible scholars still debate the accuracy of the ages provided in the Bible — such as Sarah living to age 127. Some experts claim that the Hebrew usage of exaggeration is merely a literary tool to express extreme old age, and that exact chronological age was never the intention of the sacred authors. Other scripture scholars maintain that the extremely long life spans recorded in the Bible decrease significantly as more men and women sin with more frequency and severity. The latter scholars view a shortened life span as a consequence of the accumulated sins of the human race.

Honoring Sarah

Sarah was physically unable to have children on her own. Her faith, however, is extolled even in the New Testament (she is mentioned in Romans 4:19, Romans 9:9, and 1 Peter 3:6). She never lost hope that somehow God would work things out. Divine intervention helped her get pregnant, but only after a long lifetime of barrenness and the cultural shame it brought. Her patience, despite many years of being considered barren, her perseverance despite being discarded twice by her husband, and her strength to defend her offspring and her own people are qualities that make her worthy of the title matriarch.

The memory of Sarah is still honored to this day. A mosque is built over her grave, where she lies beside her beloved husband, Abraham. According to the Qur'an (sometimes called the Koran; the sacred writings of Islam, which are believed to be the revelations of Allah to Mohammed) and Islamic tradition, Sarah is revered not because of her marriage to Abraham but because she was the "mother" of two great prophets, her son Isaac and her grandson Jacob, just as Hagar is revered for being the mother of the prophet Ishmael.

Wily Rebekah: Wife of Isaac

Rebekah, sometimes spelled Rebecca, is the daughter-in-law of Sarah, Abraham's wife. (Rebekah means means "noose" in Hebrew.) Rebekah is best known for her ingenuity, cunning, and ability to shape history — instead of allowing history to shape *her*.

We first meet Rebekah as Abraham's servant, Eliezer, comes upon her at a watering hole. Eliezer has been sent to find a suitable wife for Isaac, Abraham's son. (See more on this meeting in the next section, "From a watering hole to a wedding.")

Rebekah is at first seen as kind and beautiful. But she is also a woman of determination, which you shall later see when she schemes to secure the lineage of her younger son. Rebekah's tale serves as a reminder that all actions have consequences. Her conspiracy to steal a birthright for her younger son leads to a broken relationship with her eldest and the eventual departure of her youngest.

Nevertheless, Rebekah's actions do change the course of history, and although she uses questionable methods, her motivation isn't entirely selfish. Like her mother-in-law before her, she had a desire to preserve the fledgling Hebrew nation. She knows her sons better than anyone, even their father. She can see that the eldest is too immature, preoccupied, and disinterested to be the leader of a great people. The younger son has the determination, talent, drive, and capability to lead. It isn't his fault that his twin brother came out of the womb first, but it doesn't change the fact that whoever is born first gets the birthright.

Rebekah is as much a matriarch as Sarah in that they're mothers of great children who become leaders of the people. They're completely devoted to the family as such, and they put their personal interests behind those of their husbands, their children, and even their own people. Rebekah's intervention allows Jacob rather than Esau to continue the lineage.

From a watering hole to a wedding

Eliezer travels to Haran in search of a wife for Isaac. There, Eliezer stops at a local watering hole (literally — we're not talking about a bar here), and he prays to God. He says that whoever gives him and his camels a drink of water will be the future wife of Isaac. Rebekah soon appears, offering water to both Eliezer and his camels. Eliezer finds Isaac's match. He showers her with gifts of gold and tells her about his master, Abraham, and his master's son, Isaac.

Rebekah's family, especially her father and brothers, love her dearly, and they don't want her to leave, even though they share her joy in finding a good husband. They try to persuade her to stay in Haran rather than follow Eliezer, who seeks to bring her to Isaac in Canaan with Abraham. Besides their fondness for Rebekah, they may have been considering Isaac's inheritance as an only son. (For more details, see Genesis 24:15–55.)

If Rebekah stays with them and Isaac joins her, then their clan will benefit from the spoils of marriage. On the other hand, if she leaves, her family will not see her nor will they benefit from her husband's inheritance. Because Abraham is still alive, Isaac doesn't yet own the legacy. So perhaps Rebekah's family merely wants to wait until Isaac actually inherits the estate before they consent to the marriage. Regardless, she chooses to go with Eliezer immediately to visit Abraham and meet her future husband, Isaac. Whether she is totally motivated out of love for her fiancé or if a part of her can't wait to get away from her possessive father and brothers, no one will ever know for sure.

Although ancient weddings certainly didn't have the pomp and circumstance of today's Charles-and-Diana–style royal weddings, they were special in their own way. For example, Isaac honors Rebekah by consummating his marriage to her in the tent that belonged to his mother, Sarah. Isaac was a devoted son to his mother during her life and after her death, and this act represents a true honor to his new bride. (For more details, see Genesis 24:62–67.)

Following in Sarah's footsteps

Despite this early honor in her mother-in-law's tent, Rebekah later receives the same shabby treatment that Sarah encountered before her. Just as Abraham allowed Sarah to be taken by Pharaoh and then Abimelech under the pretense that she was merely his sister (see the section "Traveling with Abraham," earlier in this chapter), Isaac too portrays his wife, Rebekah, as his sister to guarantee protection for himself. He fears, just as his father did with Sarah, that his wife's beauty will make him a target, so he allows his wife to be taken by Abimelech (king of the Philistines) into his harem. (This Abimelech is most likely the son of the Abimelech who took Sarah.)

The famine that led Isaac to the Philistine country also makes him apprehensive about having a gorgeous bride.

The fraud is soon exposed when Abimelech catches the two lovebirds in a romantic embrace — not something a brother and sister ought to be doing. So he concludes the obvious: They're not siblings but spouses. (Read this story in Genesis 26:6–11.)

In each case, both Isaac and his father, Abraham, fear for their lives and are willing to sacrifice the virtues of their wives. Despite her husband's duplicity, Rebekah, like her mother-in-law, doesn't retaliate with infidelity or disrespect.

Rebekah shows strong character in that she is willing to endure even temporary injustice for a higher good (saving her husband's life if he was, indeed, in danger because of her beauty). Isaac most likely fears that the king will try to get him out of the way because of his marriage to the young, beautiful Rebekah. Even though nonexistent, the threat to his life is taken seriously by Isaac, enough to feign a brother-sister relationship. (For the details, see Genesis 26:6–11.)

Tricking her husband

Like her mother-in-law, Rebekah experiences infertility. But after 20 years, Isaac's prayers to God on behalf of his wife are answered, and Rebekah finally becomes pregnant — with twins.

The eldest twin, Esau, is a chip off the old block — a hunter, a jock, and an outdoorsman. Jacob, the younger son, is the tent dweller — academic, introverted, and a big thinker. Where Esau takes after dear old dad, Jacob is his mother's son, with all her wit and wisdom. Through Rebekah's prayers, God tells her that her two sons represent two nations, one stronger than the other. He also tells her that the elder, Esau, will serve the younger, Jacob. This cryptic prophecy takes time to unfold but comes to pass nonetheless.

Rebekah's two boys are the most competitive the world has ever seen. She favors the younger, Jacob, while dad gives more attention to the older son, Esau. But Esau is neither swift nor sensible when mother and son scheme to dupe the old man and cheat the birthright from him. First, sibling rivalry took a new turn among these twins when Jacob tricks Esau into surrendering his birthright as eldest son. After a long day of hunting, the elder brother (Esau) is so hungry for a hot meal that he agrees to 'sell' his birthright to his younger brother (Jacob). The price for the birthright? A bowl of porridge in exchange for the ancestral heritage! (See Genesis 25:29–34.)

Then, Rebekah hatches an *I Love Lucy* plan to have Jacob impersonate his brother. She contrives a conspiracy to dress Jacob so that the blind and hard-of-hearing Isaac, now on his deathbed, will think Esau has arrived for his final blessing. Given some animal skins and oils, nerdy Jacob is transformed into his brother Esau. Jacob brings his dad some cooked game, and although Isaac thinks he recognizes Jacob's voice, the disguise that Rebekah devised still fools the blind old man. The hairy hands (from the animal skins) and the odor (from the oils) appear to be Esau's. After supper, Jacob gives Isaac some wine and then receives the blessing intended for his brother. (For more details, see Genesis 27:1–29.)

Perhaps it's Rebekah's way of getting back at Isaac for the plot to pass her off as his sister, or perhaps it's a ruse to get the better-suited candidate, Jacob, the job as leader of the pack. Nevertheless, the plot works, and Isaac erroneously gives Jacob Esau's birthright.

As a result, Jacob must leave town for fear of Esau's revenge; Esau has vowed to kill his brother in retaliation for stealing his birthright. Jacob is sent by his father, Isaac, to stay with his Aramean uncle Laban, his mother's brother, in the town of Paddan-Aram (in Mesopotamia, near Haran). Although Rebekah doesn't want to say goodbye to Jacob, she also understands that Esau means business, so she arranges for his departure. This is the last time she will ever see her son. She spends the rest of her days with a son she betrayed and a husband she deceived, while her favorite son will not return until after she is already dead and buried. (For more details see Genesis 27:1–46.) This is the last we hear of Rebekah in the Bible.

Part of the mystery of the Bible is that it often doesn't give all the answers but many times prompts more questions. Although it was God's plan that Jacob get the blessing and birthright rather than his older brother, God didn't force or even persuade anyone to deceive or do anything immoral. Every human being has a free will, and God can use that free will to achieve his purposes even when humans go astray. The old saying "God can write straight with crooked lines or paint masterpieces with broken brushes and canvasses" is certainly true. This is the mystery — that God allows or permits evil or sin to occur because he knows that a greater good will come from it. Because God doesn't directly cause the evil, we call this his *permissive will* as opposed to his *ordained will*.

Rachel and Leah: Wives of Jacob

In addition to the fierce sibling rivalry between brothers (Esau and Jacob, discussed in the preceding section, "Tricking her husband"), the Bible also tells about the struggle between two sisters, Rachel and Leah. With the boys, competition fuels the flames; among the girls, it is daddy who is to blame. Laban, their father, uses these women to achieve his own ends and winds up pulling a fast one on Jacob. Both women eventually marry Jacob, and both will become matriarchs as a result of their offspring leading the nation. Both women also prove to be strong in character and wisdom.

Helping to shape a nation

Despite the sibling rivalry between Leah and Rachel and Jacob's obvious favoritism for Rachel, these two women helped shape the destiny of a nation and a people. Their children and the children of their servants became the foundation of the 12 tribes of Israel. Their personal struggles and challenges mirrored that of their future progeny and the subsequent kingdom. Israel as a nation, kingdom, and people later experienced similar disappointment, betrayal, rejection, and suffering but also endured as the people of the covenant, the Chosen People. Rachel and Leah helped make that happen, and their lives also reflected the growth and growing pains the nation would soon undergo. Just as there was tense rivalry between the two sisters, so there was some strong competition among the clans and tribes that composed the Israelite nation. Just as the mothers of the 12 sons of Jacob (also known as Israel) competed with each other, so, later, did the 12 tribes compete. The Danites (members of the tribe of Dan) rumbled with the Benjamites (members of the tribe of Benjamin) and so on.

Meeting Rachel; marrying Leah

When Jacob, Rebekah's son, first meets Rachel, his Uncle Laban's beautiful daughter, it is love at first sight. He even gives her a kiss (Genesis 29:11), which seals their hearts forever.

Smitten by love, Jacob makes a deal with Laban to stay and work for seven years, at the end of which he will be given the hand of his beloved Rachel in marriage. Meanwhile, it is soon clear that Laban definitely shares some family traits with his wily sister, and he begins plotting in true Rebekah style. The deception involves the beautiful Rachel and Laban's older daughter, Leah.

Seven years go quickly for a man in love, and Jacob prepares for marriage to Rachel. On the wedding night, however, Laban double-crosses Jacob, disguising his eldest daughter Leah for Jacob's true love, Rachel. Because the bride wears a veil covering her face, Jacob doesn't realize that he married the wrong sister until the morning of the honeymoon. And Laban's big con is successful.

But Jacob isn't deterred, even when Laban tries to justify his deception, explaining that custom dictates that he marry off the older daughter before the younger. Now Laban tries to use the customs of the day — which Jacob himself had formerly disregarded by tricking his brother — to rationalize his own deceitful actions. Ironic, isn't it? (For more details, see Genesis 29:21–30.)

But Jacob is still madly in love, so he commits to another seven years of service to Laban for Rachel's hand in marriage. Finally, 14 years after their first kiss, Jacob marries his first and true love, Rachel. Leah remains his first wife. Both sisters, however, will enter a sibling rivalry second to none when it comes to procreation.

Struggling for favor

Although it wasn't Leah's fault, Jacob blames Leah for Laban's deception. He offers Leah little affection while still doting on her beautiful sister, Rachel. God, however, takes pity on Leah and blesses her with fertility, giving her and Jacob six sons and a daughter, but Rachel remains barren for many years, until she finally gives birth to two sons.

The sisters also resort to using aphrodisiacs (which are called *mandrakes* in Genesis 30:14) in a contest to have Jacob's children. Leah is the first to have children, which makes her sister, Rachel, envious. Rachel at that time is unable to conceive so, to catch up with her sister, she gives her maid, Bilhah, to Jacob as a wife, who mothers two more sons for Jacob. Leah is no longer able to have her own children, so she reciprocates and has her maid, Zilpah, give birth to two sons from Jacob.

Rachel has 2 children, Leah has 7 children, and their respective servants have 4 children between them. Altogether, the four women produce 12 sons and 1 daughter for Jacob.

These 12 sons of Leah and Rachel (and their servants) become known as the 12 tribes of Israel (see Figure 9-2) after God changes Jacob's name to Israel when he wrestles an angel, as described in Genesis 32:23–32. These 12 tribes stemming from the 12 sons are the foundation of the Israelite nation and kingdom.

Escaping Laban

Neither Rachel nor Leah remains fond of their father, Laban, after his deception and the havoc he wreaked on their lives. Not only did he trick Jacob into marrying the wrong wife the first time, but after 14 years of service, neither Jacob nor his wives see a penny of his profit (the wages and livestock Jacob should have been given), which Laban has hoarded for himself. So the sisters and Jacob sneak away from Laban's house in the middle of the night. Unbeknown to Jacob, Rachel pilfers some of her dad's golden idols. (Genesis 31:1–21 provides all the details.)

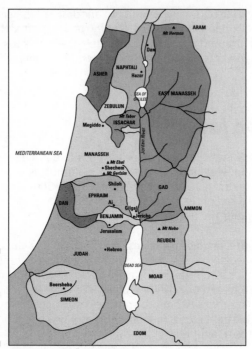

Figure 9-2:
The
territories of
the 12 tribes
of Israel.

Laban pursues his daughters and son-in-law and eventually finds them. Rachel literally sits on the idols when her father enters the tent, and makes an excuse not to get up. Several Bible commentators hypothesize that she probably hoards these for superstitious or sentimental value, rather than for their trade-in value.

Laban and Jacob eventually come to an impasse, forcing them into a peace treaty. Rachel and Leah (see Figure 9-3 for one artist's portrayal of them) and their children leave safely with their husband, Jacob, and depart from their father for a second time, never to see him again. These sisters, while different, are united in their love for their new family. Both sisters leave their father and brothers behind and move away with one husband between them. Though escaping devious dad may have held some attraction, moving away from life-long family connections will be no walk in the park. Nevertheless, Rachel and Leah come together despite their differences and do what is right — obeying the Lord, who had commanded Jacob to pack up and leave.

Rachel dies giving birth to her second son, Benjamin (Genesis 35:16–20). The Bible mentions Leah only one more, when she is buried near Jacob in the same place with Abraham and Sarah and Isaac and Rebekah (Genesis 49:31).

Figure 9-3:
Rachel and Leah by Dante Gabriel Rossetti (1828–1882).

Tate Gallery, London / Art Resource, NY

Tough Tamar: Mother of Perez

Tamar is a Canaanite woman who married Er, the eldest son of Judah (one of the 12 sons of Jacob, who came to represent one of the 12 tribes of Israel). A resourceful woman who remained courageous despite the treachery of some of her relatives and contemporaries, Tamar perseveres and becomes a matriarch whose bloodline eventually produces King David and Jesus himself. (Matthew 1:2–16 explains the family tree.)

Tamar is a woman who doesn't let human law prevent her from defending her rights and dignity. She uses her own wits and wiliness against the often corrupt, unscrupulous, and unreliable men of her time.

The relevance of her actions can't be underestimated, as she preserves the bloodline that eventually led to the birth of Jesus, whom Christians consider the Messiah — the eventual savior of all women and men, Jew and Gentile alike.

In reading about Tamar, you can see that her ingenuity and tenacity give her the strength to persevere despite almost overwhelming obstacles and disappointments. She proves that women can be as wise, astute, and clever as their male counterparts in using the system to their benefit. She is a model to anyone who experiences adversity, tragedy, opposition, and frustration, and she serves as an example of one who never gives up or becomes too discouraged. Rather, Tamar takes her destiny into her own hands and does what she needs to do to survive.

Losing two husbands

Tamar's husband, Er, does something to offend God — though the Bible doesn't say what — and Er is struck dead because of his sin, leaving Tamar childless. At the time, the law of the land, levirate law, dictates that one of her husband's brothers should marry her, becoming a surrogate father. So Er's brother Onan (another of Judah's son's) takes Tamar as his wife. Unfortunately for Tamar, Onan isn't eager to have a son because the law also dictates that any son produced is still legally considered his dead brother's. Thus, this son receives any family inheritance. With no offspring, the property goes to Er's surviving brothers, Onan being one of them. (See Genesis 38:1–9 for the story.)

Levirate marriage was a long-practiced patriarchal custom in the ancient Middle East. Some considered this practice an obligation, while others looked at it as optional. To protect the bloodline of a married man who died childless, his closest relative was supposed to marry and impregnate his widow. The first son born of this union was considered the son of the childless (dead) husband and inherited not only any property but also his name. Subsequent children belonged to the woman and her second husband.

Motivated by greed, Tamar's second husband also offends God, suffering the same fate as the first. While consummating the marriage, he performs *coitus interruptus*:

> *But since Onan knew that the offspring would not be his, he spilled his semen on the ground whenever he went in to his brother's wife, so that he would not give offspring to his brother. What he did was displeasing in the sight of the LORD, and he put him to death also.*

> —Genesis 38:9–10

Onan's legacy is not one that many men would envy. His sin before God — preventing his wife from conceiving by removing himself before the conjugal act was completed — became forever known as *onanism*. Quite a namesake.

Shelah is the next son of Judah in line to marry Tamar, but he isn't yet old enough to take over his husbandly duties when Onan is struck dead. Tamar's father-in-law, Judah, asks her to wait patiently for him and then sends Tamar to live as a widow at her parents' home (Genesis 38:11).

According to custom, if a man has no son over 10 years old, he can perform the levirate obligation himself, but if he does not, the woman is declared a free widow and may marry again. Judah could have released Tamar because two of his sons had already died and the remaining son, Shelah, is too young to marry her, but he chooses not to do so. Tamar can't remarry, and she must remain chaste. Tamar suspects that her father-in-law will never allow his remaining son to marry her, because the other two sons died soon after marrying her. Her future is up in the air.

Outsmarting Judah

Tamar takes her marital situation into her own hands, and she outsmarts Judah. During the years after his sons' deaths, Judah's wife had died as well. After a period of grieving, he takes a trip to have his sheep sheared. The trip takes him past Tamar's town, where she is still living in limbo with her parents. She forms an idea for vindication. She takes off her widow's garment and puts on a new dress and veil, positioning herself outside the temple area where Judah will pass. He sees her (see Figure 9-4 for one artist's depiction), thinks that she is a temple prostitute, and has sexual intercourse with her. He has no money with him, so he leaves her a pledge — his signet ring and a cord and staff — items of good faith akin to leaving a credit card and driver's license. (See Genesis 38:12–19 for the details.)

The next day, he sends payment with his servant, but the servant can't find the prostitute to retrieve Judah's personal effects. No one ever owns up to being the prostitute, so Judah dismisses the event and never retrieves his things. Meanwhile, Tamar soon discovers she is pregnant. Three months go by, and Judah hears through town gossip that Tamar, his daughter-in-law, is now pregnant. Judah, of course, doesn't know that he is the father or that Tamar is the woman he slept with! He shows righteous indignation and calls for her execution.

Tamar had planned for this possibility, however, and asks Judah to find the owner of the signet ring, cord, and staff from the man she had slept with. He realizes now that he is the father. He is also the one who had refused to allow Tamar to marry his son Shelah, which would have prevented this predicament. Judah now does the honorable thing and takes care of Tamar and her soon-to-be-born twins: "She is more in the right than I, since I did not give her to my son Shelah" (Genesis 38:26).

Figure 9-4:
Judah and Tamar by Gerbrand van den Eeckhout (1621–1674).

Erich Lessing/Art Resource, NY

Tamar's cleverness allows her to protect the lineage, giving birth to twins, Perez and Zerah. She thus restores two sons to Judah, who had lost Er and Onan to their sins against God. Perez will become a direct ancestor of King David and, later, Jesus Christ.

Chapter 10

Spawning a Kingdom: Women of the Hebrew Nation

In This Chapter

▶ Mothering Moses with Jochebed

▶ Playing prophetess with Miriam

▶ Saving Moses' life with Zipporah

▶ Helping save the Israelites with Rahab

▶ Going into battle with Deborah

Moses, who led his people to Israel approximately three millennia ago, had a few good women who helped him along the way. And he needed their help. After all, his trip hadn't been easy. First, he had to free his people from slavery in Egypt. Next, he endured 40 years of wandering the desert. And after that, there certainly wasn't any rest for the weary. Moses, however, did not live long enough to see or enter the Promised Land. His successor Joshua, on the other hand, led the Hebrews across the Jordan River and then had to go to war against the people of Jericho, as well as a few other cities, because they were attempting to stand in the way of God's prophecy that his people make it to the Promised Land.

Luckily for Moses, he had strong women around to help. From Moses' very first breath, his mother, Jochebed, was plotting to protect him, despite the edicts of Pharaoh. The other women who played important roles in his life were Miriam, his sister; and Zipporah, his wife. Rahab, a prostitute; and Deborah, a Judge, were other women who had pivotal parts in Hebrew history. All five of these women served to help secure Israel and defend the infant nation against invaders. In this chapter, we take a look at these women and how their actions helped to create and maintain the chosen land.

Triumphant Jochebed: Mother of Moses

Jochebed's name appears only twice in the Bible (Exodus 6:20 and Numbers 26:59), but her story is significant. It's told in Exodus 2, where she is identified merely as the wife of a Levite (Amran). She has already given birth to a daughter, Miriam, and a son, Aaron, and now she has a new baby boy.

Jochebed lives during a time in which Pharaoh, the ruler of Egypt, harbors ill will toward the Hebrews. The dynasty that ruled Egypt when the Israelites moved to the kingdom to escape famine and that welcomed them as neighbors was replaced by an unfriendly dynasty. Since Jacob's time, the 12 tribes of Israel had grown significantly (see Rachel and Leah's story in Chapter 9 for more on these tribes), and the Hebrew population had flourished.

Pharaoh views this growth as a threat, so he first enslaves the Hebrews and then issues a decree to midwives to kill newborn Hebrew males. This decree is an attempt to significantly reduce the non-Egyptian population.

Instead of blindly following Pharaoh's horrible edict, Jochebed, a Hebrew mother, places her faith in God (see Exodus 2:1–4). Her act of faith ultimately saves Moses and the future nation of Israel. Without Jochebed's courage and ingenuity, Moses would have been killed.

Jochebed's two older children, Miriam and Aaron, also play important parts in salvation history, but Moses takes center stage as the one who leads the enslaved Hebrews out of Egypt and toward the Promised Land. A devout Hebrew, Jochebed instills the love of faith and a sense of duty and responsibility in all of her children, not only in Moses.

Placing her faith in God

Jochebed is unwilling to allow her infant son to be killed per the Pharaoh's royal decree. After giving birth, she makes a bold plan to save his life: She fashions an ark from papyrus, bitumen, and pitch and places her beloved infant son in the basket. This baby boat is watertight but not airtight, so the little fellow can still breathe. With no idea what will happen, yet not wanting him to be drowned in the river by the Pharaoh, Mom sets the basket afloat in the mighty Nile River and sends daughter Miriam to follow discreetly from a safe distance. As Divine Providence would have it, that same day, the adult daughter of Pharaoh is bathing in the Nile and discovers the child. (See Exodus 2:1–6 for this story.)

Certainly the princess can deduce that this baby is a Hebrew boy whose mother is trying to save him from Pharaoh's death sentence. But the Egyptians regard the Nile as a sacred river because it brings needed water to such an arid place, allowing crops to be grown. When she finds a baby in the Nile, Pharaoh's daughter considers it an act of the gods.

Jochebed shows incredible faith when she places her beloved son into a homemade basket and sets him adrift in the crocodile-infested waters of the mightiest river of Egypt. Though she has no guarantee this scheme will work and isn't working from divine blueprints, her act is one of hope, trust, and prayer that God will spare her child the cruel fate that thousands of Hebrew infant sons have already suffered.

Reaping the rewards of selflessness

When the childless princess sees Moses floating in the river, she decides to adopt him as her own. Jochebed, however, gets the chance to act as Moses' wet nurse in place of the princess (who has no milk). After Moses is weaned, Jochebed acts selflessly again, giving Moses up to the princess to be raised. But perhaps it's their initial mother/son bond that ultimately returns Moses to his Hebrew faith, despite the fact that he lives most of his life in Pharaoh's palace.

The Hebrews view the fact that Moses was nourished by his own mother's milk as evidence of God's great plans for him to one day deliver his people from the bondage of slavery.

The Bible doesn't mention Jochebed again, but it's not improbable that she may have lived long enough to accompany her son during the great Exodus from Egypt.

Fearless Miriam: Sister of Moses

We first meet Miriam when she is sent by Jochebed to discreetly guard the basket that's carrying her baby brother, Moses, down the Nile (see the section, "Placing her faith in God," earlier in this chapter). Although a young girl, probably not yet a teenager, Miriam shows great composure and responsibility. Miriam was the eldest child of Jochebed; next came her brother, Aaron, and, finally, Moses.

Throughout her life, Miriam demonstrates religious strength. Overall, she is an obedient daughter, a devoted sister, a prophetess, and leader of worship. Indeed the last two roles were revolutionary for women of her time. Miriam shows us what family feuds can do to one's well-being, and more important, she demonstrates religious strength despite her mistakes. It isn't easy being a Hebrew slave in Egypt and still trusting that God will one day deliver his people. She possesses the moral virtue of fortitude that enables a person to be strong in times of oppression, persecution, and suffering. She also rallies the troops when her enslaved people flee their captors in the great Exodus.

Saving the day

When Moses is sent away in his floating bassinet, Miriam closely monitors his progress. She watches carefully from a distance — close enough but not too far — to ensure that neither man nor beast harms the future deliverer of the Hebrew people.

When Pharaoh's daughter finds baby Moses, Miriam springs into action. Without revealing that she is the baby's sister, Miriam offers to find a suitable wet nurse until the princess can take over as his adopted mother. By thinking on her feet, Miriam ensures that Moses is brought back to his natural mother, Jochebed, to be nursed. (See Exodus 2:5–9.) With courage and smarts, Miriam guarantees that Moses is still connected, at least for some time, to his Hebrew birthright.

The Pharaoh's daughter names the baby Moses, which means "from the water" (Exodus 2:10).

Offering her service

After Moses grows up in Pharaoh's palace, he leaves to pursue his destiny — leading the Hebrew people out of Egyptian slavery. See Figure 10-1.

At this time, Miriam and Moses are reunited. Miriam once again offers her service and shows her faith in God. Here she plays a significant role as prophetess of the Lord.

In biblical times, "prophet" or "prophetess" had a different context than it does today. Instead of meaning someone who predicts the future, as it is most commonly known today, a _prophet_ in biblical times meant one who was a messenger of God and spoke in his name. So although God blessed Miriam with this gift, she wouldn't have made it on today's psychic hotline.

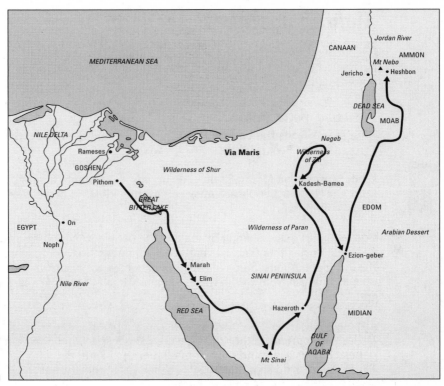

Figure 10-1:
The possible
route of the
exodus led
by Moses.

By singing an inspiring hymn to encourage the Hebrews as they flee slavery in
Egypt during the great Exodus, Miriam demonstrates her role as prophetess.
That hymn is inspired by God and is recorded in the inspired written word of
scripture. She rallies the troops and keeps them focused as they leave Egypt —
otherwise there would have been chaos, confusion, rioting, and looting. Almost
like a lighthouse that guides ships safely to shore through a treacherous fog,
Miriam sings and directs the people to follow her brother Moses. Like Moses,
Miriam gives guidance in time of need and demonstrates her faith and praise of
God.

*Then the prophet Miriam, Aaron's sister, took a tambourine in her hand;
and all the women went out after her with tambourines and with dancing.
And Miriam sang to them: "Sing to the LORD, for he has triumphed glori-
ously; horse and rider he has thrown into the sea."*

—Exodus 15:20–21

Making mistakes

Despite her heroic deeds, strong leadership, and strong faith in God, Miriam isn't perfect. And just like any imperfect human, including Moses himself, she makes mistakes.

Resenting Moses' power

After Moses leads the Chosen People from the bondage of Egyptian slavery across the Red Sea, trouble begins brewing.

While Moses is on Mount Sinai receiving the Ten Commandments from the Lord, the Hebrew people are busy committing idolatry, debauchery, and all kinds of immorality.

God punishes this evildoing by making the people wander in the desert for 40 years. During this time, the natives become restless, complaining about the living conditions. Some of the griping comes not just from the common people, but also from within the First Family itself — specifically, from Miriam and Aaron.

Although Miriam is a prophetess and Aaron a priest of the tribe of Levi, only Moses has supreme authority and enjoys the respect and obedience of the populace. This leaves no room for collaborative authority with Miriam and Aaron. There is no sign that Moses abused his authority, but the Bible does make it evident that Miriam and Aaron as sister and brother to the Lawgiver (Moses) felt slighted by the absolute authority and respect their brother receives. Even Jesus himself would say centuries later, "Prophets are not without honor, except in their hometown, and among their own kin, and in their own house" (Mark 6:4). Miriam and Aaron forget that the people hadn't chosen Moses and neither did he seek this office of leadership himself. God had chosen Moses, plain and simple.

> *While they were at Hazeroth, Miriam and Aaron spoke against Moses because of the Cushite woman whom he had married (for he had indeed married a Cushite woman); and they said, "Has the LORD spoken only through Moses? Has he not spoken through us also?"*
>
> —Numbers 12:1–2

Nevertheless, some Bible scholars speculate that Moses may have some weaknesses that his siblings exploited, out of envy that Moses is becoming too big a figure for his own good. Miriam knows his idiosyncrasies, his character flaws, his Achilles' heel. She knows better than anyone that Moses isn't perfect, that he isn't sinless, and that he does make mistakes. Despite the fact that God blesses her with her own gifts, human nature makes Miriam more than ready to knock Moses down to size — and she does so publicly. Sadly, personal pride is what motivates her to question Moses' ultimate authority in God's eyes.

Chastising Moses

Miriam also may have resented Moses' foreign wife, Zipporah. Culturally and religiously, the Hebrews mistrusted foreigners because their experience with them had been quite painful in the past. Foreigners had attacked, killed, and enslaved Hebrews. Foreigners had foreign gods, whereas the Hebrews were the Chosen People of the one true God (as they saw it, at least). Marrying outside your clan — let alone outside your faith — was considered tantamount to treason in many minds back then. Miriam's resentment toward a foreigner (Zipporah) who was the wife of her brother was understandable, considering the ways of their society. Miriam probably resented Zipporah even more because she figured that Moses, as the religious leader of the Hebrew nation, should be setting an example. Another issue was no doubt the solidarity of the Hebrews, who were all slaves in Egypt, while the foreign wife of Moses knew nothing of slavery.

The Hebrews were a minority in ancient times because of their monotheistic religion (belief in one God), as compared to the polytheistic pagan religions (belief in many gods or deities) of their contemporary neighbors. To Hebrews, religious fidelity and purity meant not diluting the religion. Mixed marriages weren't strictly forbidden, but they were discouraged due to the dangers inherent in compromising the Jewish faith.

Miriam and Aaron were concerned that Moses' foreign wife might weaken his faith, or at least encourage other Hebrews to marry foreigners instead of selecting a spouse within the same faith and ethnic background.

In any event, their outspoken dislike of Moses' wife is most likely a pretext for their resentment of his power in general. Miriam and Aaron seize the opportunity to speak against Moses for marrying this Cushite woman. "They said, 'Has the LORD spoken only through Moses? Has he not spoken through us also?' And the LORD heard it" (Numbers 12:1–2).

Moses at that time was God's spokesperson. Unlike other prophets (and prophetesses like Miriam) whom God spoke to through dreams and visions, Moses was spoken to directly, face to face by the Lord. This fact didn't go over well with Miriam and Aaron.

Not only did the Hebrew people hear them, but so did God himself. He goes about setting these two straight: "Suddenly the LORD said to Moses, Aaron, and Miriam, 'Come out, you three, to the tent of meeting'" (Numbers 12:4).

God then speaks directly to Miriam and Aaron (for the first and only time) and informs them that although he may speak to them in dreams and visions, only Moses has seen the Lord with his own eyes. Moses alone gets a face to face with the Almighty while his sister and brother must settle for indirect communications. With this explanation, God reaffirms Moses' supreme authority.

Suffering her punishment

Questioning the legitimacy of Moses' primacy means challenging God himself. Because of her prideful attack on Moses' authority, Miriam is punished with a form of leprosy. Despite their mutiny, Moses still loves his sister and brother, and he pleads with the Lord for mercy on their behalf. God does heal Miriam of her affliction, but not until she suffers for seven days, during which time the community shuns her. After the leprosy leaves her, she is reunited with the people, and they continue their journey. (This story is told in Numbers 12:10–15.)

Leprosy was considered a catastrophic illness all the way up to the early part of the twentieth century (when treatments and cures were finally developed). Before that, the illness was considered highly contagious and always lethal, so people who contracted leprosy had to be quarantined. They lived outside of towns and cities, where they had neither protection nor comforts. Lepers not only had an incurable disease, but they were also considered untouchable and thus became the ultimate social outcasts.

Miriam is only mentioned one more time, in Deuteronomy 24:9 as a warning against challenging God's prophet. Her brief period of leprosy is used as a reminder not to imitate her prideful opposition to Moses' authority. Overall, however, despite her one bad decision at the end, the Bible records most of her life as a positive one, and she remains a woman of faith — with a few spiritual blemishes and imperfections in her track record.

Virtuous Zipporah: Wife of Moses

When Moses flees into the desert after killing an Egyptian (thus proving his devotion to the Hebrew people), he runs across some daughters of Jethro (also called Reuel), a priest of Midian and of Arab descent. The daughters are tending their father's flock near a well. Some hooligans come around and harass the ladies until Moses chases them away. Jethro (Reuel) is so grateful for Moses' intervention that he gives one of his daughters, Zipporah, to Moses as his wife. The two marry and have a son, Gershom, and later another, Eliezer. (See the account of these events in Exodus 2:16–22).

Zipporah abandons her family and friends for the sake of her husband, Moses. She endures many hardships, including living with her husband's divided attention and enduring the criticism of her sister-in-law and brother-in-law. She could have retaliated against their resentment, but she doesn't. And she could have kept her old ways and traditions, but she embraces the faith and customs of Moses.

Zipporah proves to be a good, loyal, strong, and supportive spouse. Her courage may not be as obvious as that of her sister-in-law, Miriam, but Zipporah is nonetheless as courageous and steadfast in her efforts to support Moses' cause. Although Moses may be married more to the nation as the Deliverer and Lawgiver than to his wife, Zipporah is strong enough to make the necessary sacrifices for the greater good.

Circumcising Eliezer

A few years after Moses marries Zipporah, he begins his return to Egypt to attempt to free his people from slavery. Zipporah and her two boys accompany him. However, God is angry with Moses and threatens to end his life, because he has neglected to circumcise his son Eliezer as per God's covenant with Abraham generations before. (This story of the covenant is told in Genesis 17:9–14.) Moses' non-Hebrew wife, Zipporah, performs the circumcision on Eliezer. (Head to Exodus 4:24–26 for details of this.)

Zipporah's action is exceptional. Normally, Hebrew law dictates that circumcision be performed by the father and before the son is 8 days old. No other reference in the entire Bible indicates a woman performed a circumcision.

But why did Moses fail to have his son Eliezer circumcised, a rite that is a sign of the covenant? Perhaps it is because of his many years of being raised by the Pharaoh's daughter in the Egyptian tradition or the fact that he married into a non-Hebrew family.

Why Moses neglected his son's circumcision is not known. In any event, Zipporah, through God, becomes aware of her husband's religious transgression and quickly averts disaster. She becomes a mediator between God and Moses, just as Moses did when God threatened to destroy his people over idolatry. Her actions save Moses' life and his destiny to lead the Hebrews out of slavery, all of which ultimately influences the fate of the Promised Land.

Zipporah remains an enigma in the fact that she is sent away by Moses (Exodus 4:20) before the Exodus and is reunited only after the Exodus from Egypt has taken place (Exodus 18:6). The reason for the separation is never given, but some scripture scholars speculate that Zipporah's expedient move to save her husband by circumcising their son may have embarrassed Moses, because he should have done it himself long ago.

Circumcision, which refers to the practice of cutting the foreskin from the penis, was a widespread practice in the ancient Near East. In the Book of Genesis, Abraham is circumcised and so carries the sign of the covenant with God. Circumcision is also a sign of identification with and membership among the people of Israel.

Withstanding criticism

Zipporah also survives the (arguably) unfair criticism of Moses' siblings, Miriam and Aaron. (See the section "Chastising Moses," earlier in this chapter.) Although Zipporah may not have been born on the right side of the tracks for the likes of Miriam and Aaron, she nonetheless remains faithful to Moses and his cause despite what is surely an unpleasant family dynamic. It is clear that God intervenes on Zipporah's behalf and punishes Miriam (see the section "Suffering her punishment," earlier in the chapter). And after Miriam's punishment, Zipporah no longer suffers unfair criticism from Moses' siblings.

Biblical scholars debate whether it was really Zipporah (or another woman) whom Moses' siblings derided during their sibling rivalry. Some scholars propose that Moses may have eventually taken a second wife, though detractors of this theory claim that not enough evidence is available to support this fact.

This is the last we hear of Zipporah in the Bible. As the wife of Moses and the mother of his two sons, Gershom and Eliezer, she is remembered for her fidelity to her husband and family, and although not a Hebrew by birth, she is as good and loving a wife and mother as any of her contemporaries. She shows that even a "foreigner," as her in-laws called her, was capable of having faith.

Helpful Rahab: A Harlot Harbors Fugitives

We meet Rahab in the Bible as a woman of Canaan, living in Jericho during the time after the death of Moses and shortly after his successor, Joshua, leads the Hebrews across the Jordan River. There is every indication that she was a prostitute; some biblical scholars attempt to downplay or sanitize her livelihood, however, because they also know of her contributions and her ultimate lineage, which eventually traces to Jesus. Nevertheless, she is described in the Bible with the Hebrew word *zanah* and in the Greek Septuagint with the word *porne,* both of which translate into "prostitute."

Her precise occupation and her motivation for espionage still remain cause for continued debate. Was she an opportunist or a realist? Was she a pawn or a real player? Rahab was never one to kiss and tell, so you must come to your own conclusions.

Matthew 1:2–6 mentions that Jesus' lineage traces back to Rahab. The fact that a woman is mentioned in Jesus' lineage demonstrates her significance.

Rahab also plays a pivotal role in securing the Kingdom of Israel. By protecting the spies, saving herself, and ensuring a victory for the Hebrews, she sets the stage for the next crucial event. Rahab marries one of those secret agents, Salmon, and their son Boaz will later marry Ruth, the future great grandmother of David (the second King of Israel).

Assisting Hebrew spies

After Moses dies, Joshua becomes the leader who leads the Hebrew people, finally, into the Promised Land. But first he has to face some obstacles — specifically, the city of Jericho, which is blocking the Israelites from entering the Promised Land. Huge, thick walls fortify the city, so Joshua sends two spies to Jericho to gather strategic and tactical information for the ensuing battle.

The spies come upon the house of Rahab; she provides them sanctuary from the king, who knows they are somewhere in the city. Rahab makes a deal with the spies.

As described in Joshua 2:12–14, Rahab gets them to agree to repay her kindness in harboring them as fugitives by guaranteeing the safety of her family when Joshua and the Israelite army attack Jericho. The spies realize that if they refuse, she will expose them to their enemy and, if they consent, they can survive to bring back needed intelligence to Joshua and allow him to make successful attack plans). It's a win/win situation.

Surviving the fall

In return for sanctuary, the spies give Rahab a red cord to hang from her window. This symbol lets the Israelites know to pass by her house and spare her family when the walls of Jericho come tumbling down.

The Bible makes many parallels to show the hand of God. The red cord given to Rahab has historical significance going back to Moses' time. When Moses led the Hebrews out of the slavery of Egypt, the Lord instructed him to order all families to smear the blood of a lamb on the doorposts. The Angel of Death would pass over the homes marked with the red "cord" of blood on the night of the Passover meal.

The New Testament gives accolades to Rahab and her brave deeds in Paul's Epistle to the Hebrews: "By faith Rahab the prostitute did not perish with those who were disobedient, because she had received the spies in peace" (Hebrews 11:31). The Epistle of James also refers to her: "Was not Rahab the prostitute also justified by works when she welcomed the messengers and sent them out by another road?" (James 2:25).

By hiding the spies, Rahab saves her family. In turn, her help also secures the future of Israel. Her actions as an intelligent, resourceful woman, her faith in God, and her love of family save the Israelites. Her example represents the fact that you don't have to be perfect for God to use you as an instrument. (An old saying goes, "God can draw straight lines with crooked pencils," meaning that despite human weakness and imperfection, God can compensate with his grace.) Rahab certainly must not have pleased the Lord with her lifestyle beforehand, but her brave decision to hide and to assist the Hebrew spies guarantees the survival of the Israelites.

Rahab is later mentioned in the ancestry of Jesus (Matthew 1:5); she is the mother of Boaz, who is the father of Obed, who is the father of Jesse, the dad of King David. Her name also appears in the two examples mentioned earlier in the epistles of Paul and James. Her connection to the Messiah by blood and marriage doesn't overshadow, however, her act of bravery in saving the Hebrew spies and allowing a decisive victory for Joshua over Jericho.

Ruling by Example: Judge Deborah

The only woman of the Bible to wield political and religious authority by the consent of the common folk is Deborah. Other women may have been queens (Esther), princesses (Michal), royalty (Herodias), and aristocracy (Claudia), but Deborah alone holds the loftier ranks of prophetess and Judge.

Similar to a St. Joan of Arc for her day, she remains one of the exceptional figures of history. Deborah uses her charismatic charm and leadership abilities in such a way that she is even called "a mother in Israel (Judges 5:7), similar to the concept of "founding fathers" that people use today. The Bible never explains how or exactly when Deborah rises to the lofty and influential positions of Judge and prophetess. All is known is that she is the one and only woman in the history of Israel to achieve both powerful offices of leadership.

Deborah is a colorful, courageous, and committed woman of the Bible who fears no man and shows more trust in the Lord than many of her countrymen. She governs as a Judge, she teaches as a prophetess, she loves as a wife, and she fights as a patriot. Her story is exceptional because it demonstrates that the ways of the Lord are not always simply the ways of men. Women like Deborah — and also Esther, Judith, Ruth, Eve, and Mary, whose stories are told in other chapters of this book — are examples of the strength and honor shown by women, even in the predominantly patriarchal culture and society discussed in the Bible.

Meeting Deborah

Deborah is the wife of an obscure figure named Lapidoth, a name that translates into the word "torches." She lived in a time not long after (relatively speaking) Moses' followers secured the Promised Land, Israel, through seven years of war and the defeat of 31 kings and their cities. The land had been divided into the 12 tribes of Israel, which represent the 12 sons of Jacob (for more info, head to the discussion in Chapter 9).

Acting as a prophetess

During Deborah's time, Jabin of the ousted Canaanites and the king of Hazor, attempts to oppress the tribes of northern Israel. Sisera, the military commander under the king of Hazor, is ready to attack Israel with his large modern army that is equipped with the latest in military weapons — the iron chariot. Israel doesn't have these quick vehicles and so is at a distinct disadvantage. As prophetess, Deborah hears the voice of God.

Prophets and *prophetesses* were chosen by God to speak and teach his messages. Deborah's prophecies were more like an ancient-day e-mail between the Almighty and the Chosen People — she was the conduit for his communication. Acting as a prophetess was truly a vocation (from the Latin *vocare*, to call) for Deborah, whom the Lord selected to speak on his behalf to the people.

Serving as a Judge

As a Judge, Deborah gathers the men of Israel to fight. God instructs Deborah to tell the army's General Barak to take a position at Mount Tabor and bring 10,000 men from the tribes of Naphtali and Zebulun. The general agrees to go but only on the condition that Deborah accompany him and the army. She consents only because God has revealed to her that the enemy, Sisera, will be conquered, but at the hand of a woman. (See this account in Judges 4:4–9.)

The *Judges* were rulers of Israel between the period of Joshua's death and the anointing and coronation of Saul as king. They were elected for life by the people to adjudicate cases in which justice had been violated, much like court judges have done for centuries. Their authority extended only to the tribes who selected them. They settled disputes about moral, political, economic, and social concerns. Deborah as Judge was not so much a Judge Judy as she was a Judge Dredd (the comic book hero who is simultaneously a cop, judge, jury, and executioner). She heard testimony, evaluated evidence, rendered verdicts, and imposed sentences.

Ironically, Deborah isn't the woman who eventually gets Sisera, the military commander for King Jabin of Canaan. During the battle, Sisera's army is completely destroyed. He alone survives and flees to safety, or so he thinks. Sisera seeks sanctuary in the tent of Jael, the wife of Heber the Kenite. She hides him under a rug and then pounds a tent peg into his skull. Nasty, but effective. Too bad for Barak — he can't claim the victorious death of his enemy because Sisera didn't die in battle but was killed in a woman's tent. (Check out Judges 4:16–22.)

Deborah and Barak — and the Hebrew people — nonetheless are victorious against this mismatched enemy.

Experiencing praise

Judges 5:1–31 is titled the Song of Deborah. It is probably an example of early Hebrew poetry as well as a song of praise for this special woman. It tells the story of how the Hebrew people had momentarily lapsed in their faith and dabbled in other religions, something vehemently forbidden by God. The song continues with the arrival of Deborah, a devout woman who, as Judge, leads the nation's defenses to victory by securing the death of their enemy, Sisera. Deborah is forever remembered as a strong woman of faith and courage.

The men behind the women

A couple of men in the Bible are known mainly for the women they marry and nothing else.

For example, consider Lapidoth, who married Deborah. Lapidoth is referred to in the Bible as the husband of Deborah and nothing more. He is one of the few husbands known by his relationship to his wife rather than vice-versa.

Joseph, the husband of Mary, is a New Testament example of a man who is known because of his wife. He is mentioned only as the husband of the mother of Jesus because he is not the biological father. He appears a few times in the Gospels during the infancy and childhood of Jesus, and then no more is said, not even how, where, or when he died.

Chapter 11

Staying Faithful through Adversity

- -

- -

Infertility. Deaths of loved ones. You name it. The women in this chapter went through some pretty rough times in their lives. What makes them stand out, however, and what makes many people look to them for inspiration today is that, despite all odds, these women kept their faith in God.

In this chapter, we discuss Naomi, Hannah, Rizpah, Susanna, and Sarah, who meet with great hardships throughout their lives. These women continue praying, however, and believing — despite the troubles before them.

Two women covered in this chapter — Susanna and Sarah — aren't included in every Christian version of the Bible. They're included in the book of Tobit and in Chapter 13 of the book of Daniel, which are considered the Apocrypha or Deuterocanon. Head back to Chapter 2 of this book for more on these books.

Traveling Naomi: Staying Strong Despite Hardship

Naomi is the mother-in-law to Ruth, and their stories are deeply intertwined. (Check out Chapter 8 of this book for more on Ruth.) Naomi goes through major hardships — death, famine, and ostracism, to name a few — but she proves her loyalty to her family — namely to Ruth — and, ultimately, to God despite any discouragement she feels.

Naomi's husband dies. Her sons die, and she is left to care for herself. Despite her trials, she perseveres and beats the odds. Even though life was extremely trying in those days for childless widows, Naomi's faith and courage can serve as examples of how to make it through difficult times today.

Leaving her native land

Though Naomi's name means "my delight," much of her life, ironically, was filled with sadness and suffering. When the Bible first introduces Naomi, she is a Hebrew woman living in Bethlehem of Judah with her husband, not long after Moses secures the Promised Land. She leads a comfortable life as the wife of Elimelech, the brother of a prince. Unfortunately, her good fortune is short-lived. Because people are sinning greatly in the eyes of God (through idolatry or worship of false gods), a great famine embraces the land. The family is forced to uproot itself and head for foreign territory.

Naomi leaves with her husband and two sons, Mahlon and Chilion. They end up in Moab, a country east of Jordan and the Dead Sea. Although they find food and shelter there, they've still been forced to abandon their relatives, neighbors, and friends to start all over again.

Getting hit with tragedy

Here's the paradox. Her extended family has stayed behind to endure the famine, perhaps trusting that God will provide, while Naomi and her immediate family take a chance on finding better surroundings. Some would say her husband, Elimelech, had courage to brave the unknown, while others would say he lacked the trust in God, who promised to take care of his people. (In Psalm 37:19, God promises "in the days of famine they have abundance.")

Naomi wouldn't have been the one to decide whether to leave or stay. Because her husband, Elimelech, was head of the family, he had to make the decision and, therefore, be the one to suffer the guilt if his decision was sinful. Naomi is the faithful wife who accompanies her husband and sons. But she suffers — and some say it's due to their decision to leave. Soon after they arrive in Moab, Naomi's husband dies unexpectedly. Scholars debate whether Elimelech was punished for leaving Judah, instead of trusting that God would provide. In any event, Naomi's husband doesn't live long in Moab after the move from Judah.

Left a widow, Naomi must count on her two sons, who are of marrying age. Back in Judah, they would have married Jewish girls. But because the family is far from home and there aren't Jewish girls around, Mahlon and Chilion marry Moabite women, Ruth and Orpah (no, not *Oprah,* Orpah), respectively. Ten years pass, and tragedy strikes again. Both sons die as mysteriously as their father before them.

Now without a husband or sons, Naomi must fend for herself. Not permitted to earn a living independently of her husband, Naomi is forced to rely on the sympathy of others to survive, and her options include remarrying inside her husband's family or returning to her father's home.

It has been ten years since Naomi left her homeland in Bethlehem of Judah, but now that both her sons have died and news that the famine has ended has reached her, she decides to go back.

There is speculation about the death of Naomi's sons, Mahlon and Chilion, just as there was speculation about the death of their father before them. Some scholars theorize that their deaths may have been further punishment for leaving Judah and not trusting in God, and others believe their deaths may have been a sign against mixed marriages (the brothers married Moabite women and not Israelites).

Her daughters-in-law are faced with a decision. If they go with Naomi, they're unlikely to ever marry again, as Naomi has no other sons and is too old to bear more. (Ancient custom dictated that widows could marry the brothers of their deceased husbands.) If they stay in Moab, they could return to the home of their father and be cared for there. After a teary and emotional conversation, Orpah decides to stay, but Ruth remains devoted to Naomi and chooses to return to the land of Judah with her. (Ruth 1:7–14 tells this part of Naomi's story, and Chapter 8 in this book has some additional explanation.)

When Naomi returns to Bethlehem with Ruth, she is warmly greeted and explains the intervening years to the townspeople:

Call me no longer Naomi [meaning "pleasant"], call me Mara [meaning "bitter"], for the Almighty has dealt bitterly with me. I went away full, but the LORD has brought me back empty; why call me Naomi when the LORD has dealt harshly with me, and the Almighty has brought calamity upon me.

—Ruth 1:19–21

Escaping poverty

Unfortunately, even though the famine has ended in Judah and Naomi is with her native people, she is still poor, husbandless, and childless.

Ruth goes to work in the only way she can — collecting the *gleanings* from the fields for a man named Boaz, who is a relative of Elimelech, Naomi's dead husband. (Gleanings are the leftover grain that remains after reapers have harvested the field.)

As a relative of Elimelech, Boaz can legally marry Ruth, and their firstborn son would be a continuation of Ruth's dead husband's line. Ruth visits Boaz, who, impressed by her, asks her to marry him.

This marriage not only assures Ruth of a husband to care for her (and, in turn, to care for Naomi), but it also produces offspring who will be extremely important to historical lineage. Their son, Obed, becomes the father of Jesse, who in turn fathers King David of Israel, an ancestor of Jesus. Ruth 4 is the last we hear of Naomi — as a happy woman because she is a grandmother now that Ruth has given birth to a son. Although she endured a hard life, Naomi emerged a stronger woman with the help of her loyal daughter-in-law.

Barren Hannah: Praying for a Baby

Hannah's story embodies patience and faith. Through her example, it's easy to see that God acts on his own timetable and eventually answers prayers. Hannah follows through on her obligation to God, showing that when he grants you what you ask for, you're bound to serve his will and interests for the greater good. Like Sarah (see Chapter 11) and Mary, the mother of Jesus (see Chapter 6), Hannah experiences a miraculous conception, and the child that God gives to her has a major impact on the world.

Dealing with infertility

Hannah lived her life in or around the eleventh century BC, during the time after Israel was ruled by Judges, but before the time of the monarchy of King David and his predecessors. Hannah is the favorite wife of Elkanah. Unfortunately, Hannah is barren for many years, and Elkanah takes a second wife, Peninnah, who is blessed with many children. (See 1 Samuel 1:1–2.) Understandably, Hannah is distraught by her infertility.

In ancient times, women were primarily defined and fulfilled by their ability to have children; they didn't have careers or other ways to contribute to society or to create a sense of identity for themselves, as women do today.

Despite her inability to have children, Hannah remains the love of Elkanah's life, and Peninnah is jealous. She knows that she is not numero uno in Elkanah's heart, and her jealousy drives her to ridicule Hannah.

Peninnah slices and dices Hannah with her sharp words and insults her so much that Hannah becomes ashamed of her predicament, as if she somehow is being punished and deserving of her fate. The second wife misses no opportunity to rub salt in the wound, and she taunts Hannah incessantly about her condition. (See 1 Samuel 1:3–7 for the details.)

Elkanah, on the other hand, is a bit dense about the matter, as shown in this passage:

> *Hannah wept and would not eat. Her husband Elkanah said to her, "Hannah, why do you weep? Why do you not eat? Why is your heart sad? Am I not more to you than ten sons?"*
>
> —1 Samuel 1:7–8

Although Elkanah loves Hannah, he doesn't seem to fully understand her feelings about being infertile.

Reaping God's rewards

Elkanah and his two wives regularly make a pilgrimage to the temple shrine in Shiloh, where the priest Eli offers sacrifices to the Lord. Here, Hannah initiates her own version of "let's make a deal" — with God.

Deep in prayer, almost trancelike, Hannah moves her lips but makes no sound. The temple priest, Eli, eyeballs her and concludes that she has indulged in some (worldly) spirits and is drunk rather than devoted to prayer. Angry in his mistaken belief that Hannah has hit the bottle in the house of God, Eli rebukes her. (See 1 Samuel 1:9–18 for more details.)

Of course, the only thing intoxicating to Hannah is her grief and angst, and Eli soon realizes his mistake. She explains her vow to Eli. If God blesses her with a son, she will give him back to the Lord. After the child is weaned, she says, she will offer him up to be raised in the temple, where he will learn temple worship and live the Nazirite vow (no wine or alcohol, no haircuts, and no contact with dead bodies). In essence, this means she'd be giving back the son that God gave to her.

When Eli hears this story, he blesses Hannah. She leaves happy, confident, and trusting that her prayer will be answered. And it is answered. Hannah bears a son who is named Samuel, which means "heard or answered of God." Hannah believes that a deal is a deal, so after the boy is weaned, Hannah brings Samuel to Eli in order to fulfill the vow she made. (See 1 Samuel 1:19–28 for more details.)

Samuel's birth is highly significant: He becomes one of the most important prophets and leaders in the Old Testament, and one day he anoints the first king of Israel, Saul. Hannah is later blessed with several more children (three sons and two daughters); rewarded for her patience and ultimate sacrifice and service to God.

Joyful beyond belief, Hannah sings a hymn of praise and thanksgiving on the day that she presents Samuel to the temple (1 Samuel 2:1–10), which is somewhat similar to the Magnificat recited by Mary, the mother of Jesus, in Luke 1:46–55.

Although she gives Samuel up to God and to Eli, Hannah lovingly and dutifully visits every year: "His mother used to make for him a little robe and take it to him each year to year, when she went up with her husband to offer the yearly sacrifice" (1 Samuel 2:19).

Although no more is said of Hannah, her strength and faith in God during a time of adversity (being taunted about her infertility) are rewarded with a son whom she in turn gives back to God as a servant and future prophet of the Lord. Her graciousness and appreciation are equally rewarded with other children, which shows how generous God is with those who are patient and faithful like Hannah.

Devout Rizpah: A Mother Grieves

No woman suffered like Rizpah. She was a concubine to King Saul and a devoted mother to their two sons (Mephibosheth and Armoni) in life as well as after they died. Even though her boys were enemies of the state or at least political rivals of the new king, her staunch loyalty to giving them a decent and proper burial finally convinces King David to bury her sons properly as well as to give the same respect and honor for Saul and Jonathan (respectively, the former king and his eldest son by his wife, Ahinoam), whose bodies were likewise left to rot rather than be buried with dignity.

Rizpah witnessed the death of King Saul, her lover, and the gruesome extermination of their two sons, Armoni and Mephibosheth. She was also used and abused by those who saw her as an object of desire or as a political tool. First Saul uses her as a concubine rather than as a wife; after his death, she is the object of contention between Abner and Ishbaal (we get to this story later). This strong woman, however, never wavered in her fidelity as a good partner and loving mother despite the sufferings she endured.

Through her actions, Rizpah changed the course of history by influencing a mighty ruler, King David of Israel, and thus helping to turn a cycle of violence and hatred into a time of relative peace. Her life is an example of how diligence and courage can see you through daunting circumstances. Rizpah's long but persevering vigil influenced David to give respect to the bones of the former king and his son, which sealed his support with all the people of the kingdom, especially those who had been scandalized by his neglect of the memory of his predecessor (King Saul).

Losing her lover — and her sons

Rizpah was a concubine to King Saul (2 Samuel 3:7), the first king to rule over all the tribes of Israel (his reign began in approximately 1010 BC). After King Saul's death, Rizpah is comforted by the relationships with her two sons, Armoni and Mephibosheth.

In those days, being a concubine was much more respectable than the term implies today. Although she wasn't granted the full authority of a wife in a man's household, a concubine was, unlike an additional wife who is taken in to bear children if a first wife is infertile, chosen more out of love and companionship. She was second only to the wife or wives in terms of honor and respect afforded her by the servants.

Soon after Saul's death, famine devastates Israel, and King David, who now rules the land, asks God why he has punished them. God replies that he has punished the Israelites for the actions of the now deceased King Saul, who during his reign had attempted to wipe out the Gibeonite people.

King David wants to rectify the situation, so he asks the Gibeonites what they would accept as retribution. The Gibeonites answer that David must hand over Saul's heirs to be tortured and killed. The heirs to be killed included Rizpah's two sons, as well as the five sons of Saul's daughter. King David hopes that this sacrifice will placate the Gibeonites and God, thus ending the famine. (See 2 Samuel 21:1–9 for more details.)

Grieving in public

Rizpah's nightmare only gets worse. Not only are her two sons executed, but their bodies are also left outside to rot for five months. She dutifully covers them as best she can and wards off vultures and beasts of prey to protect their corpses. This lady of the court — who once wore royal purple as the king's concubine — is now covered in the penitential garb of sackcloth in public mourning of her abandoned sons. Rizpah's long vigil is possible only because of a mother's love and her personal faith.

Her long, agonizing vigil by her dead sons' bodies reaches the ears of David, who is moved by her story. In response, David finally orders the proper burial of Saul's heirs. He also orders the proper burial of Saul himself and Saul's son Jonathan, who had been killed years earlier and never been given a dignified burial. After these burials, the famine is soon lifted. (See 2 Samuel 21:10–14 for more details about these events in Rizpah's life.)

Playing the pawn

In her lifetime, Rizpah also played a part in the struggle for power within the monarchy. When the sons of Saul's wife, Queen Ahinoam, die in battle, just one legitimate heir to the throne remains — Ishbaal. He had been too young to fight and is still too young to rule, so Saul's uncle and general, Abner, comes to act as regent. When he can't control the throne as he would like, Abner takes Rizpah as his own concubine, hoping that if he can have a son with Rizpah, the royal concubine, then he has a remote claim to the throne.

Viable claimants to the throne included not only sons of kings but also other male relatives, like uncles or those by marriage or offspring. Marrying the former concubine of the king and having a son with her would get Abner's foot in the door, so to speak. (See 2 Samuel 3:7–10 for more details.)

When kings and queens died, power rarely transferred peacefully. Their children had the best claim to the throne, but other relatives and ambitious military and government officials could sneak in the back door.

Abner's move toward the throne incites tensions. Bad blood arises between Ishbaal and his uncle, ending in accusations of incest and other tawdry affairs. Abner defects to Saul's former enemy (and thus the enemy of Ishbaal), an old rival, King David.

Rizpah's desires, wishes, and welfare were never foremost in the minds of Abner, Ishbaal, or David. She was a tool to the crown and an avenue to the throne. Yet she shows strength in adversity by persevering for the burial of her dead sons' bodies. Her use as a bargaining chip is certainly demeaning, but she emerges a woman of honor, as opposed to those who sought to use her as an object rather than relate to her as a person.

The Bible doesn't mention her again, but her story and connection to the Hebrew monarchy are recorded and retold for subsequent generations to come.

Steadfast Susanna: Asking God for Help

Susanna's story is found in Daniel 13. (Daniel 13 is part of the deuterocanonical books; see Chapter 2 for more on these books.) She lived in the sixth century BC during the time of Daniel. Susanna (see Figure 11-1 for one artist's interpretation of her) spares both her virtue and her life by putting her faith in God and never giving in to the powerful men who threaten her. Although she could have easily given in to these evildoers in order to protect her life, she instead decides to act with faith and honesty to overcome evil through prayer and trust in God. Her story shows that faith and fidelity ultimately can be rewarded.

Fighting off the hounds

Susanna is a very beautiful young woman, a devoted spouse, and a virtuous and Godly woman. Like any young woman of leisure (her husband was very rich), Susanna regularly takes an afternoon walk in the garden. Unfortunately, two dirty old men soon get wind of her habit. And here the plot thickens. These men weren't only dirty and lustful — they were also quite powerful. Although their names aren't given, it is said that they are Judges. These men cast a lustful eye on Susanna and one day conspire to become peeping toms while she takes a bath on a hot day in her enclosed garden. Hiding in the garden, they lie in wait until Susanna dismisses her two maids. (See Susanna 1:1–16, or Daniel 13:1–16 in some Bibles, for a play-by-play.)

Seizing the opportunity, the codgers approach the naked beauty:

> *Look, the garden doors are shut, and no one can see us. We are burning with desire for you; so give your consent, and lie with us. If you refuse, we will testify against you that a young man was with you, and this was why you sent your maids away.*
>
> —Susanna 1:20-21 or Daniel 13:20–21

Susanna finds herself in a Catch-22. She knows that her life is at stake no matter what she does. She doesn't want to give in to these brutes, and she knows that the penalty for adultery is death by stoning. Yet if she refuses to acquiesce to their perverted designs, she's in trouble too.

Virtuous Susanna decides to take her chances and trust in the Lord. She refuses to consent to the old boys' demands. She screams and so do they, at which point the staff rushes in. Before she can defend herself, the geriatric playboys accuse her of fornicating with a young man who got away. Susanna finds herself in a situation where it is her word against theirs — two male leaders of the community. Susanna doesn't have much chance of being acquitted. (See Susanna 1:24–42, or Daniel 13:24–42 in other Bibles, for more details.)

Figure 11-1:
Susanna and the Elders by Frans Floris (1519–1570).

Scala/Art Resource, NY

Uncovering the truth

Susanna feverishly prays to God for deliverance. Lo and behold, a young man named Daniel comes to her rescue. The Lord inspires him to proclaim that he will not have anything to do with the death of this innocent woman, and because of his proclamation, the men ask him to sit in judgment. They don't yet know that he knows their dirty deed, and possibly to throw suspicion (from the crowd) off themselves, they act as innocent as can be. In their minds, Daniel is too young, immature, and inexperienced to really be a prophet with whom God communicates. So they play along and humor him in front of everyone else. The two men keep up the charade. (See Susanna 1:44–50 or Daniel 13:44–50 for more.)

According to Hebrew law, the testimony of two witnesses against one was sufficient evidence to reach a verdict. (And you think that the U.S. justice system is full of holes!) However, this law applied only if there was no other evidence or testimony.

Daniel takes on the role of an ancient Perry Mason, uncovering the truth before a riveted and mesmerized audience. He asks that the two elderly accusers be separated and then begins his interrogation of each of them (see Susanna 1:51 or Daniel 13:51).

Great mysteries are usually solved by a small but pivotal detail that the criminal considers irrelevant. Susanna's case was no exception. Daniel isolates the witnesses and asks them where they witnessed Susanna's alleged affair. The first says "under a mastic tree," while the other says "under an evergreen oak." This damning testimony cost them their very lives, because the penalty the old men had conspired to inflict upon innocent Susanna is now their own. And Susanna's virtue and reputation is spared. (You can read this part of Susanna's story in Susanna 1:52–62 or Daniel 13:52–62.)

Susanna's story ends happily ever after, because the prophet Daniel exposes her false accusers. She defends her virtue rather than give in to the men's lewd advances. Doing so almost cost her life, but she survives the adversity of lies and slander that many probably believed without any regard to what truly transpired. Her vindication by Daniel is not only good luck but also a legitimate sign of why it pays to persevere to the end.

Cursed Sarah: A Widow's Stigma

The Book of Tobit is another apocryphal, or deuterocanonical, book that tells the story of a notable woman, Sarah. (See Chapter 2 for more on these books.) Sarah is a widow seven times over — truly the black widow of her day. Although the Bible has stories of many widows, none were quite so cursed as Sarah. Despite her unlucky life, though, Sarah doesn't despair, doesn't curse God, and doesn't resort to idolatry like many of her contemporaries. She remains faithful and trusting that somehow, someday, God will deliver her, and her prayers are eventually answered.

Beating the odds

Each of Sarah's husbands dies on the wedding night. As an only child, Sarah is embarrassed for her father, Raguel, because she is unable to produce grandchildren for him, thus carrying on his family line. She feels the social stigma and shame of being a repeat widow. The text blames the unfortunate deaths of her seven husbands on the demon Asmodeus, but the kinfolk and neighbors see her as a bad omen (see Tobit 3:7–9). Needless to say, not many modern dating services would want her as a client today.

The story of Sarah tells us that she has a *diabolical obsession*, which means she is externally plagued by a demon. Being internally terrorized by a demon was — and is still — referred to as *possession*.

To add insult to injury, Raguel's maidservants begin verbally attacking Sarah. They complain that their mistress takes her frustration out on them by beating them. Faced with this shame and abuse, she makes an earnest and heartfelt plea to God to be delivered of this curse, one way or another. The Lord sends the Archangel Raphael (whose name means "God heals") to answer Sarah's plea. (See this account in Tobit 3:10–17.)

But Raphael is multitasking. God has also sent him to help an unfairly exiled Israelite named Tobit, whose son, Tobias, has been sent on a journey to help his father recover some money. Tobit had been struck blind in an accident, and God is sending help for his son, Tobias, to reward the father's faithful acts of the past.

Traveling together, Raphael and Tobias stop off in Sarah's village, where Raphael suggests that Tobias take her as his wife. Burying seven husbands, one after another, is a hard secret to keep, even before the advent of e-mail and instant messaging, and Tobias is understandably a bit skittish about the idea. As his father's only son, he has a great desire for self-preservation. (See Tobit 3:16–6:15.)

Getting blessed by an angel

But Tobias follows Raphael's guidance and decides to marry Sarah, despite her bad track record. On their wedding night, the newlyweds pray together with tenderness and affection, not just to wake up alive the next morning but to also have a long life together. This passage is often used at Catholic weddings.

Tobias began by saying, "Blessed are you, O God of our ancestors, and blessed is your name in all generations forever. Let the heavens and the whole creation bless you forever. You made Adam, and for him you made his wife Eve as a helper and support. From the two of them the human race has sprung. You said, 'It is not good that the man should be alone; let us make a helper for him like himself.' I now am taking this kinswoman of mine not because of lust, but with sincerity. Grant that she and I may find mercy and that we may grow old together." And they both said, "Amen, Amen."

—Tobit 8:5–8

Raguel (Sarah's dad) has less faith than his daughter or son-in-law and digs a grave that night, just in case. But luckily for Sarah, Raphael saves the day by releasing Sarah of the demon who cursed her. She awakens a wife and not a widow. After two weeks, the couple returns to Tobit with Raphael, who performs one more miracle, giving back sight to the old man.

Sarah and Tobias are united in love and marriage. Both of their prayers to God before the wedding night show nervousness but also trust that God will preserve them somehow or give them strength for whatever happens next. Sarah was plagued by her demon, but prayer brings her deliverance, because God heard her plea and sent Raphael to help her and her husband-to-be, Tobias.

The last we hear of Sarah is when she meets her father-in-law, Tobit. Blinded by a bizarre accident (the old bird-droppings-in-the-eye incident in Tobit 2:10), the old man is healed by the Angel Raphael (Tobit 11:7–14). After Tobit's sight is restored, he can see his son, Tobias, and Tobias's new wife, Sarah, and the old man blesses his new daughter-in-law. Sarah's name appears only one more time, when the angel reveals his identity to Tobit: "God sent me to heal you and Sarah your daughter-in-law. I am Raphael, one of the seven angels who stand ready to enter before the glory of the Lord" (Tobit 12:14–15).

Chapter 12

Ruling (and Royal) Women of the Bible

The imperial women of the Bible have vastly different backgrounds and experiences, and they prove that being royalty is often no picnic. One of these women has a royal background and is a queen in her own right (Sheba); one is the daughter and future wife of a king (Michal); and one is unexpectedly tapped as a queen (Abigail). One is even downright evil, earning the throne by eliminating her competitors (Athaliah).

In this chapter, we cover them all, noting what each of these royal women did to stand out — and leave a mark.

From Princess to Queen: Michal

Poor Michal. She is repeatedly used by the men in her life — people whom she should most trust — her father, King Saul, and her husband, the future King David. (Talk about expensive psychotherapy bills.) Her experiences as wife and daughter bear a striking resemblance to the sad story of the late Diana, Princess of Wales. Michal experiences unrequited love, political intrigue, family squabbles, and personal tragedy, all of which bring nothing but unhappiness to this young, beautiful, wealthy, and powerful woman.

Falling in love

We meet Princess Michal as the youngest daughter of King Saul of Israel. She is madly in love with the young, handsome, brave, and ambitious David, but she is from a world that is different from David's. Michal grew up in the royal court; David was a shepherd boy. She was accustomed to luxury; he was a man of simple tastes and modest living. She was cultured and refined; he was a country bumpkin. But David's bravery and manliness were too much to deny, and after he slays the giant nemesis Goliath, a Philistine who terrorized the kingdom (see 1 Samuel 17), Michal's heart belongs only to David.

Unfortunately for Michal, dear old dad had promised her older sister (and firstborn daughter), Merab, to whoever could eliminate Goliath. When this kid with a slingshot (David) turns out to be the Terminator, King Saul has second thoughts about giving his prized princess away in marriage. Threatened by David, who has won acclaim the kingdom over, Saul fears that marrying Merab to David could be a steppingstone toward the throne for David. So Saul promises Merab's hand in marriage to another man, Adriel the Meholathite, instead. (See 1 Samuel 18:17–19.)

Playing the pawn

Saul soon discovers that his younger daughter, Michal, has eyes for David. Saul wants David killed to protect his own throne, and he devises a plan. Suspecting that David has big ambitions himself, he offers Michal's hand in marriage to David in return for the foreskins of a hundred Philistine soldiers (1 Samuel 18:25). (This would be David's dowry, which in those days was offered to the father of the bride, not vice versa). Saul hopes that this mission will be too much even for tough and brave David and that he will perish on his quest.

But Saul underestimates David, who returns not with 100 foreskins, but with 200. Saul is forced to make good on his deal, and David marries Michal. Although Michal is thrilled to marry the man she is passionate about, David appears to view his marriage to Michal as more of a political move that would get him closer to the throne.

Saul doesn't give in lightly to his new son-in-law, and he continues to plot David's demise. But once again, Saul misjudges a situation. Michal, still madly in love with David, gets wind of a plot that her father has cooked up and helps David escape Saul's clutches. She shows bravery, loyalty, and quick thinking to save David's life. First, she spills the beans about the plot to David and then helps him escape out the window while dressing up an idol with goat's hair to fool Saul's soldiers (no decent mannequins back then). When asked where he is, Michal simply says he's sick. After it is discovered that David has escaped, Saul asks his daughter why she deceived her own father and why she gave sanctuary to his enemy. She simply tells her dad that as far as she is concerned, David has no deadly motives. She is standing by her man. (See this account in 1 Samuel 19:11–17.)

Abandoning Michal

Unfortunately, David doesn't take Michal with him. Poor Michal makes the ultimate sacrifice to save David's life, perhaps believing, as the saying goes, "If you love someone, set him free; if he comes back, he's yours." Unfortunately, David doesn't hurry back, nor does it appear that absence has made David's heart grow fonder. He flees to Ramah and hides with the prophet Samuel (1 Samuel 19:18).

Proof of David's disinterest in Michal comes first in the form of Abigail, whom David takes as a wife while he is on the lam. (See her story later in this chapter.) Later, he takes a third wife, Ahinoam, even though he is still married to Michal. Meanwhile, Saul gives Michal in marriage to Palti, though Michal's marriage to Palti (also called Phaltiel) is completely invalid — she was still married to David, after all. (Unfair as it was, ancient custom was that a man could have more than one wife or concubine but a woman could only have one husband.) Saul didn't much care, however, that the marriage was invalid because he hated David and regretted the marriage of his daughter to his archenemy. (See 1 Samuel 25:42–43 for the details.)

By giving his daughter Michal to Palti, he hoped to dissolve the union between Michal and David in any way he could. Saul feared a son from David and Michal would solidify David's claim to the throne after or — even worse — before Saul's death. Keeping the two apart at least bought Saul more time.

Though Palti loves Michal and treats her well, she still loves David. Sadly, during the 14 years Michal is separated from David, he makes no attempt to retrieve her or communicate with her. David takes six more wives and bears children with many of them in the meantime.

But seven years after Saul dies, David finds he needs Michal once again. Still not king of Israel, he makes a deal to have Michal forcibly removed from the sobbing Palti to be returned as David's wife (2 Samuel 3:13–14).

David understands that Michal, as the royal daughter of the former king, is a political asset and will help legitimize him as king. He needs Michal only to fulfill his true agenda: to re-establish himself as part of the royal family.

David was anointed by the prophet Samuel as king of Israel (see 1 Samuel 16:13) while Saul still lived, although David didn't assume the throne until after his death. David was king in the eyes of God by the anointing from Samuel, but for political power and acceptance outside as well as inside the realm, he needed some other link of legitimacy. Therefore, his marriage to the king's daughter was his "ace in the hole." The marriage wasn't enough in itself to make him king, but it got his foot in the door nonetheless.

Publicly berating David

Perhaps Michal had had enough of keeping quiet and playing the pawn. Or perhaps she was drawn to expose David for what he was: a selfish, self-serving husband. Maybe she was simply unhappy. She'd been taken from a husband who'd loved her for many years, and reunited with one who didn't return her love. Whatever her motivation, many scholars believe her next act may have caused God to punish her with infertility.

After the Ark of the Covenant (the receptacle containing the Ten Commandments and the holiest artifact in Judaism; the symbol of the Covenant between God and his Chosen People) is ceremoniously brought into Jerusalem, King David makes a public show of piety for the Lord, "uncovering himself today before the eyes of his servants' maids." Believing David has made a spectacle of himself, Michal reprimands him with a fierce tongue-lashing. Ironically, the one time she stands up to her poor excuse for a husband is possibly out of jealousy of his display of affection for God. Bad timing. Of all the moments to ridicule the king, she chooses the time he dances before the Lord — probably not the smoothest of moves. Michal is punished with being barren until her death. (See 2 Samuel 6:17–23 for this story.)

This is the last time Michal is mentioned except for when the Bible again mentions the story of Michal watching David dance in front of the Lord.

As the ark of the LORD came into the city of David, Michal daughter of Saul looked out of the window, and saw King David leaping and dancing before the LORD; and she despised him in her heart.

—2 Samuel 6:16

Used by her father, Saul, and then by husband David, Michal didn't love the only man who truly loved her: Palti. Unfairly treated for the most part, Michal was nevertheless a link in the chain between David and Saul, and for that she suffered.

Quick-Thinking Abigail: A Wife Saves Her Husband

Abigail is politically astute, diplomatically savvy, and strong. She is smart enough to think for herself, and she is quick on her feet — rescuing her husband, Nabal, from the hand of David. Boorish, uncouth, ill-mannered, and bad-tempered, Nabal makes Homer Simpson look like Cary Grant in comparison. And instead of blindly following after her husband, Abigail (see Figure 12-1 for one artist's view of her) violates the biblical tradition of obeying one's husband, no matter what the circumstance. Through her uncharacteristic rebelliousness, Abigail's example teaches that independent thinking — especially in the name of doing the right thing — does, in fact, get rewarded by God.

Figure 12-1: *David and Abigail,* c. 1570–1580 by Frans the Elder Pourbus (1545–1581). Located in Kunsthistorisches Museum, Vienna, Austria.

Erich Lessing/Art Resource, NY

Racketeering, Bible-style

One wonders how Nabal was lucky enough to marry Abigail, who is described as both beautiful and clever. Nabal is certainly a wealthy man, having earned his money as a successful sheep rancher. But despite his business acumen, the Bible implies that he overindulges in drink and often speaks without considering the consequences. Eventually, Nabal puts the ultimate foot in his mouth.

David and his men — still on the lam from David's murderous father-in-law, Saul — had offered "protection" to Nabal's flock (in true gangster style), when the sheep-shearing festival began.

Thieves and thugs were a problem in biblical days, just as they are today. Most were unorganized, independent crooks, but some were more sophisticated, and during the sheep-shearing festival, Nabal may have been wise to hire extra protection.

But instead of showing the proper hospitality and gratitude to David for his offer, Nabal instead displays much bravado and refuses to acknowledge or repay David's favor with food or other offerings (1 Samuel 25:10–11). Whether David's actions are virtuous is debatable; most likely, they're more like ancient racketeering. In today's language, this is like dissing Tony Soprano — a dangerous oversight, to say the least.

But no matter what David's motivations, he has plenty of power, as well as God's mandate as the future king of Israel.

Before her husband is forced to sleep with the fishes, Abigail comes to the rescue. Realizing his fatal gaffe, she slips away from her crass spouse and brings wine and food to David and his men. (We're talking *a lot* of food: two hundred loaves, two skins of wine, five sheep, five measures of parched grain, one hundred clusters of raisins, and two hundred cakes of figs.) She begs forgiveness for Nabal's bad behavior. When she returns, her husband is crocked, and she waits until morning to report what she has done to save his life. When he hears the story, though, he is so shocked that the stress causes him to have a stroke, and ten days later he keels over dead. Nabal appears doomed no matter what. Abigail could have kept her deeds secret, but she told her husband the truth, not only of what she did but that Nabal barely escaped death by offending David until she patched things up. Finding out was too much for him, however, and he died anyway. (See 1 Samuel 25:18–38 for this story.)

David hears of Nabal's demise and takes Abigail as one of his wives (1 Samuel 25:39–42). All that the Bible says after their nuptials is that they had a son, Chileab (sometimes called Daniel). Otherwise, not much more is said of her, despite the fact that she becomes a wife of a very pivotal person in scripture.

The last time we hear of Abigail is when she and David's other wife (Ahinoam) are captured by the Amalekites and held hostage until he rescues them (1 Samuel 30:5–18). Then she disappears from the radar screen.

Benefiting from Abigail

By defying her husband, Abigail validates David's kingship. She also enables David to retain his self-respect without having to senselessly kill Nabal. Her tactfulness, common sense, and propriety serve to make her the one constant in David's chaotic life. Other women were used by him or were treated as objects or pawns, whereas Abigail won his love and admiration. Her quick thinking ultimately spares her life and ensures her position as a future *queen consort* (someone who wears a crown by virtue of being married to the reigning monarch).

Of all David's wives (who also include Michal, Bathsheba, Ahinoam, Maacah, Haggith, Abital, and Eglah), Abigail earns his complete respect. Abigail is a positive influence on him, unlike his later wives.

Intelligent and Independent: The Queen of Sheba

Some of the world's smartest people know exactly how much they *don't* know. In her day, the Queen of Sheba was a good example of this.

The Queen of Sheba travels far and offers up great wealth in appreciation of King Solomon's wisdom. She is a ruling queen in her own right, and her story is significant because it sheds light on the golden era of King Solomon's reign in Israel. (King Solomon was the son of King David and Bathsheba). The Queen of Sheba's story is a testament to her own intelligence and independence, even during a time when women weren't usually afforded the same rights or respect as men.

The Hebrew word normally used in the Bible for queen is *shegal,* which means wife of the ruling king. The Queen of Sheba is referred to in Hebrew as *malkah,* which means a ruling queen in her own right, irrespective of a husband.

Can the real Queen of Sheba please stand up?

There is much speculation about the actual identity of the Queen of Sheba, because she is never mentioned by her proper name. In fact, she's probably the most famous unnamed woman in the Bible. Some scholars speculate that she may have actually been Queen Hatshepsut of Egypt, Queen Makeda of Ethiopia, or Queen Balkis of Abyssinia. Other experts point out that only the Queens of Sabean Kingdom (present-day Yemen) occupied a high place of honor that equaled that of their male (king) counterparts.

We meet the Queen of Sheba as a brave woman who travels 1,200 miles by camel caravan to see the famous King Solomon the Wise (1 Kings 10:1–13). Although other rulers send ambassadors and emissaries to visit the king of Israel, the Queen of Sheba insists on visiting him herself. This is no mere state visit, however. She comes seeking wisdom, and Solomon has by this time been identified as the world's wisest man. Sheba is indeed a true philosopher (from the Greek, *philo sophia,* meaning lover of wisdom).

She pays a visit to the world-renowned Solomon's Temple (Temple of Jerusalem) and asks Solomon hard questions — sort of like the final round of *Jeopardy.* She quickly comes to realize that the reports of his wisdom are true, and she praises his knowledge: "Not even half had been told me; your wisdom and prosperity far surpass the report that I had heard. Happy are your wives! Happy are these your servants, who continually attend you and hear your wisdom!" (1 Kings 10:7–8).

In return for this education, her majesty brings Solomon a gift of gold roughly equivalent today to $3.5 million — making even today's most expensive private universities a comparative bargain! The Queen of Sheba returns home, and we never hear of her again. Was her curiosity satisfied? Was her diplomatic mission accomplished? We don't know. She leaves as mysteriously as she appears.

Praising the queen

Jesus remembers the role of the Queen of Sheba in the Gospel of Mathew. Praising her quest for knowledge and truth, Jesus states, "The queen of the South will rise up at the judgment with this generation and condemn it, for she came from the ends of the earth to listen to the wisdom of Solomon, and see, something greater than Solomon is here!" (Matthew 12:42).

Athaliah: The Ice Queen

Athaliah, alas, is not fondly remembered. Her blind ambition and cunning are surely, in the end, her downfall. Athaliah treats human life cheaply and often with contempt. She has no loyalty to faith or family. Her brutality and ruthlessness only bring her to her own miserable end. She demonstrates how corrupt power brokers can manipulate others and how evil can lurk in almost any corridor. Although she isn't the only corrupt ruler in biblical times, she certainly isn't a good representative of her gender. If you can learn anything from her example, it's to turn away from evil — "For you reap whatever you sow" (Galatians 6:7).

Ruling Judah

Athaliah proves the apple doesn't fall far from the tree. She takes after her father, Ahab, and her mother Jezebel in promoting pagan Baal worship among her people, trying to replace and eradicate the Hebrew religion. Athaliah is the only woman of the Bible reported to have reigned as a sovereign queen of Judah, sitting on the throne of David. She lives in a time during which the 12 tribes of Israel are no longer united under one king (as they were in Saul's, David's, and Solomon's time). Rather, the tribes are ruled separately as parts of Judah and Israel, as shown in Figure 12-2.

Figure 12-2:
A map of Israel, the divided kingdom.

Unfortunately, her unique place in history isn't known for that singular fact as much as for her despicable evil, injustice, and wanton immorality. No doting grandma, she personally orders the massacre of her own grandchildren to secure her crown as queen. Athaliah truly has ice water running through her veins. After the death of her husband, King Jehoram (who reigned 12 years) and then her son, King Ahaziah (who reigned 1 year), she wants the throne so badly that she orders the execution of the royal family (all her son's children) to ensure that no opponents would prevent her from seizing the crown for herself. Fortunately, one grandson (Joash) escapes with the help of Jehosheba, his aunt and sister of the late King Ahaziah. (See this story in 2 Kings 11:1–3.)

Manipulating fate

When this grandson, Joash, is old enough, he is revealed to the people and praised and recognized as king. As punishment, Athaliah is trampled to death by horses (2 Kings 11:16).

"What goes around, comes around" is an old folk proverb that applies to Athaliah. She lived a wicked life like her evil mother, Jezebel (see Chapter 16). Both were thirsty for power and were unscrupulous in seizing and keeping it. Both died an ignominious death as well: Jezebel was eaten by dogs and Athaliah was trampled by horses. Their Machiavellian politics may have earned them the crown, but it came with a high price. History sees both women as amoral megalomaniacs who used tactics no different than those used by Hitler or Stalin. Athaliah was corrupt before she became queen, and after she claimed the throne, she continued her evil empire. After Athaliah's six-year reign of terror, the Bible says no more about her.

Chapter 13

Getting to Know the Gals of the Gospel

The women of the Gospel all had a connection to Jesus of Nazareth, either directly or indirectly. They lived at the time he did (first century AD) and in the same area (ancient Palestine). Some of the women were very prominent in the personal life of Jesus, and others were later arrivals in the early Christian Church. All of these women are in the New Testament.

In this chapter, we discuss the women who make their way into four Gospel accounts. These four books of the New Testament — called the Gospel, (from the Old English "good spiel," meaning "good news," based on the Greek word *euagelion*) — are written (and named after) "according to" Matthew, Mark, Luke, and John. (Gospel writers are often referred to as evangelists, from the same Greek word for Gospel, *euagelion*).

Christians consider these four books the most important and most sacred of all the books in the Bible because they contain the words and deeds of Jesus Christ himself. The first five books of the Bible (Genesis, Exodus, Leviticus, Numbers, and Deuteronomy), called the Torah, are the most sacred to Judaism because they contain the history of *covenant* (the sacred and perpetual oath between God and his people) from Adam to Abraham to Moses. *Torah* is Hebrew for "law" or "instruction," and the first five books of the Old Testament contain the Law of Moses, the Ten Commandments that God gave Moses on Mount Sinai after the Hebrews were delivered from their slavery in Egypt (Exodus 20:1–17 and Deuteronomy 5:1–21).

Elizabeth: Mother of John the Baptist

Elizabeth lived during the reign of Herod the Great, during the time just before Jesus was born. She was the wife of a temple priest, Zechariah. Devoutly religious, the two lived in the hill country of Judea, in close proximity to Jerusalem, where Zechariah ministered at the Temple from Sabbath to Sabbath. Elizabeth means "God is my oath" or "a worshiper of God." Both these meanings are entirely fitting for a woman who proved she had eternal trust in the Lord, even in the face of a major setback — the inability to conceive a child.

Experiencing a miracle

The Bible tells us that Elizabeth is a devout Jew and loyal wife. Although no one knows for certain, Elizabeth probably took care of the vestments and vessels for worship, typically the work done by a wife of a Temple priest. Their home became a center for prayer and talk for people to discuss God and worship with Zechariah. In fact, the evangelist (Gospel writer) Luke mentions that she and Zechariah are sinless and truly dedicated to God: "Both of them were righteous before God, living blamelessly according to all the commandments and regulations of the Lord" (Luke 1:6).

Socially and religiously, they're an important family. Unfortunately, they have one major problem — Elizabeth is barren (Luke 1:7). Like Sarah (Chapter 9) many centuries before, it initially appears that Elizabeth can't fulfill her role as mother. And in the days of patriarchal societies, in which a man's worth was defined by passing on his lineage to sons, this is a large setback.

But Zechariah and Elizabeth don't give up on each other or on God. Their relationship and love remain strong, and Elizabeth doesn't succumb to grief and remains trustful in the Lord. They continue to pray for a miracle, and eventually, they get one.

The origins of the Hail Mary

Catholic Christians use the prayer known as the Hail Mary (Ave Maria in Latin) as part of the rosary. The first part is based upon Gabriel's words to Mary in Luke 1:28: "Hail full of grace, the Lord is with you," from The Ignatius Bible, Catholic Edition: Revised Standard Version. When Elizabeth sees Mary, she exclaims in Luke 1:42: "Blessed are you among women, and blessed is the fruit of your womb." Those two lines are joined together to form the first part of the prayer known as the Hail Mary ("Hail Mary, full of grace, the Lord is with you. Blessed are you among women, and blessed is the fruit of your womb, Jesus").

Unlike today, in Elizabeth's time the possibility of influencing the natural process of reproduction through science and medical technology didn't exist. Nevertheless, God finally blesses Elizabeth with a child, despite the fact that she is elderly (some people estimate in her 80s). Elizabeth's pregnancy is a true miracle — not the result of fertility drugs or medical techniques but, according to the Bible, God's divine intervention.

An angel, Gabriel, appears to Zechariah in the Temple: "But the angel said to him, 'Do not be afraid, Zechariah, because your prayer has been heard. Your wife Elizabeth will bear you a son, and you will name him John'" (Luke 1:13). But Zechariah still has doubts. As a result, God strikes Zechariah speechless for the duration of Elizabeth's pregnancy.

Welcoming a visitor

Six months into her pregnancy with John the Baptist, Elizabeth experiences another significant event in her life. Mary, the soon-to-be mother of Jesus (and Elizabeth's cousin), comes to visit. Mary herself has just learned from the Angel Gabriel that she is pregnant with Jesus, and she also learns from the angel that Elizabeth is pregnant. (For more on Mary, mother of Jesus, see Chapter 6.)

When Mary enters the room, Elizabeth's unborn son, John the Baptist, leaps in her womb for joy. Elizabeth makes her own bold proclamation of faith when she refers to her cousin Mary as "the mother of my Lord." (See Luke 1:39–43 for more details.)

The Greek word found in Luke that Elizabeth says to Mary, "the mother of my Lord" is *Kyrios,* which is the translation for the Hebrew word *Adonai.* Only God could be addressed as Lord, *Kyrios,* or *Adonai.* Eastern Orthodox (Greek and Russian) and Byzantine Christians take Elizabeth's phrase, "mother of my Lord" to formulate the theological term *Theotokos,* which means "bearer" or "mother" of God.

The devout Elizabeth is so awed by Mary's visit that she questions how the Mother of the Savior can travel and help her. Mary, who is young, is also humble, and she knows the older Elizabeth needs her help. Unlike Mary, whose mother, St. Anne, is still alive, Elizabeth probably has no one to help her through pregnancy and childbirth. Because they're cousins, it wasn't unusual for the younger to visit her elder cousin. (See Luke 1:43 for more information.)

What joy this family receives with the granting of two miracles: the conception of John the Baptist and the conception of Jesus.

Following God's will

Jewish custom at the time was to perform a baby's circumcision eight days after his birth. It was also customary to name the boy after his father or paternal grandfather. Although Elizabeth and Zechariah adhere to the first custom, they veer from tradition with the second. Elizabeth proclaims that this child's name will be John because of the words of the Angel Gabriel. When questioned, Zechariah, who is still stricken speechless, confirms it by writing on a tablet, "His name is John." With this show of trust in his wife's decision and in the Angel Gabriel's words, Zechariah's fate suddenly changes: "Immediately his mouth was opened and his tongue freed, and he began to speak, praising God" (Luke 1:64).

Thus Elizabeth and Zechariah experience another miracle. They are filled with joy and the Holy Spirit. This joy is expressed in a beautiful prayer of Elizabeth and Zechariah known as the Benedictus, from the Latin first word of the text, "blessed." In this prophecy, found in Luke 1:68–79, Zechariah praises God for sending his son, John the Baptist, who will become a prophet and help pave the way for Jesus, the Savior.

Understanding the symbolism

The visitation of Mary and Elizabeth is heavy with symbolism. Two cousins are pregnant through divine assistance. Elizabeth is well into her 80s when she gets pregnant, so although her husband, Zechariah, fathers the child, it is God who intervenes and miraculously helps. Like the other women in the Old Testament who believed they were sterile and were eventually blessed by God (such as Sarah, discussed in Chapter 9), Elizabeth's trust in divine providence ensures that she conceives, even in old age, "for nothing will be impossible with God" (Luke 1:37).

Mary, unlike her cousin, is pregnant without the cooperation of a man. According to the Bible, she conceives her son, who is destined to be the Savior and Redeemer of the world, by the power of the Holy Spirit. Both of the women's sons are pivotal to salvation history: Elizabeth's boy will herald the coming of the Messiah, while Mary's child becomes the Messiah himself.

As soon as Mary hears the word of Elizabeth's pregnancy, she rushes to see her. And as soon as Elizabeth hears word of Mary's greeting, the baby in Elizabeth's womb stirs for joy. This fetal movement of John the Baptist within his mother is the first announcement that the Son of God (Jesus) is now here on earth, even though still in the womb of his mother (Mary) for nine more months.

Remembering Elizabeth

Elizabeth's story comes to an end as John's story is just beginning. John's religious fervor is developed first through the devout examples of his mother and father. And John's humility — reflected in his recognition that Jesus is divine and greater than he — is due certainly in part to Elizabeth's rearing. Remember, Elizabeth, the elder cousin, shows respect for Mary, who is carrying the Lord. Neither Elizabeth nor John the Baptist give any signs of jealousy. Mary stays with Elizabeth for three months until John is born and then returns home, three months pregnant with Jesus (Luke 1:56).

We hear no more of Elizabeth after the day of her son's circumcision (see the earlier section, "Following God's will").

Martha and Mary: Sisters of Lazarus

Lazarus, the brother of Martha and Mary, is a good friend of Jesus, and Jesus often stops in to see him on his journeys. Martha and Mary come to know Jesus very well themselves during his visits. The four become close friends, with Jesus often visiting their home in Bethany, a suburb of Jerusalem. The two sisters, while close, are quite opposite in personality. The one thing they do share in common, however, is their faith and devotion to Jesus, which they demonstrate on numerous occasions throughout the New Testament. This faith is ultimately rewarded when Jesus raises their brother from the dead.

Setting them straight

From her descriptions in the Bible, Martha often seems obsessed with the rules and regulations of hospitality. But her sister Mary seems quite the opposite, keeping Martha humbled, as told in a New Testament story.

While Martha was definitely a type A personality by today's standards (apparently she has more in common than just a first name with Martha Stewart), Mary was more of a type B. When Jesus comes to visit, Martha busies herself with tidying the house, sprucing up the garden, and preparing elaborate meals for the King of Kings. Meanwhile, Mary sits and attentively listens to Christ's every word. Although Mary may have assisted her sister to some extent, her work didn't seem to be up to Martha's standards.

During one particular visit, Martha switches into her usual high gear. The quintessential hostess and epitome of hospitality busies herself with last-minute details. As she meticulously prepares the food in the kitchen and the dining room for the meal, she sees her sister sitting back with Jesus, apparently taking it easy. This ignited Martha's fuse to the point that she begs Jesus to shame Mary into helping her. His response is unforgettable: "Martha, Martha, you are worried and distracted by many things; there is need of only one thing. Mary has chosen the better part, which will not be taken away from her" (Luke 10:41–42).

Some controversy surrounds the interpretation of this story. Some Bible scholars propose that Jesus' apparent rebuke is an affirmation of living a contemplative life and that spirituality is superior to the active world. Others maintain that this story simply implies that one should always see the big picture — and that Martha's preoccupation with detail is less important than Mary's appreciation for Jesus' teachings.

In addition, Luke may have been addressing a problem of the day with this analogy. At that time, the scribes, Pharisees, and Sadducees were obsessed with minute adherence to the detail of the law, while ignoring the spirit and purpose of the law. (*Scribes* were men who copied the sacred writings; *Pharisees* were lay religious leaders who used rabbinic interpretations and ancient custom, whereas the *Sadducees* were temple priests who were more fundamentalist and accepted only the written text of the Scripture as authoritative.)

Jesus often rebuked all three groups for their infighting among themselves and for their obsession and preoccupation at times for emphasizing precise observance of the laws without much concern for the spirit of and rationale behind those laws. (See Matthew 5:20 and 23:4 for more details.)

The raising of Lazarus

We next meet Martha and Mary during a more somber event. Their dear and beloved brother, Lazarus, has died. Unfortunately Jesus wasn't in town to heal Lazarus when he was sick, as he had healed many others. His absence is conspicuous — the Gospel says that when Jesus learns Lazarus is on his deathbed, he remains where he is for two more days instead of rushing to his friend's side. Some scholars believe that Jesus purposely delayed his return so as to raise Lazarus from the dead, which could happen only if he was no longer alive.

Because the Jews didn't embalm their dead, his family needs to bury the corpse immediately. When Jesus finally arrives in town, both sisters confront him. Both Martha and Mary separately say to Jesus, "Lord, if you had been here, my brother would not have died" (John 11:21 and John 11:32).

The death of such a dear friend brings tears to Jesus' eyes. This is one of only two occasions the Bible tells us that Jesus cried; the other is when he weeps over the future destruction of the city and Temple of Jerusalem.

When Jesus requests that the stone over Lazarus's tomb be rolled back, Martha, always the realist attentive to detail, reminds Jesus, "Lord, already there is a stench because he has been dead four days" (John 11:39).

Nevertheless, Jesus has the tomb opened, and he literally raises Lazarus back from the dead into the land of the living. Martha herself makes a bold proclamation of faith when she unequivocally affirms to Jesus, "I believe that you are the Messiah, the Son of God, the one coming into the world" (John 11:27). The only other such dramatic profession of such faith in the Gospel is made by Peter when he answers Jesus' question, "But who do you say that I am?" with "You are the Messiah, the Son of the living God" (Matthew 16:16 and Mark 8:29). Yet here is Martha, a woman, neither an apostle nor a disciple, making a comparable statement of belief, along with him.

Many followers of Jesus still had their doubts, and they lacked the clarity and strength of their convictions — except Martha and Peter. Mary also shows her faith, but in other ways.

Anointing the feet

Mary makes a profound show of faith when she anoints the feet of Christ with costly perfumed oil and then wipes them with her hair. This demonstration of humility is an expression of love and affection for her Lord and Savior. Although the apostles talk a good talk before Pentecost (see the Technical Stuff info later about Pentecost), Martha and Mary are the ones who actually show fidelity and faith in Jesus. For example, Judas, the apostle who turned traitor to Jesus, objects to Mary's display of emotion, asking, "Why was this perfume not sold for three hundred denarii and the money given to the poor?" (John 12:4–5). Mary, on the other hand, displays her generosity not just by the perfume she uses, but also by how she demonstrates her love.

Pentecost occurred 50 days after the Resurrection of Jesus and 10 days after his Ascension into heaven. Pentecost is the observance of the descent of the Holy Spirit upon the apostles, documented in Acts 2:1–4.

Although Mary and her sister, Martha, aren't apostles, they are disciples in that they are students seeking to learn from the teacher (Jesus). The 12 apostles would be the founding fathers of the Christian Church, but their faith was still unsteady at times, at least until the Holy Spirit confirms them with grace and truth at Pentecost.

These men and women were still in spiritual training of sorts (like religious boot camp) and therefore were not proficient yet in the faith. Peter, James, John, and the gang may have been Christ's confidants, but Martha and Mary were the ones who put their faith into practice more often than the rest. That's not to say the apostles had no or little faith or that they faltered most of time, but they were still rookies. Mary and her sister confidently lived their faith, while the men were still testing the waters.

Martha and Mary aren't mentioned again explicitly in the Bible even though some medieval and Renaissance artists often chose to insert one or both of them into scenes of the Crucifixion along with the women who are specifically named in scripture as being present.

Mary: Mother of James and Joses

Another Biblical Mary is the mother of the apostle James the Less (meaning he was chosen by Christ after James the Greater) and his brother Joses (more commonly called Joseph), a woman who proves herself through her example and devotion to Jesus by staying with him as he died on Calvary. She is also described as the wife of Clopas (also spelled Cleopas or Cleophas).

Mary makes many sacrifices for her faith in God and in Jesus. First, both her sons become disciples of Jesus, devoting their lives to him and traveling the land far and wide. Having one son leave home is hard enough, but Mary has to let both sons go. Yet she endures the hardship in the knowledge that her boys are doing the work of God. Later, Mary gives of herself by staying at Jesus' side during his darkest hour (John 19:25). She is generous, faithful, loving, and true to the Lord. She shows that love is active, not idle.

A question of sisterhood

John 19:25 says there were three Marys at the crucifixion of Jesus: his mother (Mary), his mother's "sister" (Mary, the wife of Clopas and the mother of James and Joses) and Mary Magdalene. It is unlikely, however, that the Virgin Mary's sister would also be called Mary. The more likely explanation can be determined by using the Greek translation. The Greek word originally used to refer to Mary the wife of Clopas, is *adelphe,* the feminine form of *adelphos.* This word can be translated as "sister," but it also can mean "cousin," "aunt," "niece", or other female relative, because the ancient Hebrew, from which it was translated, also had no separate words to define extended relatives. In Hebrew, *achowth* was used to mean "sister" or any female relative, including aunt, niece, or cousin. So Jesus' mother (Mary) and her "sister" Mary were probably cousins or another type of close relation.

Mary is among the faithful women from Galilee who follow Jesus to Jerusalem to witness his death on the cross. "Among them were Mary Magdalene, Mary the mother of James and Joseph, and the mother of the sons of Zebedee" (Matthew 27:56). Along with Mary Magdalene (see Chapter 7), she is among the first at the tomb on Easter Sunday when Jesus arose from the dead (Matthew 28:1–2; Luke 24:10).

Mary is also referred to in the Gospel of John, soon after the crucifixion of Jesus: "Meanwhile, standing near the cross of Jesus were his mother, and his mother's sister, Mary the wife of Clopas, and Mary Magdalene" (John 19:25).

Mary: Mother of John Mark

Yet another brave and faithful Mary shows her faith in Jesus. This Mary is the mother of Mark (the author of the second Gospel account).

Mark is Mary's son's Roman name, but he is also known by his Hebrew name that his mother bestowed upon him — John. Hence the designation "John Mark."

During Mary's lifetime, which spanned the life of Jesus and beyond, Christians had no specific buildings in which to worship and learn about Jesus. Because early Christianity was outlawed, groups were forced to be secretive for fear of persecution, and early worship took place in private homes. A Christian knew where to go to celebrate the Divine Liturgy by looking for a tracing of a fish in the dirt of the host location. (Divine Liturgy is the Christian worship service also known as the Breaking of the Bread, the Lord's Supper, Eucharistic Liturgy, and more — it had several names.) Mary provided the location and space for the weekly celebration of Christian worship just as she probably provided the room for Jesus to have his Last Supper on Holy Thursday. Scholars believe that Mary probably owned the "upper room" of the place where the Last Supper took place — and where the Holy Spirit descended at Pentecost.

Mary is believed to have been a woman of means with a spacious home, which she offered so Christians could gather in the name of Jesus:

> *As soon as he [Peter] realized this, he went to the house of Mary, the mother of John whose other name was Mark, where many had gathered and were praying.*
>
> —Acts 12:12

By giving freely of her home despite some very real risks, Mary truly leads by example. She is a woman who puts her faith in action. She could have been arrested for harboring this new religion, and she also risked losing her fortune, her home, and even her life. Yet she continues worshiping the Lord and aiding this worship by allowing believers to worship in her home. She continues to be of service to Jesus in the newly developing church. She must have felt great honor to have her Risen and Glorified Savior once again present "in the breaking of the Bread," as the early Christians first called the Eucharistic Liturgy.

Mary's home must have been a spiritual inspiration for John Mark, who comes to know Jesus through these sacred celebrations. Mary and Mark also come to know Peter, the chief apostle and first pope, in their home. One can only assume that Mary's example and upbringing are the perfect breeding ground for Mark's future work: writing the Gospel as he traveled with Peter.

Mary is mentioned for the last time in the Bible when Peter returns to her house after he has escaped the clutches of Herod (see Acts 12:12). Her generosity in providing for the early Church (also known as the assembly of the faithful) sets a standard for future believers who have been blessed with material wealth. Sharing abundance with the poor is always a laudable mission for all people of means. Mary led the way, and subsequent benefactors soon followed.

A Chance Meeting with Jesus: The Syro-Phoenician Woman

The story of the Syro-Phoenician woman (also referred to as the Canaanite woman) is a story of faith and tolerance. This woman, whose name no one knows, is described only as a Phoenician. (*Phoenicia* was an ancient civilization to the north of Israel.) Quite wealthy because they were great seafarers and traders, the Phoenicians were the envy of the ancient world. They worshiped the false god Baal, and therefore the Jews considered them heathens. Jezebel (see Chapter 16) was another Phoenician woman — not fondly remembered — in the Old Testament.

Through the story of the Syro-Phoenician woman, you can see that the New Covenant (the sacred agreement between God and His people; the first was between God and the Hebrews, the second between Christ and the Church) was designed to include all believers — not just the Jews. The implication is that God knows no racial boundaries, and every person has the chance to be saved through Jesus.

The trouble with dogs

Some Bible scholars point out that the Syro-Phoenician woman whose daughter was possessed by the devil uses the word *kunaria* (meaning dog). Phoenicians weren't well liked by the Jews, and the feeling was mutual. In fact, many of Jesus' followers considered any Gentile (non-Jew) as low as a dog or infidel. But there were two different Aramaic words for "dog." *Pariah* were the wild, often rabid, street dogs that everyone feared and avoided, and *kunaria* were the cute, cuddly puppy dogs people kept in their homes. Jesus used the more familiar and friendlier term, which the woman picks up on and uses in her counterargument.

This Syro-Phoenician woman has a daughter possessed by the devil. When she hears about the miracle worker, Jesus, and that he is traveling through her area, she seeks him out for a cure. When she encounters Jesus, she is humble and recognizes her sinfulness. Her reaction is quite striking because she has no reason to think that Jesus, a Jew, would listen to a person of her descent. It is also surprising that, with her background, this woman would have such faith in Jesus as the Savior. Nevertheless, she testifies before Christ: "Have mercy on me, Lord, Son of David! My daughter is tormented by a demon" (Matthew 15:22).

At first, Jesus appears to ignore her, but she perseveres in her pleading and kneels before him. Finally Jesus responds, and at first he sounds harsh: "It is not fair to take the children's bread and throw it to the dogs" (Matthew 15:26).

The "bread" Jesus refers to is his grace, and "children" refers to the true believers in Israel. This comment is Jesus' way of testing the woman's faith and perseverance, and she passes with wit and spirit with this quick response: "Yes, Lord, yet even the dogs eat the crumbs that fall from their masters' table" (Matthew 15:27).

All she asks is that a crumb may fall her way, despite her background. She isn't offended by Jesus' comments, and because she believes, she is determined to win Jesus' grace.

This woman's persistent faith brings its reward, and her daughter is cured: "Then Jesus answered her, 'Woman, great is your faith! Let it be done for you as you wish.' And her daughter was healed instantly" (Matthew 15:28). As a great witness to the miraculous powers of Jesus, she would later bring many others to the faith. We don't hear from the woman again, but her faith and perseverance, despite apparent obstacles, remain an example even today.

Spiritual Rebirth: The Samaritan Woman at the Well

The Samaritan woman at the well is no angel. Mixed up with a wrong crowd, this poor woman from Samaria has quite a reputation. She had been married five times and was living in sin with a man who wasn't her husband.

Through her story comes the lesson that people shouldn't live by carnal pleasure. The story also shows that a well of grace is ready to refresh the soul parched by sin and suffering and that Jesus comes to save the sick and to serve those who still need both physical and spiritual healing — not only the converted.

Her story is also relevant because it becomes an antecedent of Christian practices — that one may seek God's forgiveness for wrongdoing.

In some Christian religions, including Catholicism and Orthodox, seeking forgiveness is the basis for the sacrament of Reconciliation (confession). Every faith has a teaching and belief that God forgives sin and that repentance is always possible. The Jewish feast of Yom Kippur and Islam's Ramadan are also examples of seeking forgiveness and showing atonement for sin.

The woman at the well had her sins "washed away" by Jesus. The story shows that Jesus offers divine mercy in the living water of grace, which washes away sins and cleanses souls. The woman went to the well to get a jug of water. Instead, she got much more, including a cleansed and refreshed spiritual life.

Going to the well

Because of her lowly status, the Samaritan woman goes to the well during the hottest point of the day to avoid the wagging tongues of her fellow townspeople. Most other people were taking siestas at this time; nobody in his or her right mind is out in the noonday sun. The woman of Samaria knows this and seizes the opportunity to get water for her home without being bothered.

Jews didn't normally travel on a Samaritan road, but Jesus chose to walk this way anyway. He comes upon the well, where he meets the Samaritan woman and asks her for a drink of water. The woman, who understands her low social status in the eyes of a Jew, is astonished that this pious Jew requests water from her. (See John 4:7–9).

The rift between Jews and Samaritans

Jews didn't look upon Samaritans very favorably. Former Jews who had wandered off in the eighth century BC during the Assyrian conquest of the northern kingdom of Israel, the Samaritans had developed their own brand of Judaism that the original Jews saw as heresy. The Samaritans even built their own temple so they wouldn't have to travel to Jerusalem for ritual sacrifices (of lambs, goats, doves, and more), which didn't win them any friends, either. Most Jews wouldn't be caught dead in the company of Samaritans.

Experiencing renewed spirit

Jesus uses the water as a metaphor to teach this woman. He speaks about the living water, which gives eternal life, divine grace, or God's life within the soul. The woman craves this type of water, because she wants to have eternal life. But first Jesus has a lengthy but candid dialogue with her. He makes her understand that she needs to confess her sins and change her life before she can obtain this life-giving water — grace. Jesus shows her that he already knows she is living with a man who is not her husband. (See John 4:10–18 for more information.)

> *Jesus said to her, "Go, call your husband, and come back." The woman answered him, "I have no husband." Jesus said to her, "You are right in saying, 'I have no husband'; for you have had five husbands, and the one you have now is not your husband. What you have said is true!"*
>
> —John 4:16–18

> *The woman said to him, "I know that Messiah is coming"(who is called Christ). "When he comes, he will proclaim all things to us." Jesus said to her, "I am he, the one who is speaking to you."*
>
> —John 4:25–26

The Samaritan woman's spirit is enlightened, accelerated, and illuminated by Jesus. She now realizes what it means to take freely of the water of life, which is the spiritual refreshment that comes into her soul after her encounter and confession with Jesus. Not only was she impressed that Jesus knew all her sins, but she was also given the opportunity to have those sins forgiven. She believes he is truly the Messiah, the Anointed One. She repents of her past misdeeds and goes back to tell her family, friends, and neighbors how she met Jesus and how he revealed his knowledge of her sins and his offer of live-giving water, which brings eternal life. She went on to lead many conversions in this area through her zeal and love for God (John 4:39–42).

The Samaritan woman doesn't appear again in scripture, but for centuries afterward, numerous spiritual writers, theologians, and scholars retold and pondered her encounter with Jesus. Augustine (AD 354–430), for instance, uses the example of the woman at the well to describe the spiritual thirst the human heart has for goodness and truth and that thirst is never quenched until people are in the presence of God forever (after they die and leave this earth).

Chapter 14

Church Ladies: Women of the New Testament

*I*n this chapter, we look at some women of the New Testament — both good and bad. Although Jesus chose 12 men to be his apostles and another 70 or so to be his disciples, he also had several female followers — Christian women who had as much faith and devotion as their male counterparts. Among these women were Dorcas, Lydia, Priscilla, Phoebe, Eunice, and Lois, who all exemplified how faithful Christians should live, especially in their service to others.

We also introduce you to some women whose lives were less than exemplary: Sapphira, a Christian, and Drusilla and Bernice, both of Jewish background, who leave much to be desired as devout believers.

Sinful Sapphira: Putting Appearances First

Sapphira is one of the early Christian women who teach what *not* to do through her own wrongdoing. By offending the apostles and the early Church, she is punished in the extreme, along with her husband, Ananias. Though her biblical role is more of a cameo, the name Sapphira is widely associated with sin. And though she shares her sin with her husband, she had a chance to repent and tell the truth but rejected this opportunity. Her lie was her own, and she paid the same penalty as her spouse.

Understanding the early Church

In Acts 4:36–37, a man named Barnabas, who would later introduce Paul to the apostles in Acts 9:26–27 and then accompany him on some of his missionary journeys, sells some property and gives *all* the proceeds to the apostles, literally laying the profit at their feet. Barnabas is a perfect example of good Christian beliefs in charity. Acts 4:32 says that early assemblies of Christian believers were of one mind and heart; they shared everything. The rich shared to help the poor.

The church was no hippie commune by any means — and certainly no primitive experiment in socialism or communism. The ancient Church didn't force or compel people to surrender their wealth, property, possessions, or anything else. It did, however, encourage and promote real Christian charity — which, unlike pity, would go beyond token or symbolic donations. Real sharing and caring for one's neighbor were encouraged, because Christians were asked to view and treat their fellow human beings as brothers and sisters in Christ — one family of faith.

Getting to know Sapphira

Sapphira and Ananias are wealthy Jewish converts to Christianity. They live when the apostles themselves are still alive, around the middle of the first century AD. We don't know when they became Christians — they may have even seen or heard Jesus himself while he was alive on earth. What we do know is that they had embraced the Christian faith, at least publicly.

God blesses this couple financially and with the gift of faith, so they decide to share their wealth with those in need in the community. They aren't forced to do this but voluntarily want to give. The problem arises when they become dishonest after selling some property. No one ever said they had to give away everything or even what amount, but they chose to pretend that they gave all that they had (to look good), when actually they kept some back.

Misleading the Church

Unlike Barnabas, a man who gave all of his possessions to the apostles to promote the Christian church's spirit of sharing (see the sidebar, "Understanding the early Church"), Sapphira and Ananias withhold some of their possessions for themselves. The Bible leads us to believe that they make it appear as if they donate all the proceeds of the real estate sale, while in actuality they turn over only a portion. It's sort of like claiming a bigger charitable tax deduction on your 1040 than you actually gave — only instead of lying to the IRS, they're lying to God.

Their offense isn't the amount they gave or the fact that they withhold some of the money but that both husband and wife lie about it.

When Peter confronts Ananias to ask whether he was telling the truth — if he was misrepresenting his offering — Ananias denies it. He then falls over dead. Three hours later, his wife Sapphira enters, unaware of her husband's death. Peter then asks her if they sold the property for the price Ananias claimed. She lies as well and then drops dead herself. (See Acts 5:1–11 for the story of Sapphira and Ananias.) By claiming to turn over 100 percent of the proceeds, were they trying to make the rest of the Christian community think they were more generous than they actually were? Were they greedy in not wanting to give too much to the poor even though they may have had plenty more in reserve? We don't know for sure.

Understanding the repercussions

Sapphira and Ananias try to make themselves look good to others. If they had kept some of the loot openly, it wouldn't have resulted in such punishment. But because they pretend to donate the entire amount, they commit a sin — and they receive punishment (death!) for it.

Neglecting the poor is bad, and the Bible discourages such behavior. Yet, as Sapphira and Ananias demonstrate, merely doing good isn't enough either — especially when you do good only for appearance's sake. Doing good for the right reason is ultimately the most important act under God.

Acts 5 is the only place where Sapphira's name appears in the Bible, and like Jezebel (see Chapter 16), it's become synonymous with bad character and/or bad deeds. If Sapphira had separated herself from her husband's sin, she may have saved her life and her soul. She instead chose a different path, which ultimately led to her ruin.

Devout Dorcas (Tabitha): Doing Good for Others

Dorcas (who lived in the early first century AD) demonstrates that just as bad deeds are punished, good deeds can bring the ultimate reward. Called Tabitha by the Jews and Dorcas by the Greeks, this woman of Joppa is known for her generosity, kindness, compassion, and charitable works. Unlike Sapphira, Dorcas does good not to impress others but because she truly loves God and her neighbor.

We learn of Dorcas, who practices real Christian charity by giving her time, talent, and treasure to the poor, in Acts 9. She is also called a female disciple (*mathetria* in Greek).

A female disciple was not the same as a male disciple (*mathetes* in Greek). When the New Testament merely refers to "the disciples," it can mean the 12 apostles before the Resurrection, or it can refer to the 70 or 72 male disciples who followed Jesus but were not apostles. The men who were called apostles and disciples later became the religious leaders of the early Christian Church (apostles as bishops and disciples as priests or elders). The women named as female disciples listened to Jesus preach and teach, and they supported him and the male apostles by their prayers and sometimes by financial support as well, but they didn't take on formal leadership roles in the Church.

A dressmaker and seamstress by trade, Dorcas uses her talents and resources to help unfortunate and needy widows by making and donating clothing for them. In those days, widows who had no inheritance or adult children to support them often had no means to support themselves and were destitute. (See Chapter 21 for more on widows.)

After years of doing good works, one day Dorcas becomes ill and dies. When Peter hears this news from one of the many people who love her, he quickly goes to her home (because he is the visible leader of the Christian community after Jesus' resurrection and ascension to heaven) and enters the upper room where her dead body is laid. "Tabitha, get up" (Acts 9:40), he commands the corpse. Miraculously, she opens her eyes and rises from her deathbed. Coincidentally, this is the same Peter whose deathly sick mother had been miraculously healed by Jesus earlier in the Gospel (Luke 4:38–39).

The contrast between Dorcas (Tabitha) and Sapphira is obvious. A good woman helps others for good reasons, and when she dies, she is raised from the dead. A bad woman helps others merely to look good to others, and she drops dead when caught in her attempted deception. Dorcas is an example of a supporting character of the Bible — one who has only a cameo appearance in the Bible but whose example still resonates to this day.

Self-Made Lydia

Lydia is referred to as the first Christian convert of Europe. Lydia and others like her demonstrate that you can have wealth, power, position, and influence, and be a devout Christian, as long as you recognize the plight of the disenfranchised and powerless and do something to help them. She is able to be poor in spirit by not allowing her material possessions to possess her.

Lydia shares generously and joyfully, and her kindness helps key figures like the apostle Paul and Silas (a Christian leader from Jerusalem) when they need a place to stay after being released from prison in Philippi.

Lydia is a self-made woman and a very successful businessperson who is referred to in the Bible as a "dealer in purple." This term means that she sold and traded purple linens and was involved in the dyeing process, which was a profitable enterprise.

Purple at that time signified status and wealth. The Romans used purple and the various shades of it to designate and differentiate the aristocracy (senators) and royalty (emperor) in the empire. Greeks used purple to symbolize the rich and powerful. Wearing purple then was like wearing the Rolex watches, Gucci bags, and Armani suits of today.

Lydia comes from Thyatira in Asia Minor, and later she moves and works in the city of Philippi in Macedonia. As a Gentile who was attracted to Judaism and attended the synagogue but never formally converted to Judaism (often called a God fearer, *theos phobeo* in Greek; Acts 13:16), Lydia seeks to grow in her faith. Providentially, she hears Paul and Silas preaching, which converts her and her entire household to Christianity, and she then uses her wealth and position to assist the infant church. (Acts 16:14–15; 40 tells the story of Lydia.)

She provides lodging and accommodations for Christian missionaries on their many travels. Her generosity and thoughtfulness go beyond occasional charitable feelings and acts. Instead, Lydia personifies that ideal of noblesse oblige, the obligation and duty of society's elite to help the less fortunate. She sets a good example by using her home and her money for the sake of those in need and for the spread of the faith. Although some renounce their earthly treasures for the sake of serving God, others use the blessings they have in the forms of wealth and possessions and power or influence to also serve God by helping those less fortunate. Although this is the last we hear of Lydia in the Bible, her example carries on through teachings today.

Pious Priscilla

Priscilla (also called Prisca) plays a highly influential role in the early church as educator and gatherer of early Christians. She and her husband, Aquila, are always mentioned together as a couple (Acts 18:2, 26; Romans 16:3; 2 Timothy 4:19), but three out of five times Priscilla's name is mentioned first. This order is highly uncommon, as a husband's name ordinarily is mentioned first in a patriarchal society. This fact is testament to her influence and her devoted witness to God and early Christianity.

Meeting up with Paul

Originally from Rome, the couple leaves the city when the Emperor Claudius expels the Jews in AD 49. They flee to Corinth, where they meet the apostle Paul who helped establish the Christian faith in the town. It appears as if they had already converted to Christianity before this meeting in AD 50. (Acts 18:2).

Priscilla and Aquila are tentmakers, and Paul approaches them about gaining part-time employment with them so he doesn't have to burden the church by asking for financial support to obtain room and board. Paul becomes an employee, friend, and tenant, when the couple provide a place for him to live as well. We assume that this is when Priscilla's devotion to Christianity blossomed. She puts her faith into practice, and so her deeds and her words coincide and reflect the Christian belief in her heart. She and her husband later accompany Paul to Ephesus.

Priscilla's homes in both Corinth and Ephesus are gathering places for early Christians to hear about and celebrate the faith. Over time, both places become centers for Christianity, as evidenced by the letters (epistles) that Paul later writes to each community (Romans 16:3–4; 1 Corinthians 16:19; 2 Timothy 4:19). Paul is so grateful and indebted to this couple that he says in his Epistle to the Romans: "Greet Prisca and Aquila, who work with me in Christ Jesus, and who risked their necks for my life, to whom not only I give thanks, but also all the assemblies of the Gentiles" (Romans 16:3–4).

Teaching Apollos

When Apollos, an eloquent Jewish Christian preacher from Alexandria who is well schooled in the Old Testament arrives in Ephesus, Priscilla takes him under her tutelage. She offers him mentoring in the oral tradition (what the apostles preached about Jesus) and early gospels (what the evangelists actually wrote about Jesus) to enable him to be an even more effective preacher. Apollos had learned about Christ from John the Baptist, but he doesn't have full knowledge of the Christian Word. The Bible says that Priscilla and Aquila "explained the Way of God to him more accurately" (Acts 18:26). This verse shows that she is an astute student of the scriptures and capable of teaching even a respected teacher.

Priscilla and her husband are true lay missionaries in that they help spread the new Christian faith but are not full-time church workers like Paul and Silas. We don't hear again about them, but their example inspires people today.

Phoebe (Phebe): A Trustworthy Messenger

The scatter-brained character from the TV show *Friends* has quite a noble namesake: Phoebe, a deaconess in the New Testament. Phoebe (also spelled Phebe) is considered an important and trustworthy messenger for Paul. At one point he calls her *prostatis,* which is often translated as "patroness" or "a woman of high esteem and respect."

Phoebe lives in Cenchreae, a port city near Corinth, when Paul sends her to Rome to deliver a letter to the church (his Epistle to the Romans). Such an assignment is a big responsibility; sending her on this mission implies that Phoebe is trustworthy and highly capable.

Phoebe's influence and status are revealed when Paul refers to her in Romans 16:1 (see the Revised Standard Version Bible) as a deaconess, *diakonissa* in some Greek manuscripts. His words say that by serving Paul, she also serves her Church, God, and early Christianity.

Several Protestant Christian churches consider Phoebe's example — and the fact that Paul called Phoebe a "deaconess" — as a basis for ordained ministry for both men and women. They use Phoebe as an example of women who participated in Christian liturgical worship, which had not been done in the Jewish temple. For more on this topic, see the sidebar, "Implications of 'deaconess.'"

Implications of "deaconess"

Some denominations have extended women's roles in recent decades to include the higher offices of pastor and even bishop (beyond their roles as deaconesses). Eastern Orthodox and Catholic Christians, however, believe the ceremonial *deaconesses* (female) to be separate and distinct from the official public office of *deacons* (male), who assist the *priests* (presbyters or elders) and the *bishops* in the three-fold ordained ministry. They believe that female deacons were used in order to baptize women. (It was judged inappropriate for men to get too close to loosely clothed women who would be fully immersed in water during the baptism process.) Outside of this assistance at the baptism of adult women, Catholic and Orthodox scholars claim that no deaconess was ever promoted to *presbuteros* (priest) or *episkopos* (bishop), nor did they preach or hold official office like male deacons *(diakonos).* They further justify women's exclusion from higher ministry through Paul's first epistle to Timothy: "Let deacons be married only once" (1 Timothy 3:12). The implication is that only a male deacon could have a "wife," and the Greek word *gyne* (wife) can't be translated merely as spouse, which could be either gender.

Phoebe isn't mentioned again in the Bible, but her service to the ancient church — to the early Christian faith community —is still honored today. Her generosity in her material support as a patroness and her spiritual assistance to Paul and the church in Rome by personally delivering an important message epitomizes what the Greek word *diakonia* (service ministry) truly means.

Drusilla and Bernice: Spoiled Sisters

Drusilla (Acts 24:24) and Bernice (Acts 25:13, 23; 26:30) are sisters who lived during the first century AD. As the granddaughters of Herod the Great, the man who had ordered all infant boys slaughtered when Jesus was born, and the daughters of Herod Agrippa I, a persecutor of early Christians, these sisters appear in the Bible as they come to see Paul in the courts of Caesarea, where he has been imprisoned.

Paul previously had been arrested and imprisoned in Jerusalem by the Jewish religious leaders for preaching about Jesus of Nazareth. Some 40 zealots plot to kill him, and Paul's sister learns about it and tips off the Romans — Paul is a Roman citizen and legally can't be executed by non-Roman authorities. Paul invokes his citizenship rights and appeals to Caesar, which eventually lands him in Rome where he is martyred at the order of Emperor Nero.

Before their encounter with Paul, neither Drusilla nor Bernice has led God-fearing lives. They both have had multiple marriages and have engaged in illicit relationships, and they live the typical scandalous lives of the rich, powerful, and well-to-do of their time. With inherited wealth and almost no supervision, guidance, or direction, they grow up expecting that the world owes them. Privileged, spoiled, and overly indulged, they may have had Jewish background, but they show no religious devotion whatsoever to the Hebrew faith.

Drusilla's encounter with Paul (see Acts 24:24) comes via her second husband, Felix, who is the procurator (a Roman financial officer, in charge of collecting imperial taxes) of Judea when Paul was imprisoned in Caesarea. (Her first husband was King Azizus of Emesa, whom she abandons to live with Felix, in defiance of Jewish law. The facts of her prior marriage are mentioned in the *Harper's Bible Dictionary, Easton's Bible Dictionary,* and the *Tyndale Bible Dictionary,* which all base their information on the historical record of Flavius Josephus in his work, *The Antiquities.*)

When Paul is brought before Felix and Drusilla (several days after his arrest by the Romans), his response is "It is about the resurrection of the dead that

I am on trial before you today" (Acts 24:21). He speaks of justice, self-control, and faith in Jesus Christ. But Drusilla isn't impressed. She casually suggests that he be left in jail. Even after hearing his teachings, she doesn't repent for adultery. (The *Codex Bezae* is an ancient manuscript containing the text of Acts of the Apostles, which adds a few lines to Acts 24:27 saying it was Drusilla's suggestion that Paul stay in prison.)

Her sister, Bernice, is no more open to Paul's word. After two years in prison, Paul appears before Bernice when she comes to Caesarea with her brother, Agrippa II, from Rome. Allegedly, this brother is also her lover. After her first husband, Marcus died, she married her uncle, King Herod of Chalcis, and after he died, she got involved with Agrippa.

Paul tells the court his conversion story about beginning as a zealous and devout Jew named Saul of Tarsus, rising to the high levels of being a Pharisee, and spending time and effort persecuting Christians as enemies of the Hebrew faith. While en route to Damascus, Paul encounters a voice that cries out, "Saul, Saul, why are you persecuting me?" The voice identifies himself as Jesus, and from that moment on he becomes Paul the Christian Apostle. (See Acts 26:12–18.)

He points out that he was a devout Pharisee, and unlike the Sadducees who denied the resurrection of the dead, he believed like his fellow Pharisees that there was life after death. In fact, he believes not only in the general concept of the dead being raised at the end of time, but now as a Christian, he also believes that Jesus died and rose by himself from the dead. (See Acts 26:19–23.)

But like Drusilla before her, Bernice isn't moved by the words of faith and truth that Paul speaks. Festus thinks Paul is insane, but Agrippa is not so inclined to believe that; he remarks to Festus, "This man could have been set free if he had not appealed to the emperor" (Acts 26:32). The wheels are set in motion, however, and Paul's case must now go before Caesar, so he is put on a ship headed to Rome (where he eventually is martyred by the Emperor Nero around AD 67). Bernice apparently believed as Festus did, viewing Paul as a religious nut. Her husband, Agrippa, on the other hand, sees him as an innocent man being persecuted for his faith.

We hear no more of Bernice, and this one encounter with Paul was much like the visit her sister Drusilla had earlier with Paul. Both sisters heard the preaching of this apostle, but neither one of them embraced his words. Both sisters had lived notorious lives, and both are given the opportunity to listen to the apostle, yet neither sister allows his words to have any effect. We don't hear of them again, but they epitomize people who lead sinful lives, have a chance to repent, and ignore that chance.

Eunice and Lois: Fostering Faith

Eunice and Lois symbolize how mothers and grandmothers can positively influence their children to do great things. These women of the first century AD were raised as Jews and converted to Christianity during one of the apostle Paul's missionary trips to their home in Lystra. Despite a patriarchal system and male-dominated society, Timothy (a convert and companion of Paul) isn't identified by the name of his father, but instead by his mother, Eunice. Although Eunice and her mother, Lois, are referenced only briefly in the Bible, the context in which their names appear speaks volumes. The implication is that Eunice and Lois together lay the foundation for Timothy's faith (2 Timothy 1:5).

It is through Timothy's mother that we see such a strong practice in the faith. Paul alludes to this when he says:

> *But as for you, continue in what you have learned and firmly believed, knowing from whom you learned it, and how from childhood you have known the sacred writings that are able to instruct you for salvation through faith in Christ Jesus.*

> —2 Timothy 3:14–15

Lois, Timothy's maternal grandmother, also is credited for her impact and influence on Timothy. Although the Bible mentions many grandmothers (like Sarah and her grandson Jacob), the word *grandmother* itself — *mamme* in Greek — appears only once, in reference to Lois. Paul wrote to Timothy "I am reminded of your sincere faith, a faith that lived first in your grandmother Lois and your mother Eunice and now, I am sure, lives in you" (2 Timothy 1:5).

This mother and daughter are known only by their relationship to Timothy. But the very mention of their names in the New Testament verifies that mothers and grandmothers can have a vital role in the spiritual development of their youth.

As devout Jews, Eunice and Lois know all the stories of the Old Testament, and they share their Hebrew faith with Timothy. Then Paul leads all of them to convert. It was Paul to whom they entrusted Timothy's future. And Paul, who has no wife or children of his own, looks upon Timothy as a beloved and spiritual son — one he can be proud of, thanks to the fine religious foundation these two women gave him.

This mother-and-daughter team isn't mentioned again in the Bible, but they shine as beacons to all mothers and grandmothers, inspiring them to give good examples, sound teaching, and lots of love to their children so they may grow up to be vibrant believers and teachers.

Part IV
Women of Public Debate . . . or Disdain

Delilah discovers the source of Samson's strength and meets with the Philistines.

©RICHTENNANT

"...but before you render him weak and helpless, I need him to move some bedroom furniture, haul a bunch of junk out of the basement, my vomitorium needs repainting..."

In this part . . .

You encounter in this part the women of mystery in the Bible — the obscure, the controversial, and the dangerous. The Bible is not a biography or a history book, and many of the people in it, like the women we look at here, have mysterious origins, unknown endings, and questionable motives. These women spark debate and discussion among scripture scholars and Bible readers alike. Yet they, too, influenced the course of history, either directly or indirectly.

Chapter 15

Hiding in Obscurity: Important Yet Overlooked Women

Certain women in the Bible were often overlooked although their stories are relevant and should be viewed more prominently. These women were active participants — not mere spectators — but over time, they have been largely ignored in favor of more flamboyant biblical characters.

In this chapter, we discuss women like Hagar, who bore a son to Abraham when his wife Sarah couldn't conceive (Chapter 11), and Dinah, who was defiled by a man, an act that caused an outbreak of violence. We also look at Lot's wife, who looked back upon the city of Sodom and was turned into a pillar of salt. We delve into the lives of Potiphar's wife and Huldah, who — in their own ways — impacted history. These women continue to spark theological interest and debate . . . even today.

Mothering Ishmael: Sarah's Handmaid, Hagar

Hagar lived at the time of the patriarch Abram (later to be renamed Abraham) around 1800 BC. She was born in Egypt but then lived in Canaan as a maidservant to Sarah. Her name in her native tongue means "flight" or "fugitive." The scriptures don't tell us anything of her background, history, or genealogy, but according to the *midrash* (rabbinic teaching on scripture), she was the daughter of Pharaoh. The midrash also says she was given as a recompense for the embarrassment caused when the king of Egypt (her father perhaps) mistakenly took Sarah for his wife, believing she was Abraham's sister rather than his wife, a story told in Genesis 12:10–20. See Chapter 11 of this book for more details about Abraham, Sarah, and the Pharaoh.

Midrash is a Hebrew word that means a method of interpreting Biblical text.

Acting as surrogate

Hagar first appears in Genesis 16. Sarah, who has been unable to bear children with Abraham, proposes that he have a child with her handmaid, Hagar, instead (Genesis 16:1–3).

This idea, which may seem peculiar by today's Western standards, wasn't uncommon at that time. The Code of Hammurabi (Babylonian law), the Nuzi tablets, and old Assyrian marriage contracts allowed a barren woman to give her maid to her husband as a second wife or concubine in order to perpetuate the lineage. Although Sarah is the one who suggests this option, she later regrets it. Hagar has a change of heart toward Sarah too: "When she saw that she had conceived, she looked with contempt on her mistress" (Genesis 16:4).

No one really knows why Hagar felt this way and how she expressed it. In any event, the pregnancy causes bad blood between the two women. Perhaps Sarah sees Hagar as a rival for Abraham's affection. Perhaps Hagar resents the status Sarah enjoyed as wife, while she has to be content as a concubine.

Regardless, after Sarah detects Hagar's contempt, she begins to mistreat and abuse her, spurring the pregnant Hagar to escape and flee into the wilderness (see Genesis 16:6). God sends an angel, however, to speak with Hagar and encourage her to return to her mistress despite the abuse. The angel also tells Hagar that she will conceive and give birth to a son whom she is to call Ishmael, which means "God hears" (Genesis 16:11). Hagar finds out that this son will be the origin of many peoples.

Overcoming family dysfunction

Ironically, an 80-something Sarah finally becomes pregnant herself about ten years later, after a lifetime of being barren. She conceives a son, a fact also foretold by an angel of the Lord. This son is named Isaac and is chosen by God as the one to carry on God's covenant with his father, Abraham, because he is the son of Sarah. This means that Hagar's son, Ishmael, though firstborn to Abraham, will not receive his father's birthright.

When Isaac is a baby and Ishmael is about 13, Sarah sees the two half brothers together. The Bible is ambiguous about exactly what transpires. Some translations say that Ishmael is playing with Isaac, and others say that he is mocking or teasing him. Whatever happened, Sarah becomes very protective and defensive and insists that Abraham expel the child and his mother.

If Ishmael was just playing, perhaps Sarah was nervous that the boys would become too close later in life, which would complicate matters when Isaac claimed the birthright in place of his older brother. Or maybe Ishmael was making sport of his little brother, and Sarah simply took innocent fooling around too seriously. Whatever the motive, and despite not knowing the exact details of Ishmael's actions, we do know that he and his mom, Hagar, are thrown out of the camp and cast into the desert. (Genesis 21:8–14 describes this incident.)

As described in Genesis 21:15–20, God doesn't forget the promise he made to Hagar, however. An angel comes to her again (see a painting of this scene in Figure 15-1), reminds her that God will make a great nation out of her son, and leads them to fresh water in the desert. Both mother and son survive, and eventually Hagar finds an Egyptian wife for Ishmael.

Figure 15-1:
Hagar rescued by the angel, by Giambattista Tiepolo (1696–1770).

Scala/Art Resource, NY

Two covenants

In his New Testament Epistle to the Galatians, Paul sees an allegory in Hagar and Sarah. To him, the former represents the earthly Jerusalem and the Jewish community, whereas the latter represents the heavenly Jerusalem and the Christian church: "Now this is an allegory: these women are two covenants. One woman, in fact, is Hagar, from Mount Sinai, bearing children for slavery. Now Hagar is Mount Sinai in Arabia and corresponds to the present Jerusalem, for she is in slavery with her children. But the other woman corresponds to the Jerusalem above; she is free, and she is our mother" (Galatians 4:24–26).

Ishmael becomes progenitor of the Ishmaelites, from whom most Arab peoples descend. Hagar, his mother, is only mentioned once again — allegorically by Paul in his Epistle to the Galatians.

Looking Back: The Demise of Lot's Wife

Lot's wife, who also lived at the time of Abraham — nineteenth century BC — is never identified by name in the inspired canonical books of the Bible (these are the books officially recognized by Jewish and Christian authorities, as opposed to the noncanonical books, which are not included in the Bible — see Chapter 2 for more on these). Some Hebrew midrash refer to Lot's wife as "Idis" or "Edis," but she is most often known by the simple moniker of "Lot's wife," and most people remember her for the way she died.

A few Bible commentaries propose that Lot's wife was a native of the town of Sodom, the same place from where his sons-in-law came. Sodom was the "twin" city (close by and built around the same time) of Gomorrah, both of which were filled with sin and sexual depravity. God doesn't look favorably upon these cities and sends two angels to Lot's house to warn him and his family.

The angels tell Lot and his wife, two daughters, and their husbands to flee because God is about to punish the evil cities with utter and total annihilation. (See Genesis 19:12–13 for more details.) Before they leave, the sin and depravity that was so rampant in these cities appear at Lot's doorstep. The men of Sodom see the angels enter Lot's home, believing them to be human men. These men demand access to these two "male" visitors so they can "know" them (a Biblical euphemism for having sex). Lot instead offers them his two daughters (see more on the daughters in Chapter 20), but they aren't interested in women. So one of the angels momentarily blinds them, and the family makes its escape.

Before they leave, the angels also warn them: "Do not look back" (Genesis 19:17). As they flee, the Biblical equivalent to an H-bomb rains down from the skies — fire and brimstone (sulfur) shower down upon the cities of Sodom and Gomorrah. The sins of these two places were so great, so heinous, and so frequent that chastisement was inevitable. The sexual depravity had become so rampant, perverted, and promiscuous that an example had to be made. To this day, people still speak of the doomed fate of Sodom and Gomorrah. (You can find the story of these two cities in Genesis 19:1–29.)

But as they flee, Lot's wife doesn't heed the angels' warnings: "But Lot's wife, behind him, looked back, and she became a pillar of salt" (Genesis 19:26). Was Lot's wife cruelly punished merely for curiosity — the kind of curiosity that today's motorists encounter when they slow down to gawk at an auto accident on the side of the road? Scripture scholars attest that her action represented more than mere curiosity. If Lot's wife had been a native of Sodom, perhaps part of her couldn't leave, even though it meant risking her safety. Maybe she was still attached to the decadent lifestyle and opulence to which she had been accustomed. Maybe she wanted to see the horrible catastrophe with her own eyes, like a crowd or mob at a public execution. If that was the reason for Lot's wife to turn around and look, then she was indeed punished for her sin.

Some people today use the story of Lot's wife as a metaphor to refrain from looking backward at what has happened in their lives and to instead always look forward. That interpretation seems too benign. The woman was turned into a pillar of salt. By turning around, it meant turning her back to Lot and their two daughters so she could face the cities of Sodom and Gomorrah, despite the angels' warning. The smell of the sulfur and the intense heat from the fire from the sky should have been more than enough evidence of the devastation. Why did she have to *see* the two cities destroyed? No one knows for sure, but she did, and she suffered the consequences.

Even Jesus uses this woman as an example. When Jesus speaks of Judgment Day, the end of the world, he refers to the sheep being separated from the goats (the good from the bad). He says the evil people will be punished like Sodom and Gomorrah were, and the good, who will be rewarded, should not look back to see what happens. To illustrate his point, Jesus says, "Remember Lot's wife" (Luke 17:32).

Dinah's Dismay: The Daughter of Jacob and Leah

Leah and Jacob's only daughter, Dinah, is a key figure who alters the course of history. Dinah lives sometime between the sixteenth and fifteenth centuries BC in the land of Canaan. Curious and self-assured, Dinah is a real daddy's girl, and Jacob has deep affection for her. The lone female among 12 brothers, Dinah is also impetuous and used to having her own way. Her beauty and vulnerability in a strange land — the land of Shechem in the city of Samaria, part of Canaan — and the lack of sophistication of the townsfolk would prove a dangerous combination.

Dinah defiled

While exploring her new homeland alone one day, the lovely Dinah catches the eye of Shechem, the son of Hamor the Hivite, the ruler of Shechem. (Shechem is both the name of the place, 41 miles north of Jerusalem, and the name of Hamor's son.) Motivated by lust, the playboy prince rapes her. Afterward, some vestige of decency returns, and he repents for his heinous crime and even falls in love with Dinah. He asks his father if he can take her in marriage. Word, however, of the crime has since gotten back to Dinah's brothers and her father, Jacob, who are outraged that she has been defiled. Bloody revenge fills their hearts. (See Genesis 34:1–7 for more details.)

Hamor and Shechem, on the other hand, begin making plans to ask Jacob for Dinah's hand in marriage. The family hopes to rectify Shechem's horrible deed by uniting the two families and attempting to restore some modicum of justice. Once stolen, however, Dinah's virtue can't be returned. Her brothers vow that those responsible will pay dearly.

Dinah avenged

The brothers initially play along with Hamor's request, making a deal. They ask that in exchange for Dinah's hand in marriage, all male Hivites be circumcised, in order for them to share the same religion. Circumcision is the sign of the covenant of God and his people, the brothers tell Hamor, who believes that the brothers are making a spiritual and godly request.

Genesis 17:10 tells of God's command to Abraham to be circumcised, as well as all males after eight days of their birth as a sign of the covenant. Abraham was 99 and Ishmael 13 when they were circumcised, and every Jewish male since then is circumcised by the eighth day as a sign of that same covenant between God and the children of Abraham.

Getting circumcised seemed a fair price — a few days of painful discomfort was worth the peace and prosperity that would be created between the two nations. What the Shechemites don't know and what will hurt more than the circumcision is the plot hatched by Jacob's sons, Levi and Simeon.

Dinah's brothers' darker motivations soon come to light, however. During circumcision, the brothers know that the Hivite males will be incapacitated and unable to defend themselves. The brothers can then take advantage of the situation. Indeed that is just what they do.

Once the circumcised men are recovering, every single male in the country is killed by the Israelites as a vendetta for the rape of Dinah. Not only were all the men of Shechem killed, including Hamor and his son, but the Israelites plundered and looted as well. Jacob reprimands his sons because everyone had given his word that the Shechemites would be safe if their men were circumcised. The boys had taken advantage of the situation, and Jacob was concerned that breaking their word would have repercussions. He worried that other nations would hear of their lies and not trust any agreement or treaty from the Hebrew nation. (See Genesis 34:20–31 for more details.)

Jacob wasn't proud of his sons. While, as a father, he despised the horrible crime that befell his beloved daughter, he was also the patriarch of a people — the Hebrew nation — and any attempts to establish a peaceful coexistence between Hamor's people and his own people were now impossible. Plus, Jacob knew that using religion as a decoy to trap and slay people who had willingly submitted to the sign of the covenant was a sacrilege, no matter what the motivation.

Dinah's brothers, as it turned out, had viewed her rape as more of a personal insult to themselves and to their family honor, rather than a gross injustice to her. Unlike Rachel's brothers, who consulted their sister when she wanted to leave for her new home with husband Jacob, Dinah's brothers never considered her feelings. They were more concerned with revenge.

This crime tarnishes the integrity of the Israelite people, as the story will be told and retold among the neighboring peoples. Hence, Dinah's curiosity and her horrible rape incited her brothers to react with a vengeance never before seen, and its consequences were devastating.

The rape of Dinah can also be interpreted as an illicit seduction, which was — in those days — considered just as heinous an action as rape. Dinah was probably only 14 or 15 years old when Prince Shechem stole her innocence. Many cite the following quote as evidence that Schechem's actions were more of a seduction, rather than a violent rape. "And his soul was drawn to Dinah daughter of Jacob; he loved the girl, and spoke tenderly to her. So Shechem spoke to his father Hamor, saying, 'Get me this girl to be my wife' " (Genesis 34:3–4). What exactly took place, however, didn't much matter. In ancient times, fathers and brothers saw any seduction as they would a rape: a dishonor to their daughter, sister, and, ultimately, to their clan.

It appears that Dinah never married. She is listed among the names of those who later traveled to Egypt where Joseph, her brother, lived under the rule of the Pharaoh (Genesis 46:15). We hear no more of her after that. Jacob, however, still laments the revenge of Dinah's brothers to the Shechemites many years later (Genesis 49:5–7).

Plotting Against Joseph: Potiphar's Wife

Potiphar's wife, otherwise nameless in the Bible, lived in Egypt in approximately the sixteenth century BC. Her husband was the captain of the guard for Pharaoh — sort of like the head of the secret service, someone who protected the monarch and kept an eye on possible traitors, dissidents, and troublemakers.

Potiphar buys Joseph, the son of Rachel and Jacob, as a slave from the Ishmaelites, who had previously purchased Joseph from his ten older brothers. These brothers sold Joseph into slavery out of jealousy, and then explained his disappearance by saying Joseph was killed by a wild animal. (You can read all about this part of Joseph's life in Genesis 37:12–36.)

Potiphar makes Joseph a domestic servant, and he proves himself to such an extent that Potiphar promotes him to be head of the entire estate. Meanwhile, Joseph doesn't go unnoticed by Potiphar's wife, who has a very sensual appetite and sees how young, handsome, and virile Joseph is.

She soon attempts to seduce him. But Joseph resists her luring enticements ("lie with me"), day after day, as he is an honorable young man who avoids sin and the betrayal of his master: "Look, with me here, my master has no concern about anything in the house, and he has put everything that he has in my hand. He is not greater in this house than I am, nor has he kept back anything from me except yourself, because you are his wife. How then could I do this great wickedness, and sin against God?" (Genesis 39:8–9). His refusal of her advances, of course, only angers Potiphar's wife. So Joseph leaves in a hurry, and Potiphar's wife keeps part of his cloak, which falls off in his hasty retreat, as shown in one artist's rendering in Figure 15-2.

The vixen then lies to her husband, claiming that Joseph tried to rape her. She shows him the garment as evidence. Potiphar has Joseph immediately imprisoned, with no interrogation, let alone a trial.

Potiphar's wife had tried to seduce Joseph into an adulterous affair, and failing that, she then lied and slandered the poor man into jail. We hear no more of her even though Joseph's time in the big house is not permanent. The wife of Potiphar is remembered only for her lustful advances toward a chaste and honorable man. The seductress loses on all accounts. Not only does she not become the illicit lover of Joseph, but Joseph eventually rises to a royal appointment in the Pharaoh's court that is higher than even her husband's position. The ironic twist: Joseph's high position in court may have never happened had it not been for his time in jail. While he was imprisoned, Joseph was summoned to interpret a dream of Pharaoh (because he did so for his fellow inmates), and that won him Pharaoh's favor and position as governor. (See Genesis 41 for more details.)

Figure 15-2:
Joseph fleeing Potiphar's wife, from the school of Raphael (1483–1520).

Heeding Advice from a Prophetess: Huldah

Although her name means "weasel," Huldah is anything but. She lived in Jerusalem during the seventh century BC, during the reign of King Josiah. The wife of Shallum, she is one of only three women named in the Old Testament as a prophetess (Miriam in Exodus 15:20 and Deborah in Judges 4:4 are the other two; Chapter 10 has the details on these women). Even the King recognizes Huldah's reputation as a holy and wise woman.

King Josiah initiates reforms in Judah, one of which is the restoration of the Temple of Jerusalem, which had fallen into disrepair during the reign of previous kings. During the project, some ancient scrolls are found, probably from Deuteronomy, written in Hebrew. Because there was no carbon dating back then, the only way to ascertain whether the documents were real was to take them to a holy person — a prophet — who can ask the Lord directly.

King Josiah could have gone to the prophet Jeremiah, a contemporary of Huldah. Instead he goes to the prophetess. A few scholars speculate that the king had hoped a female prophet would be more disposed to ask for mercy for the king than a male prophet. But most scholars believe it is because Huldah, also the keeper of the royal wardrobe, had earned a reputation for holiness, wisdom, and intelligence that even surpassed Jeremiah's — especially on a matter such as verifying the authenticity of a sacred scroll.

So the high priest Hilkiah brings Huldah the scrolls — the book of the Law — that King Josiah had excavated at the Temple (2 Kings 22:14–20; 2 Chronicles 34:22–28). She attests that the scrolls are genuine, but she also gives a dire prophecy:

> *Thus says the LORD, "I will indeed bring disaster on this place and on its inhabitants — all the words of the book that the king of Judah has read. Because they have abandoned me and have made offerings to other gods, so that they have provoked me to anger with all the work of their hands, therefore my wrath will be kindled against this place, and it will not be quenched."*
>
> —2 Kings 22:16–17

She adds some words of comfort, however, saying that the current king will not live to see the destruction of the kingdom. Because he had been so devout and pious during his reign, he will be spared that disgrace. But after his death, the nation will be punished for religious infidelity — their pagan worship of false gods. Huldah's prophecy indeed comes to pass after Josiah's peaceful death. This incident is also mentioned later in Chronicles, and then we don't hear about her again. Her dire prediction sadly came to fruition and vindicated her authenticity as a prophetess.

Chapter 16

Getting Wise to the Connivers: Biblical Femme Fatales

Several notorious women in the Bible are shrouded in intrigue and mystery. Whereas the women of the previous three chapters are powerful and faithful, these women are influential and often dangerous. These women portray the dark side of human nature, displaying traits like lust, misguided ambition, political intrigue, and more. Although not all these women are entirely bad or morally evil, they show the same vulnerability as their male counterparts who often equally share the blame.

In this chapter, we discuss two-faced Delilah, adulterous Bathsheba, the notorious witch of Endor, blasphemous and manipulative Jezebel, and the unfaithful and weak Gomer.

Double Agent Delilah: Sapping Sampson's Strength

Delilah, who lived in the thirteenth century BC, breaks the heart of her lover, Samson, a man who devoted his life to fighting the enemies of the Israelites. In fact, she even betrays him to these enemies, the Philistines. She is the poster child of femme fatales for her intrigue, seductiveness, and treachery toward her lover, the iron man of the ancient world. In her story, she is the only woman in a numerous cast of characters who is identified by name.

Delilah is perceived by many as the Mata Hari of her day — a double agent who worked both sides of the fence. (Mata Hari was accused of being a double-agent spy for both the French and the Germans during World War I.) Because of her behavior, Delilah is now a name used to refer to any treacherous and cunning woman.

Playing Samson

Samson, Delilah's "prey," is one of the Judges of Israel, a ruler who led the nation before the monarchy. Like Deborah, who had also been a Judge (see Chapter 10 for more on her), Samson guides and governs the Hebrew people. Unlike Deborah, though, he is a bit of a loose cannon. He often loses his temper and shows a similar lack of control over his passions. Shortly before he meets Delilah, Samson visits a prostitute — a reward, perhaps, for slaying a thousand Philistines, his sworn enemies (Judges 16:1).

Delilah herself is a Philistine, the last in a string of Philistine women whom Samson seemingly can't resist. The Philistines were traditional rivals and enemies of the Hebrews for centuries. Although Samson is blessed with extraordinary physical strength, he suffers great weakness when it comes to Delilah. His first wife, also a Philistine, had perished as a result of Samson's conflict with these people. (See more on Samson's first wife in Chapter 18.)

When he meets Delilah, it's clear he hasn't learned from his previous mistake. Samson has a thing for Philistine women — and usually for women who are not totally devoted to him, either. His first wife was killed when, at the prenuptial party, a silly bet is made that no one can answer his famous riddles. The Philistine guests get Samson's Philistine wife to trick the answer out of him. She tells her countrymen the answer, and Samson loses the bet. In a rage to pay his debt, Samson slays 30 Philistines and takes their garments. The result is that his wife-to-be is given by her father to Samson's best man. He angrily goes out and destroys the grain fields of the Philistines, and they retaliate by burning his home with his former betrothed and her father inside.

Although he is physically the strongest man on earth, when it comes to Philistine women, Samson has weak knees. He acts impetuously and blabs secrets to them. He fails to learn from his experience with the first wife, and he soon makes a similar mistake with his lover, Delilah.

Understanding Samson's strength

Samson kills a lion with his bare hands and slays a thousand Philistines with just the jawbone of an ass that had been lying on the ground. His very name intimidates and infuriates the Philistine men.

Soon after Samson and Delilah meet, the Philistine overlords ask Delilah to discover the enigma of Samson's strength, unbeknownst to Samson. Being superstitious pagans, they suspect the secret to his strength is some magic amulet or talisman or perhaps some potion or spell. Whatever it is, they need to know so they can capture and destroy their archnemesis.

But Samson's strength comes from God, and it will remain only as long as Samson stays faithful to his Nazirite vow, one part of which means never cutting his hair. No one knows this source of his strength except the man of steel himself. The Nazirite (from the Hebrew word *Nazir,* meaning "dedicated one") vow was made first for Samson by his mother and then by Samson himself. Taking the vow means that he won't consume strong drink (wine with high alcohol content), won't contaminate himself by touching a dead body (animal or human), and won't ever cut the hair on his head. These external signs represent a special relationship of the person with the Lord God.

Delilah was to be Samson's ultimate downfall. For 1,100 pieces of silver she agrees to spy on her boyfriend and learn his secret, going to work as an undercover agent for her people.

Finding Samson's Achilles' heel

The Bible recounts three occasions when Delilah unsuccessfully attempts to learn the mystery of Samson's strength.

"If you *really* loved me. . . ." How many times has that line been spoken by women and men throughout history in an effort to get their beloved to do, show, or prove something? Delilah is no different. She comes right out and asks Samson: "Please tell me what makes your strength so great, and how you could be bound, so that one could subdue you" (Judges 16:6). No secrets between lovers, right?

Her tactic was simple but brilliant. Instead of plying him with booze to get him to tell all, and knowing she was no physical match for his strength, she takes the direct approach, which seems most logical. By explicitly asking him, Delilah thinks that it seems too obvious that she wants nothing more than a demonstration that he loves and trusts her.

Samson, for his part, must see through her wily ruse — at least at first. So he tells her that the only way to subdue him is to bind his hands with seven green bowstrings. She relays the secret to the Philistines, who obtain some of these ripe vines, and she ties Samson's hands while he sleeps. When the soldiers come to capture him, she yells and wakes him, "The Philistines are here!" But he easily snaps the chords. Obviously, he hadn't divulged the correct answer (Judges 16:6–9).

Delilah rebukes him for lying to her and asks him again. He gives her another answer, telling her that only unused rope can restrain him. She believes him and tells the Philistines, and once again an ambush is staged. And once again, Samson snaps the ropes as if they were a single thread (Judges 16:10–12).

Third time's the charm, right? Delilah thinks so. One more time she harangues Samson for mocking her. He never inquires as to why she keeps tying him up or how the Philistines keep popping up in his bedroom. Instead, he again answers her. The third reply gets closest to the truth. He tells Delilah that his capture requires seven locks of his hair to be woven together and fashioned into bands to bind his hands and feet (Judges 16:13–14).

For a third time, however, Samson breaks free and foils his attempted capture. Delilah resorts to nagging him incessantly until he relents and spills the beans.

Ensuring his capture

Was it the nagging that caused Samson to tell the truth, or did the game master enjoy the game too much, raising the stakes higher than he could handle? In any event, Samson finally reveals his secret to Delilah — that God is the source of his strength and that violating his Nazirite vow by shaving his head would be the cause of his downfall (Judges 16:15–17).

Delilah uses this information and takes matters into her own hands. She lulls him to sleep in her lap, and a servant cuts his hair. The hair wasn't the true source of his power, but it was a sign of his personal covenant with God as a Nazirite. For violating the confidentiality and thus allowing his vow to be broken, God takes away Samson's Herculean strength.

The Philistines, in turn, bind Samson and gouge out his eyes — both to ensure that his power is gone (there's nothing weaker than a man who can't see) and to engage in some personal sport (taunting him like a sick child would torment a fly by pulling off its wings). Humiliated, betrayed, and captured like an animal, he is dragged away in shame. Because they know his superhuman strength is no longer with him, the Philistines do to him what they never could do before — sort of like Lex Luthor beating up Superman after exposing him to kryptonite. Delilah is paid her betrayal money (Judges 16:18–21).

Although the Bible makes no more mention of Delilah after this treacherous betrayal, many scripture scholars suspect she went to the Philistine temple of Dagon, where Samson had been put on display before 3,000 people. Samson, in the meantime, repents and asks God's forgiveness. His last prayer is for enough strength to punish the Philistines, even if it means his own death (Judges 16:28).

As his hair begins to grow back and God answers his final prayer, Samson secretly pushes on the pillars to which he is chained. Unfortunately for the Philistines, these columns hold up the ceiling. Samson regains enough strength to tear down the entire building, killing himself and all 3,000 Philistines (Judges 16:30). We don't know whether Delilah was there too, but some people speculate that she may have been killed along with the Philistines.

Bathing Bathsheba: King David's Secret Lover

Bathsheba is the wife of Uriah, a loyal soldier in King David's army. She is first discussed in the Bible when she has an adulterous affair with King David.

Although Bathsheba gets a bad reputation because of this affair, David is the one who pursues her. She may have willingly cooperated in the adultery, but this is the worst of her sins, and some people question whether it was truly a sin. She lived, after all, in a time when women were expected to obey the commands of the king. She later suffers because of the king's actions, as well: King David ultimately has her husband killed, and she loses her first child as punishment for David's sin.

Bathsheba is described as *maod towb* in Hebrew (*sphodra kalos* in Greek), which translates into "very beautiful." She is the only one in the Bible who is described this way, and a few versions of the Bible even say she is gorgeous (2 Samuel 11:2). This extremely attractive woman doesn't go unnoticed by the king, who has an eye for such things.

Lying begets lying

One day King David wakes from a nap and takes a walk on the roof of his palace, an imperial penthouse of sorts, which overlooks the city of Jerusalem. He sees Bathsheba bathing on her roof. Noticing how lovely she looks, he inquires into her identity and summons her to the royal residence (2 Samuel 11:2–3).

While her husband is busy fighting for the kingdom, the king seduces Bathsheba. She becomes pregnant and sends word to David that he is the father of the unborn child. The king acts quickly to cover up his tracks and prevent a scandal. He commands his general, Joab, to order Bathsheba's husband, Uriah, to take a leave and come home.

David meets Bathsheba's husband and pretends to be interested in the progress of the war. He then sends him to his home in the hopes that he will have relations with his wife. David wants people to see Uriah visiting so that, when it becomes obvious that Bathsheba is pregnant, people will conclude that the child was conceived when Uriah was home on leave (2 Samuel 11:6–8).

Uriah, however, is uncomfortable about enjoying his wife's intimacy while his brave men suffer hardship during a war. He decides to sleep at the entrance of the palace with the other servants instead. When David learns of this, he summons Uriah and invites him to dinner. The king liquors him up, hoping that he'll finally weaken and go home for a conjugal visit with his wife. Even inebriated, though, Uriah thinks of his comrades in arms and can't indulge in this legitimate pleasure while his pals are battling for their lives.

Disgusted with such a display of integrity, King David resorts to plan B. He issues secret written orders to his general, Joab, to be hand delivered by Uriah. In those orders, David instructs Joab to send Uriah to the front lines of the fighting, thereby ensuring that the enemy kills Uriah. Thus, this honorable soldier delivers his own death sentence to General Joab, who obeys the king's immoral command. After Uriah is dead, King David knows that Uriah can never dispute the paternity of Bathsheba's baby.

Sure enough, Uriah is killed. At this point, King David has broken three commandments: Thou shall not kill, thou shall not covet thy neighbor's wife, and thou shall not commit adultery. After Bathsheba observes the normal period of mourning as a widow, King David takes her into the palace as his wife, and she gives birth to their son (2 Samuel 11:26–27).

Repenting for sin

After David's machinations, the prophet Nathan confronts him with a story. Nathan tells of a rich man and a poor man. The rich man has lots of money, land, and livestock. The poor man has but one lamb, which he cares for and becomes attached to — it's like one of the family. When a visitor comes to the rich man, he kills the one and only lamb of the poor man rather than one from his large flock, serving it for dinner to his out-of-town guest (2 Samuel 12:1–6).

Outraged, David says that whoever did such a dastardly deed deserves death. "You are the man!" responds Nathan. He then reveals that he knows David's dirty secrets. Consequently, Nathan prophesies that their infant son will die for his father's sins.

Despite the seven days that King David spent in extreme penance, prayer, and fasting, the baby dies. King David realizes he is totally responsible. He consoles Bathsheba, and she conceives another child through David, this time legitimately. The child is Solomon, whom the prophet Nathan names Jedidiah, which means "beloved of the LORD." (You can read this story in 2 Samuel 12:7–25.)

Living the royal life

As the eighth wife of King David, Bathsheba becomes the queen and the mother of the future king (Solomon). As such, she will also deal with the further machinations of the royal family.

Bathsheba reappears in the first Book of Kings. When David is old and ready to cash in his chips, his fourth son, Adonijah (whose mother was Haggith), assumes the throne after the death of his older brothers (Amnon, the eldest son, whose mother was Ahinoam, and Absalom, whose mother was Maacah). King David, however, indicates that he wants Solomon — Adonijah's younger brother — to become king (1 Kings 1:1–8).

So the prophet Nathan goes to Queen Bathsheba and convinces her to approach her dying husband, David. Bathsheba informs David of Adonijah's actions and explains that she fears his next move will be to kill her and Solomon. The prophet Nathan then joins Bathsheba and encourages King David to send for Zadok the priest to anoint Solomon king. Bathsheba, with the assistance of Nathan, is able to secure the throne for her son, Solomon (1 Kings 1:11–31).

The queen is accorded all the honors and dignities befitting her office as Queen Mother of the reigning King Solomon. The next and last time she appears in the Bible is in a peculiar encounter with the now-estranged Adonijah. He asks Bathsheba to approach King Solomon with a special request. "Please ask King Solomon — he will not refuse you —to give me Abishag the Shunammite as my wife" (1 Kings 2:17).

Solomon, however, isn't tricked by Adonijah's request. Although Bathsheba sees no harm in asking, the wise king can smell a plot a mile away. Abishag had been a concubine of King David and was part of his harem. Marrying her would give Adonijah the legal right to lay claim to the throne.

Solomon orders the execution of his treasonous brother, and we hear no more of his mother, Bathsheba, until the New Testament, when Matthew 1:6 gives the genealogy of Jesus. Listing his ancestors, the Gospel writer mentions that David was the father of Solomon by "the wife of Uriah" (but doesn't refer to her by her proper name of Bathsheba). With this verbiage, her indiscretion is made clear. Yet it also shows that the fruit of her union and love with David was Solomon, who continued the Davidic lineage and thus ensured the ancestry of the Messiah.

Witch of Endor: Summoning the Dead

The woman of Endor is another woman whose story poses more questions than it answers. While the Bible leaves her nameless, rabbinical midrash (commentaries on scripture) suggests that she was Zephaniah. She lived in the eleventh century B.C. four miles south of Mount Tabor in a town called Endor. This woman is described in 1 Samuel 28.

She is a fortuneteller, which is a profession that the Bible certainly refuses to endorse, yet she isn't personally condemned for it either. King Saul approaches her in desperation, looking for insight into his future, and she helps him not only by summoning the dead but also by caring for him when he becomes ill.

Although the Bible doesn't condone her day job, neither is the woman of Endor punished for violating the law of the Lord. Some scholars believe it is because she is not a Hebrew and that her talents are in actuality a misreading of the real work of the divine — she had erroneously concluded that her premonitions were of her own making instead of originating from the Lord God.

Depending on the translation and version of your Bible, the witch of Endor is called many things: witch, medium, oracle, fortuneteller, clairvoyant, spiritualist, seer, soothsayer, psychic, enchantress, and sorceress. Although the Greek word *manteúomai* has a benign meaning of an oracle or fortuneteller, the original Hebrew word *baalat-owb* has a more sinister and diabolical connotation to it, such as *necromancer,* meaning one who summons and communicates with the dead. This word is also interchangeable with *kashaph,* a word that means witch or sorceress. The Bible (see Leviticus 19:31, Leviticus 20:6, and Deuteronomy 18:11) condemns such activity.

Advising Saul

King Saul must have been desperate to seek out this woman. But Samuel, the prophet upon whose advice he relied, had recently died. There was only one way to communicate with the dead (a practice called necromancy), which was forbidden by the Ten Commandments. Ironically, before Samuel died, "Saul had expelled the mediums and the wizards from the land" (1 Samuel 28:3)." But now, ironically, he needed one to communicate with Samuel. Saul is desperate for Samuel's advice, even if it means breaking the holiest commandment (no idolatry, false religion, or occult practices practi) — and his own previous laws — to do it.

Seeing an approaching army of Philistine troops, King Saul becomes very nervous. He prays to God but gets no answer. He then instructs his soldiers to fetch him a fortuneteller. One of the troopers reveals that he has heard of medium in Endor. (See 1 Samuel 28:1–7).

Saul takes the information, disguises himself, and travels to Endor to see her. When he asks her to summon the dead, she replies, "Surely you know what Saul has done, how he has cut off the mediums and the wizards from the land. Why then are you laying a snare for my life to bring about my death?" (1 Samuel 28:9). He assures her that no harm will come to her, so she begins her trance to speak to the netherworld. When she asks Saul whom to invoke, he answers, Samuel the prophet.

As soon as Saul asks for Samuel, the woman screeches with horror and asks Saul by name why he has deceived her by disguising his appearance. The Bible doesn't explain how she knows it's Saul, though readers can guess that she has figured it out because of his request (and his well-known previous friendship with Samuel), or perhaps through some information she was receiving from Samuel. Saul doesn't answer her question as to why he is incognito. Samuel appears and has a conversation with King Saul through the woman.

What happens next is described in 1 Samuel 28:15–19. The deceased prophet asks why his eternal rest is being disturbed. Saul starts whining about the Philistines and how God no longer listens to his prayers. Samuel rebukes him, telling him bad news — that Saul will lose his kingdom, his throne, and his life for his disobedience to God. He will be punished for disobeying God's request to completely destroy a former enemy; Saul had kept the best sheep, oxen, and booty as plunder even though he was told not to do so.

Caring for Saul

Overcome with fear, stress, and hunger, Saul falls to the ground. The witch of Endor tells the demoralized king that up to now she has obeyed him, so now he must obey her and take some nourishment. She slaughters a fatted calf and cooks it with some unleavened cakes. Although not asked to, the woman shows hospitality to a man she knows is doomed (1 Samuel 28:20–25). Saul dies the next day in battle against the Philistines. While retreating, he is wounded by an arrow and begs his aide to end his misery with his sword lest the enemy make sport of him, but the soldier can't do it. So Saul falls on his own sword to prevent himself from being tortured and toyed with by the Philistine enemy.

Bible scholars debate whether the witch of Endor actually conjured Samuel or a demon impersonating him. Did she summon the dead by divine or diabolical power? Did God use her despite her belief that she had the gift of second sight? If summoning dead spirits is so virulently condemned in the Law of Moses, then why does she escape punishment? There are no answers, only plenty of questions surrounding the tale of this woman. After this mysterious story, we hear of her no more.

Infamous Jezebel: Cunning and Unholy

Jezebel lived in Phoenicia (circa 874–853 BC) and first appears in the Bible in 1 Kings 16:31. She was the daughter of King Ethbaal of the Sidonians, a people who worshiped false gods. Nevertheless, she married King Ahab of the northern kingdom of Israel. This unholy alliance between the Israelites and the Phoenicians (or Sidonians) proves disastrous in the end. Time and time again, God warned Hebrew leaders to avoid marrying foreigners, lest they introduce their pagan ways to the people.

As queen, Jezebel serves as a strong-willed and independent woman who co-rules with the king and shares in the power and decision making. Queen Jezebel seeks to establish an absolute monarchy, which was in stark contrast to the beliefs of the Chosen People: bound by sacred oath to one another and to the Lord. The covenant (a sacred oath that united people) meant that only God was supreme and absolute and that the law of the Lord — not the king or queen's whim or will alone — was to be the final word.

To this day, call a woman "Jezebel," and you won't get a pretty reaction. Her name has become synonymous with impudent, shameless, and morally reprehensible women. No girls are being baptized Jezebel these days, any more than boys are being given the name Judas. Not only does she worship Baal, a false god, but while serving as queen, she also promotes this worship among her people. And when things don't go her way, she resorts to lying and murder to achieve material ends. Eventually, she is punished and comes to a grisly end. Through Jezebel, we learn what *not* to do.

Worshiping pagan idols

Jezebel worships the pagan god Baal and convinces her Jewish husband, Ahab, to do likewise, turning his back on his Hebrew faith. Although he doesn't completely surrender to the pagan religion, King Ahab does allow Baal worship to be protected and encouraged in the northern kingdom. Because of this, pagan idols and rituals often appeared alongside holy places where Jewish ceremonies were celebrated in the name of the one true God.

As queen, Jezebel brings 450 priests of Baal into the northern kingdom of Israel with King Ahab's full consent. She was responsible for the murder of many prophets of the Lord during her infamous reign (1 Kings 18:4). This bad apple does anything she can to slowly but surely eradicate the Hebrew religion, which she detests. Her goal is to replace it with her own Baal worship.

Baal worship was the worst sin a Jew could commit against God and was repugnant to God in the same way that Christians regard Satan worship today. It was the most extreme violation of the first commandment against idolatry. Baal was a pagan fertility god whose companion was Ashtaroth, the mother goddess of the earth. The religion glorified human sexuality and reproduction as literally having an effect on the planet, everything from weather to agriculture. Ritual sex and temple prostitution were integral components to ensure a bountiful harvest and success of the crops.

Standing up for Baal

God soon punishes Ahab for his reliance on pagan fertility rites by inflicting a three-year drought and famine in the land — what better way to expose the false religion than by showing it has no power. Not only are the priests of Baal unable to end the agricultural desolation, but the Lord and his prophet are going to show who's boss.

God sends the prophet Elijah, who had survived Jezebel's former bloodbath against prophets, to King Ahab. He admonishes the monarch for his idolatry and blames him for the plight of the nation. Elijah infuriates Jezebel by demanding a contest between Baal and the Lord God. The 450 priests whom the queen has been keeping in the palace are asked to meet Elijah at Mount Carmel for the match of the ages. (See 1 Kings 18:17–19 for this information.)

Elijah instructs the people to get two bulls, slaughter them, and place them on a pile of wood. The competition goes like this: The 450 priests of Baal invoke their deity to ignite the fire by supernatural means, and Elijah prays to the Lord God to do the same. Whoever is able to burn the bull completely without a human lighting the fire is the winner and follower of the true God.

Jezebel is confident that her pagan god and priests of that god can easily win this contest. From morning to noon the pagan priests chant and pray, "O Baal, answer us!" At midday Elijah taunts them to cry louder because their god must be meditating, on a journey, or possibly asleep. These Baal worshipers even slash themselves with swords and lances, drawing their own blood. But it's all to no avail. (See 1 Kings 18:20–29 for the details.)

Finally, at the end of the afternoon, Elijah places 12 stones around his bull to represent the tribes of Israel. He digs a trench around the altar of sacrifice and has water poured three times over the bull, the wood, and ground, soaking the bull and the wood. Then the prophet invokes the God of Abraham, the God of Isaac, and the God of Jacob — the one true God, the Lord.

Suddenly, out of heaven comes a fire that descends upon the earth and consumes the bull, the wood, the dirt, and the water in the trench. The people realize that the Lord is God, and Baal is a fake. Elijah orders the execution of the 450 priests of Baal. This is the final straw for Jezebel, who vows to see Elijah die for his actions. (Check out 1 Kings 18:30–40.)

Manipulating murder

After her 450 pagan priests are killed, Jezebel still clings to her false religion, and her hatred for Elijah and his Hebrew faith only intensifies. The next incident involving Jezebel concerns a vineyard owned by a man named Naboth. Her husband, Ahab, wants to plant a garden there and offers Naboth a parcel of his own land or money in exchange for it. But Naboth refuses because when he dies his sons will inherit what he himself inherited from his ancestors before him (1 Kings 21:1–4).

Dejected, Ahab goes home and sulks until Jezebel sticks her nose into the matter. She tells her husband that as king he should do as he pleases. Then she conspires to have Naboth wrongly accused of blasphemy by two false witnesses, a crime for which he is then stoned to death. After he is dead, Queen Jezebel tells her husband to go take his vineyard, which he does. (See 1 Kings 21:5–16 for this story.)

For this heinous crime and gross injustice, Elijah prophesies to Ahab that the Lord will punish him. He also tells Ahab that dogs will eat Jezebel. Ahab is so overwhelmed by the news that he puts on sackcloth and ashes and fasts. God is pleased to see him repent, so he tells Elijah that he will not bring disaster on Ahab's house until after his death. Instead, God's punishment will arrive upon his sons. (You can read this account in 1 Kings 21:20–29.)

When Ahab dies bravely and honorably in battle, he is succeeded by Ahaziah, his son from Jezebel. Ahaziah soon dies and is succeeded by brother Jehoram, another of Jezebel's sons. When Jehoram is killed by Jehu, who seeks the throne for himself, Jezebel goes on the lam.

When Jehu arrives at the capital to be crowned king after the prophet Elisha (the successor to Elijah) anoints him, Jezebel heckles Jehu from a window. Jehu commands two eunuchs to throw her out of it. She falls to her death, only to have her dead corpse devoured by dogs, as Elijah had foretold — an ignominious death for a horrible and despicable woman. (Check out the story in 2 Kings 9:28–37.)

The last biblical reference to Jezebel comes in Revelation (also known as the Apocalypse) 2:20, when the name Jezebel is used as a synonym for a wicked woman.

Old Habits Are Hard to Break: Gomer

Although her name doesn't sound very feminine, Gomer is indeed a biblical woman, described in the Book of Hosea (*Osee* is the Greek spelling). In fact, she is a harlot who becomes the wife of the prophet Hosea. They lived around 790–686 BC in the northern kingdom of Israel. God instructs Hosea to marry this woman (Hosea 1:2). Their marriage is meant to personify the relationship between God and Israel. Hosea is the God-like figure: the ever faithful husband who is always ready to forgive. Gomer symbolizes Israel, who, despite being loved, keeps prostituting herself.

Gomer has three children: two sons, Jezreel and Lo-ammi, and one daughter, Lo-ruhamah. Hosea is identified as the father of Jezreel, but the other two are never confirmed as being his, so they may be the offspring resulting from Gomer's nighttime activities.

The marriage of the prophet and the prostitute reflects the reality that God remained faithful no matter how often Israel compromised the faith. The relationship of husband and wife, so intimate and personal, transcends a mere Creator-creature relationship that the Lord has with all his people.

Israel prostitutes the faith by assimilating idolatry, especially Baal worship, from the king down to the ordinary person. As the kingdom becomes economically prosperous and makes political alliances, the Hebrew faith becomes more and more compromised, diluted, and violated. Each time the people are unfaithful to the covenant, it is like a spouse being unfaithful to his or her mate.

The infidelity of the northern kingdom of Israel was eventually punished by the collapse and conquest by the Assyrians in the eighth century BC. The southern kingdom of Judah fared only slightly better, lasting until the Babylonians conquered it in the sixth century BC.

Gomer wants to be faithful, but old habits are hard to break. Despite her best efforts, she keeps slipping back into her old ways (prostitution). Similarly, Israel wants to be faithful. But, like Gomer, the people keep giving in to weakness and continue flirting with phony ideologies and false religions.

Instead of casually ignoring her repeated infidelity, Hosea challenges his wife to better herself and return to a faithful relationship. He never gives up on her, but neither does he give her a green light to pursue a promiscuous and adulterous lifestyle. Similarly, God never gives up on Israel, his beloved spouse, no matter how many times she gives in to the temptation of idolatry. (See Hosea 2:1–23.)

Whenever Gomer misbehaves and falls back into her old lifestyle, Hosea patiently waits for her to return, forgiving her and taking her back. At one point she leaves and ends up the slave of one of her paramours, and Hosea has to buy her back with pieces of silver. But to Hosea, she is worth it, in the same way that God shows unfaithful Israel he will ransom her and pay to get her back. (See Hosea 3:1–5.) Hosea's action can be seen as a foreshadowing of the price of redemption that Jesus offered on behalf of the whole human race.

Gomer is not the model wife, but her willingness to try to do better — as well as Hosea's constant love and willingness to take her back — represents the relationship between the Lord and his people. Weak and vulnerable, Gomer doesn't make excuses or rationalize or glamorize her infidelity. No matter how often she falls, she keeps getting back up.

Chapter 17

Causing Controversy: Intriguing Biblical Women

In This Chapter

▶ Viewing the evil acts of Herodias and Salome

▶ Seeing how Pilate's wife tries to save Jesus

▶ Glimpsing the hospitality of Simon Peter's mother-in-law

▶ Understanding the concept behind the whore of Babylon

The stories of several mysterious women in the Bible still cause controversy, even today. Because of their actions, words, or just their very existences, they have been the focus of questions that have sparked much discussion and debate over the years among people with opposing positions.

In this chapter, we look at such women by examining the actions of Herodias and Pilate's wife, the very existence of Simon Peter's mother-in-law, and the concept behind the whore of Babylon.

Vengeful Herodias and Her Dancing Daughter, Salome

The quintessence of evil and personification of malice in the New Testament has to be Herodias (Matthew 14:3–11; Mark 6:17–28; and Luke 3:19). Like Jezebel (see Chapter 16) in the Old Testament, the very name Herodias conjures up images of a vindictive, vile, and venomous woman. She is the person primarily responsible for the beheading of John the Baptist (more on him in the sidebar "Was John a Baptist?" in this chapter), and the method by which Herodias accomplishes this task proves the depth of her depravity. Whereas Queen Athaliah went so far as to murder her own grandchildren to seize the throne (see Chapter 12), Herodias uses her own daughter, Salome, to make a disgusting seduction toward her own husband, Salome's stepfather.

Mother and daughter both abuse their position and influence to attain selfish and wicked goals. They have opportunity, privilege, wealth, and power, but instead of using them for good, they selfishly use them for personal gain and revenge.

Following in familiar footsteps

Herodias was certainly influenced by her environment. She hailed from notoriously wicked people. Her grandfather was Herod the Great, the former king who had ordered the slaughter of the Holy Innocents (Hebrew male infants) in futile hopes of killing the Christ Child. Born between 9 and 7 BC, Herodias was the sister of Herod Agrippa I (grandson of Herod the Great; he executed James the brother of John and he had Peter imprisoned). While she was an infant, good old granddad arranged her marriage to her uncle, Herod Philip, with whom she has a daughter. The Bible doesn't give the name of that daughter, but the Jewish historian Flavius Josephus (AD 37–100) identifies this child as Salome, and he is the one who provides most of what we know of the family history of Herod.

This is where the story begins to sound like a Jerry Springer episode. When Salome is about 10 years old, Herodias and Herod Philip are living in Rome. Another uncle, Herod Antipas, comes to visit. More visits follow. Herodias and Herod Antipas engage in an affair, and there is speculation that she pursues him because he is more powerful than her current husband, Herod Philip. (The historian Flavius Josephus is also the primary source of information about this bizarre family.)

Herodias can't stand Herod Antipas's first wife, the daughter of King Aretas of Arabia. Herodias dislikes the wife because she is an Arab and there is bad blood between the Kingdom of Arabia and Herodias's family, known as the Hasmoneans. So by plotting with Antipas to divorce his first wife, Herodias not only leaves her husband to marry her lover (also an uncle), but she also boots out an enemy (Herod Antipas's first wife). The unnamed wife flees to her daddy, and hostility between Herod Antipas and King Aretas escalates over time because of this insult. They finally go to war with each other in AD 36.

Even though Jews were allowed to remarry according to Mosaic law (the laws Moses gave to the Hebrew people, especially as found in the Book of Deuteronomy and as interpreted by the Talmud, the commentaries and opinions of respected rabbis), there were limits. This bizarre relationship — an uncle marrying his half brother's former wife — is just too much for the devout Hebrews to stomach.

Was John a Baptist?

The Bible calls John the Baptist a "baptizer" in some translations and a "baptist" in others. The word "baptist" in this context merely means one who washes or dips in water, from the Greek work *baptizein*. It doesn't mean that John belonged to the Christian Baptist Church. (The Baptist Church wasn't even established until AD 1612, when John Smyth and his entire congregation separated from the Church of England, which was Anglican.) John the Baptist, however, was a Jew. His father, Zechariah, was a priest of the Temple in Jerusalem and of the Hebrew tribe of Levi. He gets the name *baptist* because he dipped people in the Jordan River as a symbolic gesture of being spiritually washed clean for repentance for one's sins.

Avenging her reputation

John the Baptist was Jesus' cousin, a prophet, and holy man who spoke with conviction. John denounces Herod for marrying his brother's wife, Herodias: "It is not lawful for you to have her" (Matthew 14:4). The Gospel of Mark says that Herodias doesn't take lightly to this criticism, bearing a grudge against John so serious she wants to kill him (Mark 6:19). Her only stumbling block is that in spite of the fact that John denounced Herod's marriage, Herod Antipas likes to listen to John. And there is the problem of John's popularity. The crowds like John, and Herod is afraid of inciting a riot if he casually orders his execution.

So Herodias has to endure the public ridicule and repudiation of her illicit marriage until she can spring her trap. The cunning and crafty Herodias sees an opportunity to rid herself of the nuisance and embarrassment of John the Baptist. When her husband, Herod Antipas, throws a formal birthday party for himself with local dignitaries, Herodias gets her only daughter involved in the nefarious plan. She knows that her husband has a lustful eye for his stepdaughter, Salome, and instead of rebuking him, Herodias uses his behavior for personal advantage.

At the party, Salome dances an elaborate and provocative dance. This seductive routine has been called the "dance of the seven veils" by Oscar Wilde in his play *Salome* and by Richard Strauss in his operatic version, even though the Bible itself never uses that term.

According to legend, Salome dances and gyrates, removing layers of veils until she is scantily clad, if not scandalously naked at the end of the dance. Her stepfather is so excited that he promises her a gift of anything — she only needs to ask! And Salome falls right into her mother's grand plan. "She went out, and said to her mother, 'What shall I ask?' She replied, 'The head of John the baptizer' " (Mark 6:24). The trap had been sprung. Herodias had patiently waited until the right day, time, and occasion. She stoops to using her own flesh and blood as means to an end. Worse yet, she encourages her daughter to flirt with her husband just to lure him to make an irresistible offer.

Because Herod Antipas makes the oath to grant Salome's any request in front of political dignitaries, public officials, and local aristocrats, protocol demands that he keep his word. Neglecting to do so would have been worse than embarrassing; it would have been an attack on his authority and his manhood. Although the Bible says he is deeply grieved over the request, he nevertheless orders his soldiers to bring the head of John the Baptist on a platter.

The Bible mentions no more about Salome, and the Jewish historian Flavius Josephus says only that she later married Philip the Tetrarch, who was also her uncle (like mother, like daughter). Herodias disappears from the radar screen as well, even though she most likely was in court when Jesus was brought before her husband, Herod Antipas (Luke 23:6–12). Roman Governor Pontius Pilate had sent Jesus there, hoping Herod would keep the prisoner, but instead Herod sent Christ back to Pilate, who finally had Jesus crucified.

Secular history does say that Herodias becomes jealous of her brother, Agrippa, whom Caesar had made king, while her husband remains a *tetrarch* (one of four governors of a divided province).

Again Herodias shows her power-hungry nature. She foolishly gets Herod Antipas to complain to Emperor Caesar Caligula. Agrippa informs Caligula of the political maneuverings of the tetrarch and banishes Herod to Gaul (modern-day France). Because she is Agrippa's sister, Caesar offers sanctuary to Herodias, but she turns it down and joins her exiled husband.

Daughter of Herodias

Salome is never mentioned by proper name in the Bible — she is referred to only as the daughter of Herodias from Herodias's first marriage to Herod Philip. The Jewish historian Flavius Josephus (first century AD) first identifies the daughter as Salome, a name that has stuck as a result of plays, operas, and movie adaptations over the centuries. One legend from the historian Nicephorus claims that Salome died tragically in the same way John the Baptist died. Allegedly, she was walking on a frozen lake one day when the ice beneath her broke. She fell in up to her neck and was decapitated by the ice fragments.

The Bible, and history for that matter, doesn't paint a pretty picture of Herodias. She uses her office and her marriages as tools for her own agenda. Even her daughter is fair game. John the Baptist was scratching the conscience of Herod, rebuking him for his adulterous marriage to Herodias, who made sure the voice of morality got squelched. But imprisoning the prophet isn't enough, so Herodias enlists the aid of her own daughter.

While Herodias seems to most people to be a reprehensible person, her daughter, Salome, is more mysterious. The mother had reason to hate John because he denounced her illicit relationship with Herod. Salome, however, wasn't a target of John the Baptist's criticism.

But Salome was no innocent bystander. She did participate in a scheme with Herodias to have John killed. Conspiracy to commit murder is what the police would call it today. Whatever her motivation, Salome cooperates in the evil done that day as much as her mother, Herodias, and Herod himself, who finally issued the order to execute John the Baptist.

Speaking Out: Pilate's Wife

Although Pilate's wife is mentioned only briefly in the Bible — and never by name — her story is no less significant. Her memory and example live on in the hearts of many, and the Greek Orthodox religion even considers her a saint, celebrating her in a feast day on October 27. She is beloved because she had the courage to stand up for what she believed to be right — opposing the persecution of an innocent man, Jesus.

In the Bible, Pilate's wife wakes quite upset one day because of a disturbing dream. The Romans believed dreams had profound meanings. She had dreamed that Jesus was arrested and brought before her husband, Pilate, the governor of Judea (Matthew 27:19).

Based on her dream, she feels an urgency to tell her husband to not pronounce judgment on an innocent man. Pilate himself believes that Jesus is innocent, but he also wants to avoid embarrassment and possible displeasure from Caesar should the crowd in Jerusalem get out of control. (Tiberius was Caesar at the time, and he had reprimanded Pilate on two previous occasions for instigating a riot among the Jews. Pilate was therefore not eager to have another incident occur that could further irritate Tiberius.)

Jesus' political and religious enemies are inciting the crowd to demand the release of Barabbas, a common criminal, rather than demanding Jesus' release (Luke 23:18–23). Pilate's wife tries to warn her husband that it is unwise to have innocent blood on his hands. During the turmoil and upheaval of political and religious unrest that was brewing among many in Jerusalem, the wife of Pilate gives a brief warning, which is crucial, though ignored: "Have nothing to do with that innocent man" (Matthew 27:19). Disregarding his wife, Pilate literally washes his hands of responsibility and condemns to death a man he knows is innocent, turning him over for crucifixion (Matthew 27:24–25).

The apocryphal (see Chapter 2) Gospel of Nicodemus, which has never been considered canonical by any Christian religion, identifies Pilate's wife as Claudia Procula, the granddaughter of the Emperor Caesar Augustus and the illegitimate daughter of the Emperor Caesar Tiberias and his (Tiberias's) third wife (Augustus's daughter). Although the Bible never mentions her by name, she is still commonly referred to as Claudia today.

Pilate's wife is remembered as someone who tried to intervene in Jesus' crucifixion, though it was to no avail. She wasn't content to sit silently and witness injustice. Many others who had influence or authority said and did nothing, despite, perhaps, their private reservations about what was happening. The wife of Pilate used whatever influence she had, offering wise counsel to her husband.

Some Bible scholars think Pilate's wife was merely superstitious, as most Romans were back then, and reacted to the dream she had the night before. Others see her as a good woman wanting her husband to do the right thing and avoid having innocent blood on his hands (despite Pilate's ceremonial washing of them).

If Pilate's wife is indeed the Claudia who was the granddaughter of Caesar Augustus, she would have been raised and exposed to the politics in Rome, especially among the imperial family and the Roman Senate. She could have been savvy enough to know that getting rid of Jesus would not be the panacea to calm the crowds. One day it is Jesus' blood they demand; the next it is someone else's. We'll never know her complete motivation or all the circumstances, but the Bible does show that she made an attempt to save Jesus, which is more than others did. The Bible doesn't mention her again.

The Enigmatic Mother-in-Law of Simon Peter

Another intriguing woman is referred to in the Bible only as the mother-in-law of Simon Peter, the fisherman and later chief apostle (Mark 1:29–34; Matthew 8:14–17; Luke 4:38–41). Simon Peter's mother-in-law shows selflessness and service even under difficult circumstances. Although mentioned in only a few lines of the Gospel, she is intriguing for what she reveals just by her very existence.

Peter and his brother, Andrew, were fishermen when Jesus called them to follow him and be his disciples (see Mark 1:16–18), but no mention is ever made of Peter being married and having a wife. We find out that he was married only when the existence of a mother-in-law is revealed by her miraculous healing from Jesus. This then raises the question: Who was the wife of Peter? Does she accompany Simon Peter on his missionary work or does she stay home? Is she even alive when Jesus calls him? Could Peter be a widower? These logical questions arise as soon as the mother-in-law appears.

Peter's mother-in-law shows up in the Bible briefly when she is sick and in need of healing:

> *Now Simon's mother-in-law was in bed with a fever, and they told him about her at once. He came and took her by the hand and lifted her up. Then the fever left her, and she began to serve them.*

—Mark 1:30–31

The original Greek text uses the word *diakoneo,* meaning that Simon Peter's mother-in-law "ministered" to Jesus, Peter, and his brother Andrew, with James and his brother John, as soon as she was miraculously cured. While the context of the passage indicates that Peter's mother-in-law ministered by attending to the protocols of hospitality (a very big thing back then), the same Greek word *diakoneo* is used by the early church to identify the seven men who are called to "minister" to the poor, the sick, the orphans, and the widows (see Acts 6:1–6).

To show her gratitude for being healed and to show respect to Christ as a guest in her home, Peter's mother-in-law waits on everyone in the house, even though she had up until then been on her sickbed. The scriptures portray this woman as someone who immediately takes on the role of a good hostess as soon as she is well. This is more than just good manners for Peter's mother-in-law. In ancient times, hospitality to guests was a sign of respect for the other person and almost a religious duty because you never knew whether an angel of the Lord in disguise might show up as a guest one day. Showing kindness to guests gives us a small glimpse into what kind of woman she was, even though we don't hear of her again.

The appearance of this mother-in-law is important because her presence creates big questions about Peter's marital status. On the one hand, Peter's wife is conspicuously absent (not mentioned at all) during the scene where Jesus comes to the house and cures the sick mother-in-law and she immediately waits on them (Mark 1:30–31). On the other hand, there is an interesting subtle reference in Paul's first letter to the Corinthians (1 Corinthians 9:5) where he says: "Do we not have the right to be accompanied by a believing wife, as do the other apostles and the brothers of the Lord and Cephas?"

Cephas is the Aramaic name for Peter (*Petros* in Greek and *Petrus* in Latin — see also John 1:42). The implication of Paul's statement could be that Peter's wife was still very much alive and accompanied him. The debate still continues among scholars.

Will the real whore of Babylon please stand up?

The Great Whore of Babylon is mentioned in the last book of the Bible, called the Apocalypse or Revelation: "Come, I will show you the judgment of the great whore who is seated on many waters" (Revelation 17:1) and "Babylon the great, mother of whores and of earth's abominations" (Revelation 17:5). Earlier in the New Testament (1 Peter 5:13), Peter uses the word Babylon as a metaphor for the city and the empire of Rome: "Your sister church in Babylon." Because ancient Babylon was synonymous with imperialism, unbridled power, arrogance, and the persecution of Christian believers, the Roman Empire seemed almost like a reincarnation of the Babylonian Empire for many from the first century AD until the legalization of Christianity by the Emperor Constantine in AD 313 with the Edict of Milan.

There is no actual "whore of Babylon." Rather this term is a concept, just as Lady Wisdom is (see Chapter 4). Whereas Wisdom is described as a gentle, loving, intelligent, and beautiful lady, the whore of Babylon is associated with infidelity, fornication, lying, cheating, stealing, and idolatry. In essence, the whore prostitutes the faith by ignoring truth and by disregarding God's religious and moral laws.

The Book of Revelation says that the whore of Babylon will eventually be defeated, as will the Antichrist (Revelation 18:1–24). Bible commentaries and scholars believe that, as a place, Babylon usually represents the city of Rome, the Roman Empire, or the secular world at large. When referring to a person, especially in the case of the whore of Babylon, Babylon refers to the believers who have abandoned their faith and polluted their religion with false teaching and the worship of false gods.

Over the course of history, several individuals and even entire religions have been unjustly and unfairly identified by their opponents as being the Whore of Babylon or the Antichrist (called the beast in Revelation 13:1 and 17:3). For the most part, however, biblical scholars and theologians consider the whore of Babylon to be a metaphor for only those believers who have lost or given up the faith. These include men and women and their assemblies that no longer preach the Gospel, no longer teach the truth, and no longer practice the Christian faith (by following Christ's commands to love thy neighbor, turn the other cheek, and so on).

Part V
The Nameless: Wives, Mothers, Daughters, and Widows

The 5th Wave   By Rich Tennant

©RICHTENNANT

"Lots of women in the Bible were never even mentioned by name. I figure you've got to dress the part to get people to remember you."

In this part . . .

Here come the wives, mothers, daughters, and widows of the Bible, along with a few other unnamed ladies. You meet the many unnamed, anonymous women in the Bible who are identified by their relationships, their roles, and the regions where they live. Some of these women are very courageous, faithful, and remarkable, while others are nasty, vengeful, or downright dangerous. Although the Bible doesn't have a lot of info about them, what is in there is still interesting. We show you why.

Chapter 18

Walking the Walk: The Wives

. . . .

In This Chapter

▶ Encountering women about whom little is known

▶ Meeting women of strong faith in troubled times

▶ Witnessing the lives of wives who suffered

▶ Getting to know some tragic figures

. . . .

*T*he nameless women of the Bible identified by their relationships as wives are discussed in this chapter. These women are known by the fame of their husbands or by their own words and deeds recorded in Scripture. Some of them are faithful to their spouses and to the Lord, while others are almost adversarial — if not confrontational with either or both. We see the best and the worst of the wives here — as well as those who fall in between.

Cain's Wife: Mystery Woman

The single biblical reference to Cain's wife raises more questions than it answers, but they are nonetheless interesting points to ponder.

Cain, the son of Adam and Eve who killed his brother, Abel, takes a wife. As the first murderer recorded in the Bible (and in the human race), Cain also is the first fugitive, and it is during his exile that presumably he met his wife. Together they have a son, Enoch, and build a city (east of Eden in the land of Nod) named for him. (Genesis 4:17 is where you can find these details of Cain's life.)

Pondering whom Cain's wife could have been is interesting. After all, if Adam and Eve were the first human beings and they produced only two children — Cain and Abel — where did this mystery woman come from?

The story of Cain is an example of where the Bible demonstrates it isn't a history or science book. Mystery is prolific in the Bible, and those who read it must also embrace the mysterious, such as Cain's wife's identity.

According to Genesis 5:4, Adam and Eve had "other sons and daughters" after Cain and Abel, including Seth and more (unnamed children). But unless Cain's wife was one of his sisters, no one really knows who she is.

A second question regards whether Cain's wife knew that her husband was the world's first murderer — and that he had murdered his own brother. God put a mark on Cain after he killed Abel to warn anyone not to seek vengeance by killing Cain (Genesis 4:15). His wife must have seen this mark and knew what it meant. Many theologians propose that Cain did regret his heinous sin and asked for God's mercy — and that his wife and son signify this fact. Had Cain not repented, his punishment would have been more severe, possibly never finding a wife and not ever having any children.

Though barely mentioned in the Bible, Mrs. Cain, whoever she was, must have seen some intrinsic good in the man reviled throughout history for murdering his only brother. Something in Cain was lovable, and his wife may have recognized it.

Noah's Wife: Faithful in the Flood

Noah's wife presents more biblical mystery. She and Noah lived in what is called the *antediluvian era,* which is a fancy way of saying "before the flood." People in the Bible before Abraham and Sarah (going all the way back to Adam and Eve) do not have a definite historical chronology; in other words, we're not sure when they lived because no other nonbiblical historical references identify the time period.

She is briefly mentioned in Genesis 6:18 when God instructs Noah to bring two of every animal, plus his wife and children to the ark, which Noah has built in order to escape the divine punishment meant to rid the earth of wicked and evil. Although Noah's wife's name is never given, she must have been a righteous and virtuous woman. Otherwise, she would have been left behind with all the evil and unrepentant people who perished in 40 days and 40 nights of torrential rain. The wife of Noah is mentioned only five times in the Bible (Genesis 6:18; 7:7; 7:13; 8:16; and 8:18) and always as a member of the family with Noah and their children — never alone as an individual.

She also must have been courageous and strong to contend with a boatload of animals for more than a month. Imagine the smell alone on that damp and confined vessel, not to mention the responsibility of feeding and caring for the menagerie. Noah and the human race greatly depend upon her even after the rains subside and the ark lands. Noah and his wife, along with their sons and daughters, must repopulate the world because all the other people have perished in the flood. Noah's wife obviously didn't know beforehand how God's plan for them would play out, yet she and her husband trust that God knows what he is doing, thus proving that she is a woman of faith.

The last time we hear of Noah's wife is when the flood stops (after 40 days), the dry land appears, the ark lands, and the family and animals disembark (see Genesis 8:18). She is conspicuously missing or at least not mentioned when Noah was discovered naked by his son Ham, getting drunk on some wine he made from grapes he had cultivated (see Genesis 9:20–22). Ham's sin was that he went out and told his brothers, Shem and Japheth. When they find Noah, they show modesty and respect by covering him up, whereas Ham just went out and let his brothers know that their dad was in an embarrassing situation. The Bible doesn't say when the wife of Noah died, but it does say that he lived to be 950 years old, 350 of those after the flood (Genesis 9:28–29). We're not sure if Noah's wife died before the wine incident or later, but the Bible doesn't mention her after the animals leave the ark.

Judah's Wife: Famous for Her Death

Judah and his wife lived sometime during the seventeenth or sixteenth century BC. He was one of the 12 sons of Israel (also known as Jacob), and we hear of his wife for the first time in Genesis 38:1–5 (see more two paragraphs below). They were living in Canaan at this time, but later, Jacob (Judah's father) and his sons (including Judah and his wife) move to Egypt to escape famine.

The most significant aspect of Judah's wife, as recorded in the Bible, isn't her life; it's her death. As the wife of Judah, she had given birth to three sons: Er, Onan, and Shelah. Unfortunately, the two elder sons die, one after another, each leaving the same widow, Tamar. Childless Tamar presumes she can marry the third son, Shelah, but his father, Judah, says no. (See Tamar's full story in Chapter 9.)

Most translations of the Bible present Judah's wife as nameless, merely identifying her as the "Shua's daughter, the wife of Judah" (Genesis 38:12). A few translations give the original Hebrew for "daughter of Shua" as if it's her proper name: Bath-shua. What we do know for sure is that she was a Canaanite and her father was Shua.

The death of Judah's wife is significant because it allows Tamar to move in and trick Judah into becoming the father of her twin sons, Zerah and Perez (the ancestor of King David and also of Jesus). Had Judah's wife not died when she did, Judah would never have been involved with Tamar, and the lineage would have ended there. The Bible never says when the wife of Judah dies nor how. The Book of Jubilees, which is not in the Bible but part of the noninspired books of the Old Testament era (called the Pseudepigrapha by Protestants and the Apocrypha by Catholics and Eastern Orthodox), does claim that she died soon after refusing to allow Shelah to marry Tamar, as Judah had previously promised. Due to the questionable authenticity, authorship, and origins of the Pseudepigrapha, facts found in the Book of Jubilees aren't considered reliable, however, so no one knows for sure.

Manoah's Wife: Obeying an Angel

This woman who lived around the twelfth century BC is best known for having a famous son, Samson (the strongest man on earth who could single-handedly wipe out a thousand Philistines), but the Bible identifies her only as the wife of Manoah (see Judges 13 for more details). Manoah and his wife live in Zorah and are of the tribe of Dan. This Danite couple is, unfortunately, childless until an angel of the Lord appears to the barren wife to tell her that she will conceive and bear a son.

Sarah, Rebekah, Rachel (read more about them in Chapter 9), and Hannah (see Chapter 11) all were blessed with children after the embarrassment of many years of childlessness. When the wife of Manoah gets pregnant with Samson, she joins their ranks. The angel tells her, however, that she must avoid wine and liquor and all unclean foods during the pregnancy, because she will give birth to a son who will be a Nazirite (see more on this in the Technical Stuff information later). Today, most people would consider the angel's advice as merely good prenatal care.

Back at the time of Manoah's wife, though, following such instructions was a real act of faith. Water, wine, salt, and bread were the staples of life in the ancient world. Wine symbolized both physical and spiritual life. Potable water wasn't always accessible, and wine often served as a good substitute. Religious rituals involved wine libations poured over altars and consumed by worshipers.

A *Nazirite* is someone consecrated to God who doesn't drink alcohol, touch dead bodies, or get a haircut. The prohibition against drinking wine and liquor, touching corpses, and cutting one's hair as a sign of the vow can be traced to Numbers 6:1–8.

After the angel tells Manoah's wife's of her coming pregnancy, the couple offers to make a meal for the angel, which he refuses, instead asking that they take the goat they would have cooked to eat and burn it as an offering to God.

They comply with the request, the offering's fire rises to the sky, and the angel went with it. Manoah and his wife then realize that it is an angel who had visited them, and they fall to their knees with their faces toward the ground. Manoah fears they will surely die for having seen an angel. (See Judges 13:3–22 for more details.) Unlike the naked babies with wings you see on Valentine's Day cards, angels in Biblical times didn't appear as cute little infant cherubs. Angels are powerful beings with enormous strength, intelligence, and beauty far beyond what any human being could ever achieve. Seeing an angel was a fearful event for many Jews and early Christians because the angelic messenger usually brought important news that was not always happy. For example, angels could bring a warning about imminent disaster, death, or disease. Manoah's wife, however, reassures him:

> *If the LORD had meant to kill us, he would not have accepted a burnt offering and a grain offering at our hands, or shown us all these things, or now announced to us such things as these.*

> —Judges 13:23

And right she was. The wife of Manoah does as the angel instructs and has a son that she and her husband name Samson. Even though both husband and wife listen to and obey the divine message, the woman is the one who shows a great religious insight. Manoah's wife appears one more time in Scripture when her son, Samson, is grown. She protests the wife her son chooses because the woman is a Philistine (Judges 14:3). Philistines were the enemies of Israel, and Samson, a Danite, was to deliver his people from them. Yet he falls in love with someone from the other side.

Samson's Wife: The Answer to a Riddle

Like Samson's mother, the wife of Samson is also nameless. This Philistine woman lives in Timnah (20 miles west of Jerusalem) during the eleventh century BC. She had been criticized by Samson's own mother as unsuitable — after all, Samson devotes his life to fighting the Philistines — and some scholars speculate that Samson uses her to get back at her people. Judges 14:4 says "he was seeking a pretext to act against the Philistines" when Samson told his parents about the woman he intended to marry.

Her significance lies in the fact that she serves as a pawn between Samson and her father, as well as within Samson's war on the Philistines. But she doesn't just sit back and take it. She may have figured out he was marrying her only to use her, and so she does something that could have been conceived as revenge. Before the marriage is consummated, Samson gives a riddle to his Philistine guests, which was common wedding reception entertainment in those days:

Let me now put a riddle to you. If you can explain it to me within the seven days of the feast, and find it out, then I will give you thirty linen garments and thirty festal garments. But if you cannot explain it to me, then you shall give me thirty linen garments and thirty festal garments.

—Judges 14:12–13

Thirty of the guests accept the bet. The riddle Samson tells is, "Out of the eater came something to eat. Out of the strong came something sweet" (Judges 14:14). They are stumped and can't solve the puzzle, but the guests convince his fiancée to lure the answer from him. She weeps for seven days until he breaks down and tells her the solution: "What is sweeter than honey? What is stronger than a lion?" (Judges 14:18).

Previous to his engagement, Samson had slain a lion with his bare hands and later that day came upon the dead carcass to find bees making honey within the dead beast. The *eater* is the bee who makes something to *eat,* honey. The *strong* is the lion, now dead, but from within his carcass came the *sweet* honey. Then she tells the guests, who are able to solve the riddle. Samson becomes infuriated and says, "If you had not plowed with my heifer, you would not have found out my riddle" (Judges 14:18). Outraged, Samson kills 30 Philistines and takes their cloaks and uses them to pay off the gambling debt he has just lost.

When Samson leaves, the father of his bride is so embarrassed he gives his daughter to Samson's best man, and when he returns to find his wife given to another, it spawns a series of escalating violent incidents. The father then tries to substitute his younger daughter for the one Samson had wanted. Samson replies: "This time, when I do mischief to the Philistines, I will be without blame" (Judges 15:3). Samson gets creative. Using foxes, he ties torches to their tails and sets them loose to burn the standing grain of the Philistines.

The Philistines retaliate by burning Samson's wife, her sister, and her father to death in their own home. His wife's gruesome demise angers him, so he slays a thousand Philistines with a donkey's jawbone that he found on the roadside. Whether he truly loved her or not, Samson was outraged that his father-in-law gave his wife to the best man and was even more livid when his mortal enemies kill them. He avenged their deaths and defended his honor. (See Judges 15:4–15 for this story.) Samson's wife is never mentioned again.

Solomon's Wives: A Kingdom's Downfall

King Solomon of the unified Kingdom of Israel (tenth century BC) had 700 wives and 300 concubines (30 times more than his dad, King David) during his reign (1 Kings 11:3). Used as political bargaining chips rather than as loving partners in a marriage covenant, the wives of Solomon may have lived in material opulence but were romantically impoverished. His wives were a virtual rainbow of ancient ethnicities and included a daughter of Pharaoh along with Moabite, Sidonian, Edomite, and Hittite women.

Marrying a king's daughter was the best insurance for global peace in those days, and many of Solomon's wives were offered as flesh-and-blood treaties by their fathers, foreign rulers with whom Solomon chose to make peace. Solomon's wives are relevant because they lead him into alien religions, which were not only taboo but also spelled disaster for the throne and the kingdom.

For when Solomon was old, his wives turned away his heart after other gods; and his heart was not true to the LORD *his God, as was the heart of his father David. For Solomon followed Astarte the goddess of the Sidonians, and Milcom the abomination of the Ammonites.*

—1 Kings 11:4–5

By worshiping the false gods of his wives, Solomon offended God greatly. His punishment would not be seen in his lifetime, however, out of God's respect for King David, Solomon's father (1 Kings 11:9, 11–12).

Punishment came when the Promised Land was later split into two kingdoms: north (Israel) and south (Judah). This was the end of the great kingdom of Israel (only 99 years old) that Moses had helped secure. No longer a single, unified kingdom, it would become two separate entities in 922 BC only to be conquered later on by the Assyrians in 721 BC (Israel) and then by the Babylonians in 587 BC (Judah).

Jeroboam's Wife: Suffering for Her Spouse's Sins

Jeroboam's wife was the queen to a king who ruled northern Israel from 928–907 BC. Discussed in 1 Kings 14:1–17, Jeroboam's wife was a tragic figure who suffered because of her husband's sins.

King Jeroboam I worships foreign gods, makes molten images of calves in shrines, and persecutes the priests of the true religion of Judaism. His son becomes quite ill, so thinking that God may heal his son despite his infidelity, he sends his wife the queen to the prophet Ahijah for a cure.

Cognizant of his sins, Jeroboam instructs the queen to disguise herself and bring gifts to the prophet that would befit a commoner. He hopes that the prophet, who has bad sight, won't recognize her and therefore will grant her the request.

When Ahijah hears the sound of her footsteps, he greets her: "Come in, you wife of Jeroboam! Why do you pretend to be another?" (1 Kings 14:6). Unfortunately, he doesn't grant her wish. Instead, he instructs her to tell Jeroboam that God intends to punish him for idolatry and other abominations against the Hebrew religion. Her son won't be cured but will die as a result of his father's sins.

Imagine a mother hearing such a prophecy? She says nothing in reply. The dutiful wife instead returns home to find her son already dead. Jeroboam's wife and her son are innocent victims. Her husband is the one who violated the Mosaic law (Ten Commandments) by erecting golden calf idols and promoting pagan worship, but she must pay the price for his sins through the death of a son.

Not mentioned again in the Bible, this dutiful wife and loving mother may have been comforted that her son is at least buried with dignity . . . unlike the dire prediction "Anyone belonging to Jeroboam who dies in the city, the dogs shall eat; and anyone who dies in the open country, the birds of the air shall eat; for the LORD has spoken" (1 Kings 14:11).

Job's Wife: Giving Up on God

The Book of Job was written sometime between the seventh and fifth centuries BC, but we don't know the time period in which Job himself lived. Many Bible scholars speculate that it was sometime before the Exodus and after Abraham lived. Job's wife plays a very brief role in the Bible. They live somewhere in Arabia, and the Book of Job opens with the wealth they initially enjoyed: seven sons, three daughters, 7,000 sheep, 3,000 camels, 500 oxen, and 500 donkeys. Job's luck, however, turns suddenly and sharply, and his wife's doubts are in stark contrast to Job's eternal patience and faith in God.

Job becomes the subject of debate between Satan and God. The Evil One says Job is faithful only because everything was going his way. He claims that if Job's luck turned, he eventually would curse God for falling upon hard times. (See the Job 1:6–12 for more details.)

But Satan is proved wrong. Even when Job's children die and he is struck with leprosy, he remains faithful to God. At no point does he give in and blame God for his predicament. He utters this memorable response, "Naked I came from my mother's womb, and naked shall I return there; the LORD gave, and the LORD has taken away; blessed be the name of the LORD" (Job 1:21).

Job's wife, of course, is suffering along with him, because her sons and daughters died, too. When she has finally had enough, she questions Job: "Do you still persist in your integrity? Curse God, and die" (Job 2:9). This could be a means to an end — blaspheming the Lord usually results in being struck dead. She may also just be saying that only one other thing could possibly happen: After all the bad luck and suffering both Job and his wife have thus suffered, his own death is all that's left to endure. We don't know exactly what she meant by this statement.

Is she fed up with all the suffering? Or is it just that she can't stand to see her loved ones suffer anymore? Whatever her motivation, Job doesn't accept her questioning and rebukes her. He asks why, if they receive good things from the Lord, should they not also receive the bad. The Bible never explains the mystery of why there is evil in the world or why the innocent rather than the guilty are the ones who often suffer.

Although his wife doesn't appear again, Job curses, not God, but his own life. His friends try to tell him he must have done something evil to deserve such suffering or that he must need to be chastised or corrected by the Lord. Job just wants his life to end and curses the day he was born. Yet, he never curses God, and for this he is ultimately rewarded at the end of the book with twice as much as he had before he was an object of mischief from the devil.

The entire Book of Job focuses on innocent suffering. Job isn't punished because he said or did anything wrong, immoral, or sinful. The point of his story is that bad things happen to good people, too. The presumption that only the evil suffer and the good are rewarded in this life is a spinoff from the *lex talionis* (the law of retribution, or "eye for eye, tooth for tooth," in the words of Deuteronomy 19:21), which presumes that suffering is a punishment for a wrongdoing. In reality, the law of retribution was a crude form of commutative justice in which each person was rewarded for his goodness or punished for his evil. The *lex talionis,* however, never was meant to be a way of explaining why people suffer in the world.

Ezekiel's Wife: A Symbol of the Temple

Ezekiel, a prophet in the sixth century BC, is married to the love of his life, a woman whom God even called "the desire of your eyes" (Ezekiel 24:16). Because of her beauty and importance to Ezekiel, God uses her as a symbol of the Temple of Jerusalem. Unfortunately, like the Temple, this woman meets a tragic fate.

The couple lived during the time of the Babylonian captivity and exile after the southern kingdom of Judah fell in 587 BC. In a dream, Ezekiel is told that his beloved wife is soon to die. Worse yet, he is forbidden to show any external mourning for her — no tears and no public grieving.

Mortal, with one blow I am about to take away from you the delight of your eyes; yet you shall not mourn or weep, nor shall your tears run down. Sigh, but not aloud; make no mourning for the dead. Bind on your turban, and put your sandals on your feet; do not cover your upper lip or eat the bread of mourners. So I spoke to the people in the morning, and at evening my wife died. And on the next morning I did as I was commanded.

—Ezekiel 24:16–18

Her death symbolizes the fulfillment of a prophecy. The Temple of Jerusalem is the pride and joy of the Hebrew people, but because of their sins, the Temple will be destroyed. Just as Ezekiel isn't allowed to publicly mourn the death of his beloved wife, the Jewish people, who were at that time in exile, have to refrain from mourning the destruction of the Temple by King Nebuchadnezzar in AD 586 and the slaughter of the Jews in Jerusalem by the Babylonians. Ezekiel's wife was as dear to his heart as the Temple of Jerusalem was to every Jew, especially those in captivity who longed for their release. When Ezekiel has to deal with the sudden and unexpected death of his wife, it is a symbol of what the exiled Jews would feel and experience when they received the news of the ruin of Jerusalem and the desecration of the Temple.

In both situations, the response is utter shock and horror, with no public mourning to adequately express the enormous loss. God took away Ezekiel's wife the day before he speaks to the people so he could adequately prophesy to them the great loss they were about to experience: the destruction of the beloved Temple, a loss as painful as losing a spouse. Just as Ezekiel was told by God not to show any public mourning for his recently deceased beloved wife, the Israelites were told to not mourn the loss of their beloved Temple — no crying and no outward sign of grief. The pain of losing something beloved was compounded by the fact that the people were forbidden to express their misery. This was the punishment the people received for their sins against religion. The analogy of husband-wife recurs in the Bible again and again to describe the relationship of God and the Hebrew People in the Old Testament and between Jesus Christ and the Church in the New Testament.

Chapter 19

Mothering Worth Mentioning

Many women of the Bible are described simply as mothers, without being named. The mothers we discuss in this chapter span the spectrum of good and evil, with some falling smack in the middle of mediocrity. Some women exhibit great faith in God and love for their children, and others show the worst of fallen human nature. Wise or foolish, generous or selfish, prideful or humble, these nameless women of the Bible are known by their roles as mothers.

Material Minded: Sisera's Mother

Sisera's mother was a woman whose priorities in life seem a bit skewed. She lived in the twelfth century BC. While her son Sisera, a Canaanite general, is away in battle, she has thoughts that seem out of place for a mother in her situation. Instead of typically worrying about his safety, the mother of Sisera is preoccupied with thoughts of the spoils of war he will bring her. She thinks of herself more than of her son. Ultimately, her story is sadly ironic — while she hopes and wonders about his return from battle for selfish reasons, she doesn't know that he is already dead.

Sisera's mother is waiting for him to return home from a war her son has lost. The Israelites, led by Deborah the Judge (see Chapter 10 for more on her), have defeated the Canaanites in an epic battle, conquering 100,000 Canaanite troops, led by Sisera, with only 10,000 of their own Israelite men. (See Judges 4:12–17 for more details.)

The mother of Sisera could have represented the pains and casualties of war, waiting and worrying about her son's safety. But she doesn't know her son has been defeated, and one night she peers out a window and wonders if her boy is late because his chariot is stuck. She wishes him home, not for his safety but for the gifts she hopes he will bring her. She eagerly anticipates the booty Sisera has captured: "Spoil of dyed stuffs for Sisera, spoil of dyed stuffs embroidered, two pieces of dyed work embroidered for my neck as spoil?" (Judges 5:30).

Meanwhile, Sisera has already been killed — and not honorably or for a good cause, the Bible says. After Sisera loses the war and becomes a cowardly fugitive, a woman named Jael tricks him into hiding in her tent. While Sisera is asleep, she pounds a wood stake into his head, fastening him to the ground. This gruesome death is contrasted with irony in the Song of Deborah in the Book of Judges. "Out of the window she peered, the mother of Sisera gazed through the lattice: 'Why is his chariot so long in coming? Why tarry the hoofbeats of his chariots?' " (Judges 5:28). While Sisera's mother impatiently awaits the return of her son, primarily for the nice gifts he will bring her, she has no idea that he has already died a gruesome death.

The Bible doesn't mention Sisera's mother after his death, and it doesn't say when she discovers the bad news or what her reaction was. You can imagine the sadness, shock, and then guilt she must have felt when, after spending so much time and energy fantasizing about the goodies Sisera was going to bring her, she finds out that the most valuable prize, his very life, was taken from him.

Falsely Religious: Micah's Mother

The story of Micah and his mother, who lives in the twelfth century BC, is a paradox of absurdities. The story of this nameless woman, mentioned briefly in Judges 17:1–4, goes something like this: When 1,100 silver shekels are stolen from Micah's mother, she utters a curse upon anyone involved with the theft. Micah soon confesses that he stole the money. His mother then blesses him with the same lips that had just cursed him. And when the money is returned, she takes 200 of the 1,100 silver pieces to pay a smith to make an idol of the Lord God, a practice vehemently forbidden by the Mosaic law.

Many contradictory elements are at work in this story:

✔ Micah breaks a commandment: "Thou shalt not steal."

✔ His mother does worse by cursing the thief, her own son, and practicing idolatry (Judges 17: 4–6).

✔ Micah is repentant and confesses his actions, and his mother blesses him.

Their behavior shows moral and spiritual confusion on the part of both mother and son, and it's a confusion that was heavily present during the time that they lived. Because there was no king, the land lacked a moral and spiritual leader, leaving the people to make their own decisions — often the wrong decisions.

The sin of Micah's mother is one of false religion. The reason why the Hebrews were forbidden to make any images or idols of God is the same reason why they were forbidden to speak the sacred proper name of God. (**YHWH,** from the verbal root meaning "to be." Thus God's name seems to mean "He who is" or "He who causes to be.") Unlike the pagans who uttered names and made idols of their false gods in order to control or manipulate them, Jews were to trust completely in the God who can't be seen and whose name they could not speak.

Zeus and Jupiter, Hera and Juno, Isis, and more had names and images, and if you had both, you could persuade the deities to grant any request. God, however, was so almighty and powerful that no one could control him, and no one dared say his name. The mother of Micah didn't have a pagan idol, but one of the Living God. Yet, he forbade such things. Based on her cursing and idol use, she is shown to be — not a devout Hebrew — but someone of superstition.

Morally Influential: The Woman of Tekoa

Through an Oscar-worthy performance made for the greater good, the woman of Tekoa (described in 2 Samuel 14:1–20) played a part in securing Israel — at least for a short time. She lives in Israel in the tenth century BC, when David was king, and she is renowned for being a wise person, a devout Jew, and a moral influencer on a par with the likes of Mother Teresa of Calcutta.

The woman of Tekoa is called into service by King David's general, Joab. She must travel from her home in Tekoa (approximately 12 miles from Jerusalem) to help address a situation in the royal family. King David's son, Absalom (son of David and Maacah), had gone into exile for killing his brother Amnon (son of David and Ahinoam) in retribution for Amnon's part in the rape of Absalom's sister (and Amnon's half sister), Tamar. The Law of Moses (Exodus 20:13; Deuteronomy 5:17) required the death penalty for *fratricide* (bumping off your own brother). After three years, General Joab is afraid that if David dies, while his heir Absalom is banished and Prince Solomon (son of David and Bathsheba) is still a boy; then the kingdom is in jeopardy with no ruler.

Joab asks the woman of Tekoa to go to King David and pretend to be in mourning. The woman must present herself as a mother of two sons — one of whom has killed the other. She tells King David that her family is seeking justice and wants her only surviving son to be punished, according to the Law of Moses. (See 2 Samuel 14:5–7.)

But even though she mourns the unjust death of her son, she doesn't want her other and only remaining son to die as well. She begs the king for his wise counsel and royal authority to prevent the destruction of her family.

The woman's story is actually a parable about King David's own family, and it serves its purpose well. It gets King David thinking about his own family's situation. Soon David sees that he must rescind the exile order and forgive his older son, for the greater good of the nation of Israel, in spite of his anger at his son's deed.

The Bible doesn't say whether the woman of Tekoa actually has any children. But some scholars believe that only a mother could be as convincing in this role.

In any event, she speaks her words with conviction and intensity — and changes history in doing so.

Conflicted: The Two Mothers and King Solomon

The story of these two nameless mothers (see 1 Kings 3:16–28) has been told and retold through the centuries. These mothers go before the wise and clever King Solomon to solve a conflict. Their story sounds like an exaggerated episode of Judge Judy — except that these mothers can rely on the renowned wisdom of Solomon to decide their case.

The unwed women work as prostitutes in the same brothel and have recently given birth to sons. Unfortunately, one of their infant boys has died. Both women now appear before the king, claiming to be the mother of the surviving infant.

The first mother tells Solomon that on the night of the infant's death, their babies were switched. She claims that her son is still alive and that she woke up with the other woman's dead baby next to her side.

The second mother says that she is the mother of the living child now before the king. She claims that Mother #1 simply can't accept that fact, which is why she has created the bizarre story of midnight baby swapping. Because both are ladies of the evening who live in a house of ill repute, no one can corroborate either one's story.

Cannibalism in the Bible

In 2 Kings 6:26–30, a bizarre Bible story deals with two mothers during a horrible famine. They both make a pact to kill their sons and share in eating them to stay alive. After the first mother does the unspeakable and both partake in cannibalism, the second one changes her mind and refuses to kill, let alone eat, her son, even though she joined the other mother the day before. The first cannibal mother approaches King Jehoram of Israel, complaining that her accomplice has broken their pact to mutually kill and consume their offspring to survive the famine. This Bible story isn't one you'd tell little children, that's for sure.

This macabre tale shows the absolute lowest level to which a mother could slip: survival by killing and consuming your own child. It is as revolting and reprehensible now as it was then. The fact that the Bible contains such a story is testimony that human beings are capable of great good and holiness or great evil and wickedness. Thankfully, the majority of mothers in Scripture are too decent and good to ever commit such heinous acts.

With no DNA tests as evidence, all King Solomon had to go on was literally one mother's word against the other's — quite a pickle for even wise King Solomon. So the king, who had formerly asked God for the gift of wisdom to rule Israel, now tests his mettle. He orders a soldier to take his sword and cut the infant in half, giving each mother an equal part.

This peculiar command is not one that judges today would be issuing in court. Before the deed is done, the first mother shouts to stop the soldier before his sword can touch the child: "Please, my lord, give her the living boy; certainly do not kill him!"(1 Kings 3:26). The second mother responds, "It shall be neither mine nor yours; divide it" (1 Kings 3:26).

Solomon uses their reactions to figure out the real mother. He knows that the child's real mother is the one willing to give him up rather than see him die. Solomon's tactic is meant to elicit the maternal instincts of the real mom, and he succeeds.

The story and the solution still intrigue people thousands of years later. Solomon has shown great wisdom in being certain that the real mother would make the sacrifice of renouncing her claim in order that the child might live. He knows a mother's love is this strong. While these two harlot mothers are not mentioned again in Scripture, the scene of them before Solomon has been portrayed in art throughout the centuries. Artists who have portrayed this scene include Bartholomäus Bruyn the Elder, *Solomon's Judgment*, 1532; Nikolay Gay, *The Judgment of King Solomon*, 1854; and William Blake, *Judgment of Solomon*, 1827.

Voice of Reason: Belshazzar's Mother

The mother of King Belshazzar (wife of King Nebuchadnezzar; seventh century BC) is not named in the Bible. As Queen Mother, however, she has significant influence and rules indirectly as regent while her son was too young to be king. As he grows up, Belshazzar proves to be a bit of a playboy who indulges himself too much and too often. His mother is a voice of reason and wisdom in the Babylonian kingdom, second only to that of the prophet Daniel.

The mother of Belshazzar may have regretted getting involved in her son's affairs, because doing so spelled disaster for her people. But she was an honest and upright woman who preferred knowing the truth, no matter how painful. On one occasion, King Belshazzar invites 1,000 aristocratic guests to the palace and defiles the sacred gold cups his father King Nebuchadnezzar had stolen from the Temple of Jerusalem. While they guzzle wine and engage in debauchery, a dismembered hand appears out of nowhere and begins writing on the wall. Scared silly, the king pleads for anyone to interpret the foreign message. He promises to clothe this able man in purple, put a gold chain around his neck, and rank him third in the kingdom. (See Daniel 5:1–7 for the details.)

Belshazzar's mother, the queen, enters the scene. She utters eloquent and wise advice to her no-good son. She suggests that he ask the person who gave sound counsel to his father before him, the man who interpreted the dream of Nebuchadnezzar when no one else was able. (Daniel 5:10–12 gives the account of the queen's remarks to her son.)

"Mene, mene, tekel, peres" was the message written by the mysterious hand, which no one could translate. Heeding his mother, Belshazzar calls for Daniel, who immediately understands the cryptic note on the wall. *Mene* comes from the verb "to number"; *tekel* comes from the verb "to weigh"; and *peres* comes from the verb "to divide." Thus Daniel interprets the message to mean the following: God has numbered the days of the kingdom and weighed King Belshazzar on the scales of justice. God has found him guilty, and he will divide the Babylonian Empire among the Persians and the Medes.

This prophecy came to pass. If her son had half of his mother's integrity, his kingdom might never have been destroyed. That very night King Belshazzar died. His mother was mentioned in only these three verses and then no more. (See Daniel 5:24–31 for more details.)

Chapter 20

Darling Daughters of the Bible

In This Chapter

▶ Meeting the daughters in the Old Testament

▶ Getting to know the New Testament daughters

*W*hen people today research their family trees and do extensive genealogies, they can trace both the men and women in their families. But in ancient times, only the bloodlines of males were recorded — unless, of course, you were royalty. Wives may have merited a mention, but daughters were almost never listed at all, especially if they were married. It wasn't that their families didn't love them or that they didn't play important roles as daughters. They just weren't mentioned much in reference to their immediate families. After marrying, a woman became part of her husband's clan, tribe, or family, whereas a son continued the lineage of his father. Sadly, this practice meant that many wives and most daughters were omitted from biblical history.

Despite their undervalued status, the Bible still refers to a number of specific women as daughters, and approximately 200 references to daughters are peppered throughout. The apocryphal/pseudepigraphical Book of Adam and the Apocalypse of Moses claim that Adam and Eve had 30 daughters, but the inspired, canonical scriptures mention only that they "had other sons and daughters" (Genesis 5:4). (These books aren't found in any Bible because they were never considered inspired text. Protestants refer to these books as the *Pseudepigrapha,* meaning "false writings," whereas Catholics refer to them as the *Apocrypha.* What Protestants call the Old Testament Apocrypha, Catholics and Eastern Orthodox Christians call the *Deuterocanon,* meaning "second canon.") Because only Cain, Abel, and Seth were mentioned by name, we don't know much about any of these other children.

Also in Genesis, the Bible makes reference to the "daughters of men" (*benot ha'adam* in Hebrew) having relations with the "sons of god" (*beney ha'elohim* in Hebrew) (see Genesis 6:4). Some biblical scholars consider the men's daughters to be the descendants of Cain, whereas the sons of God were the descendants of Seth. Other scripture scholars see the sons of men as angelic (fallen or otherwise) or as intelligent, but nonhuman (Homo sapiens), beings.

In this chapter, we take a look at the several other daughters from the Old and New Testaments. Some of these nameless daughters are famous because of their dads, like the daughters of Lot or the daughters of Jethro. Others are a classification of women, such as the daughters of Jerusalem or the daughters of Zion. In every case, however, we look at women whose identities are linked to the roles of being daughters only — as their proper names are not given.

Interestingly, the Bible explicitly differentiates daughters (*benot* in Hebrew) from sons (*beney* in Hebrew), even though it doesn't give proper names to many of the daughters, as it does the sons.

Meeting the Daughters of the Old Testament

Being a daughter meant a few different (and very accepted) things during the times of the Old Testament:

✔ Daughters were not considered "daddy's little girls." Patriarchal societies, especially nomadic and tribal ones, prized sons more than daughters because the boys would inherit the birthright and property and the girls had to become part of their husband's family and clan.

That doesn't mean that fathers in ancient times didn't love their daughters as much as they do today. It just means that, socially and culturally, a man with several daughters wasn't considered as prosperous and secure as a man with several sons.

✔ When daughters were of age, mom and dad usually planned their union with an eligible man (who may or may not have been young, handsome, and unmarried).

Daughters in the Old Testament weren't considered property, but custom was that a dowry was given to the father by the groom or the groom's family, rather than the later Christian-era custom in which the father of the bride paid a dowry to the new husband when he married the daughter.

Life wasn't always easy for daughters. They knew they would someday be married off (and it often wasn't for love). While not completely ostracized, these young ladies often felt like they were being yanked from their families and taken to distant lands — without the frequent flier miles to easily return for the holidays. And these women weren't very highly respected either; their brothers, who would carry on the lineage, were the prized offspring in every family.

Sodom and Gomorrah

Sodom and Gomorrah were two cities in ancient times that were known to revel in decadent and sinful behavior (especially sexual perversion) that was abhorrent to God. The cities' destruction became a biblical example of how God judges sin. In Genesis, God rains down sulfur out of the heavens, which leads to the cities' destruction.

Shameless nameless: Daughters of Lot

The two daughters of Lot are nameless in the Bible, but their deeds are notorious. Lot, their father, doesn't lead such a fabulous example, but some Bible commentators call his daughters the "shameless nameless." Lot decides to get cozy in Sodom, the ancient city that God is said to have destroyed due to sin, and his daughters follow this early lead. (See the sidebar, "Sodom and Gomorrah," earlier in this chapter for more details on this sin city.) The daughters of Lot lived around the time of their grand uncle Abraham, which was about the eighteenth century BC. (Their notorious mother — who turned to a pillar of salt — is mentioned in Chapter 17.)

According to the Book of Genesis, one day, two angels come to Lot in the form of men to warn him to leave the evil city. But the perverted inhabitants of Sodom soon learn of the two angels' arrival and seek to have their way with them. The men of Sodom go to Lot's home and demand that he turn over the two men (the angels) for illicit sex. Instead, Lot offers the Sodomites his two virginal daughters. (Nice dad, huh?)

But the men outside don't want women; they want men. The angels save Lot and his family by momentarily blinding the deviant men at the door of Lot's house, allowing him and his family to escape.

That Lot offers his own flesh and blood — his daughters — rather than turn over the two men (who are really angels) shows the extreme expression of hospitality. The two men are Lot's guests, and he's responsible for their comfort and safety. He's also responsible for the welfare of his own daughters, but he places them after the guests. The Bible never condones his actions or behavior but merely states what happens.

After Lot and his two daughters leave Sodom to escape the destruction, they live in caves. The daughters believe they have little chance of procreating — their fiancés died when the sulfur and brimstone rained from heaven, and no marital prospects were lining up at the door to their caves — so they devise a plan of their own. They conspire to liquor up their dad to trick him into having relations with them. Sure enough, their vile plan works, and they both become pregnant. To read the biblical account of this story, see Genesis 19:30–38.

One daughter becomes the mother of Moab, the ancestor of the Moabites, while the other daughter mothers Benamni, the father of the Ammonites. Both groups become fierce enemies of the Hebrew Israelites. These women aren't mentioned again in the Bible. Posterity and history will merely remember them as the daughters of Lot who intoxicated their father in order to get themselves pregnant.

Caring for Moses: Daughter of Pharaoh

Although a pagan, the daughter of Pharaoh plays an instrumental part in saving the Hebrew people. She's the princess who finds baby Moses floating in a basket in the Nile River after his mother, Jochebed (see Chapter 10), places him there to save his life following Pharaoh's order that all male Hebrew infants be killed.

Pharaoh decrees the death sentence on Hebrew males because he fears the Hebrews will outnumber and overrun their Egyptian slave masters.

When the princess finds Moses, she admits, "This must be one of the Hebrews' children" (Exodus 2:6). She knows about the royal order her father issued to kill all male Hebrew babies. She asks Miriam (see Chapter 10), Moses' sister who is watching his progress along the river, for a wet nurse to care for the child until the princess can care for him. Miriam, of course, takes little Moses back to their own mother, Jochebed. Later, Moses returns to the princess as her adopted son, making him royalty.

Pharaoh's daughter saves the man who later saves the Hebrews from Egyptian tyranny and slavery. In addition, Moses' position in the royal court gives him an education and training he later uses after the Hebrews escape the slavery of Egypt, seeking the Promised Land. There was no guarantee that when she first found baby Moses she would not have immediately had him killed out of loyalty to her father. Perhaps she kept him just to be a little rebellious, or as most scripture commentaries speculate, she had a warm spot in her heart that God took advantage of and used her to effect his will of preserving the Deliverer (the one who would free the Hebrews from their bondage). The Pharaoh's daughter isn't mentioned again in the Bible, so we're never really sure of her exact reasons for hiding his identity. All we do know is that she chooses to keep Moses' Hebrew origins a secret, thus changing history.

Getting water for their flock: Daughters of Jethro

After Moses grows up with his adopted mother — the daughter of Pharaoh (see the preceding section) — he kills an Egyptian and has to flee into the desert. While a fugitive, he meets the seven enchanting daughters of Jethro, who is also known as Reuel, a priest of Midian. Jethro's unmarried daughters are nomads who are tending sheep when Moses encounters them at a well. As Moses enters the scene, several shepherds are harassing the ladies. See Exodus 2:16–20 for the story.

Moses chases the men away. The ladies then invite Moses to meet their father, who is so grateful that he offers one of his daughters to be Moses' wife. Moses chooses Zipporah (see Chapter 10) as his bride, with whom he spends 40 years until he encounters a burning bush and leaves to free the Hebrew slaves in Egypt.

A fresco by Botticelli (1485) in the Vatican's Sistine Chapel depicts the daughters of Jethro as young and beautiful, yet strong and in command as shepherds to their flock. These ladies enter the Bible briefly only to have Moses arrive in the nick of time as their hero. Only one of them is named: Zipporah, the one who later becomes Mrs. Moses. If nothing else, these daughters of Jethro also become sisters-in-law to Moses, and in those days being related even by marriage meant you were family, with established bonds stronger than often recognized today. As easily as they slip into the Bible, these women slip out, not to be heard from again.

Showing bad behavior: Daughters of Zion

The phrase "daughter (or daughters) of Zion" appears 32 times in the Bible. But the word daughters doesn't exactly refer to someone's physical offspring.

In the Old Testament, the phrase "daughters of Zion" has been used to mean all of the following:

> ✔ **Israelites:** Hebrew often uses the word *bat* (meaning "daughter") juxtaposed with the name of city or nation to refer to the people or citizens who live there. "Daughter Zion" and "Daughters of Zion" are phrases used to refer to the Israelites — they are the folks who live in Zion (another name for the city of Jerusalem). Because Jerusalem was the ancient capital of the Kingdom of Israel, all Israelites could be considered "daughters of Zion," not just the people who live in Jerusalem.

✔ **Gentiles who show respect and give comfort in Zion:** Anyone who didn't live in Israel or who wasn't of the Jewish faith was called a Gentile by the Jews. The Gentiles sympathetic to the Hebrew religion or who demonstrated fairness, justice, and even compassion to Jews and to the Jewish nation were often called "Daughters of Zion" because of their kindness to Zion, the nation and the people of Israel.

✔ **Small towns on the outskirts of bigger cities:** These towns often were the first to meet with disaster when enemies invaded or attacked. Larger cities, such as Jerusalem (also called Zion), had neighboring towns and villages, which were called the "daughters of Zion" because of their proximity and connection to the holy city.

The prophet Isaiah also uses this phrase to describe the women of Jerusalem. Unfortunately, these women aren't being complimented; rather, they're being reprimanded and chastised for their misbehavior (Isaiah 3:16).

These women of high society not only spend too much time and money on adorning themselves with expensive jewelry, clothing, and perfume, but they're also very snooty and snobbish, acting superior to others. Worse yet, they flirt with men, especially husbands of other women. They give more importance to appearance than to substance. Social status means more to them than their spiritual relationship with God.

Isaiah warns the daughters of Zion that their riches will be stripped away by incoming invaders like the Assyrians and Babylonians. Their possessions will be taken from them, and with no faith, they'll have little to cling to in their desperation:

The LORD said: Because the daughters of Zion are haughty and walk with outstretched necks, glancing wantonly with their eyes, mincing along as they go, tinkling with their feet; the LORD will afflict with scabs the heads of the daughters of Zion, and the LORD will lay bare their secret parts.

—Isaiah 3:16–17

The case of the sizzling shrub

This strange phenomenon of a sizzling shrub is a not so subtle way that God gets Moses' attention and then communicates to him the divine plan to deliver the Chosen People from their captivity.

The fact that the bush burns but is not consumed by the flames is mystery in itself, but when Moses hears the voice of God, it dispels any doubt about the importance of this message (Exodus 3:2).

Daughters of Zion in the New Testament

The New Testament uses the term "daughter (or daughters) of Zion (or Jerusalem)" as a positive one.

You can find this phrase in Matthew 21:5: "Tell the daughter of Zion, Look, your king is coming to you, humble, and mounted on a donkey, and on a colt, the foal of a donkey." The last time this phrase appears is in the Gospel of John, when Jesus is about to enter Jerusalem on Palm Sunday and sits upon a donkey: "Do not be afraid, daughter of Zion. Look, your king is coming, sitting on a donkey's colt" (John 12:15).

Find out more about the New Testament's daughters of Jerusalem in the section "Looking at the Daughters of the New Testament" in this chapter.

Many prophets denounced the greed and avarice of their time, especially when so many other people were poor, homeless, and destitute. Social justice wasn't seen as an option but rather a sacred duty, which these unfortunate women of the world found out the hard way. Israel was invaded and conquered time and time again, and the former glory and opulence became only a fading memory of the past.

The daughters of Zion are cited only parenthetically in the prophets other than Isaiah. For example, in Jeremiah 6:2, God says he will destroy the "daughter of Zion," and Zechariah 9:9 says, "Rejoice greatly O daughter Zion."

Isaiah, Jeremiah, Micah, Zephaniah, and Zechariah mention at least once if not more "daughter" or "daughters" of Zion. When used in conjunction with "daughter of Jerusalem," then "daughter of Zion" symbolizes the nation, whereas the former represents the inhabitants of the city of Jerusalem. The language can get confusing because often the Bible uses Zion and Jerusalem interchangeably.

Zion can be another name for Jerusalem because the original Jerusalem or City of David was built on Mount Zion.

Looking at the Daughters of the New Testament

The nameless daughters of the New Testament aren't much different from those of the Old Testament in terms of social and cultural treatment of them.

These women are often associated exclusively with their fathers, as in the case of the daughter of Jairus. The New Testament also uses a euphemistic saying like the Old Testament's "daughters of Zion," discussed earlier in this chapter. In the New Testament, the more common phrase is the "daughters of Jerusalem."

Rising from the dead: Daughter of Jairus

You meet the daughter of Jairus in the New Testament during Jesus' time, in the Gospel of Mark. This 12-year-old girl is gravely ill and suffering, which deeply troubles her father. Jairus, a leading member of the synagogue, desperately seeks the miraculous healing power of Jesus:

> *My little daughter is at the point of death. Come and lay your hands on her, so that she may be made well, and live.*

> —Mark 5:23

While Jesus is en route, the daughter succumbs to her illness. Jairus is told that his little girl is dead, and the people ask him, "Why trouble the teacher any further?" (Mark 5:35). Jesus overhears this statement and tells the father to not be afraid, but to believe. Christ then takes Peter, James, and John to the house of Jairus, where they're met by relatives who are weeping and wailing. Jesus questions the commotion and boldly proclaims that the girl isn't dead but asleep. The bystanders laugh and mock him.

Jesus enters the home and tells the daughter of Jairus in Aramaic (his native dialect), "Little girl, get up" (Mark 5:41). The girl immediately sits up and is reunited with her jubilant father. Everyone is amazed, and a joyful family reunion replaces the tragic scene of a dead daughter.

The curing of the daughter of Jairus is a moving scene and is depicted in several works of art, including pieces by Rembrant, 1660; Vasiliy Polenov, 1871; Ilya Repin, 1871; and Gustave Dore, 1865, all titled *The Raising of Jairus' Daughter*. Though she is never mentioned again, this brief but powerful story shows the tenderness of Jesus, helping a desperate father who so loves his gravely ill daughter.

Remaining faithful: Daughters of Jerusalem

Like the daughters of Zion described earlier in this chapter, "daughters of Jerusalem" is a euphemism for a group of women. But that's where the similarity ends. Although the daughters of Zion are greedy, egotistical, and selfish women, the daughters of Jerusalem are devout, faithful, and loving women who follow Jesus to his passion and death on the cross at Calvary on Good Friday. Some of these women could've been the same ladies who regularly followed the condemned to their place of execution.

Jewish custom at that time included formal or designated mourners, especially when a family wasn't large enough to have enough mourners. Most, if not all, of these daughters of Jerusalem, however, are believed to be friends of Jesus and/or his mother, Mary. Their sorrow and agony as he walks the *via dolorosa* (road of sorrow) to his crucifixion prompt him to say, "Daughters of Jerusalem, do not weep for me, but weep for yourselves and for your children" (Luke 23:28).

Jesus is prophesying the imminent destruction of the Temple of Jerusalem, which happens 37 years later (in AD 70) when the Temple of Jerusalem is destroyed by the Romans in retaliation for acts of subversion against the empire. The Wailing Wall of Jerusalem is the only remaining structure of the Temple today, and faithful Jews still literally wail and weep before it for the destruction of their Temple nearly two millennia ago.

These women aren't referred to again in the scriptures. Their name, however, continues as a reference to compassionate women in general.

Chapter 21

Widows and Other Women without Names

. . . .

In This Chapter

▶ Understanding the needs of widows

▶ Recognizing the lessons of other nameless women

. . . .

The Bible is filled with women without names, including many widows who are mentioned because of their marital status or because of their deeds, actions, and faith. The nameless women in sacred scripture who are merely identified as widows aren't as numerous as the mothers, wives, and daughters of the Bible, but they do have an important part to play in the life of faith as portrayed in the Bible. Their examples offer encouragement even today.

Most of the widows, through their actions, didn't consider themselves to be victims of society — though their culture certainly didn't make things easier for them. Instead, most of these widows overcame their bleak situations by trusting that the Lord would keep his word, rewarding the good and punishing the bad. Certainly, none of these women were perfect or sinless (just as no biblical men were). But their unwillingness to give up and their commitment to try to do better are what distinguish these women, ultimately explaining why they're mentioned in the Bible.

But the Bible includes other nameless women — women who are described by their actions, personal characteristics, or even by where they lived. Like the widows, these nameless women are mentioned in the Bible because of what they did, said or represented that believers remember and pass on through the ages.

In this chapter, we examine both — the widows and the nameless women who had a significant impact, despite not being referred to by name.

Understanding the Culture of Widows

Because ancient societies were predominantly patriarchal, most women and children depended exclusively on husbands and fathers to provide food, clothing, shelter, and safety. When a man died and left behind a wife — either with children or without — she was usually unable to support herself financially. Unlike today, when women are an integral part of the workforce, in ancient times, women and children couldn't normally get employment. Without a husband and/or father, widows and orphans often had to beg for their survival.

Taking care of the physical needs of widows wasn't something the secular government saw as its duty or responsibility. Practically no kingdom or republic back then had any type of social services. Individuals and/or the local synagogue or church were the usual places you'd find charity toward one's neighbor. Rather than being an optional gesture of kindness, however, providing for those in need was seen as an imperative of love and faith. The Bible teaches that caring for the temporal needs of widows and orphans is a necessary practice of justice.

For instance, individuals were encouraged to give alms to widows who begged for them, usually outside the temple or synagogue area. Christianity extended this to a broader application when the entire faith community (congregation or parish) raised funds or collected food and clothing for widows and orphans. They also distributed or disbursed the collections to make it easier for those in need.

In one specific instance, the Book of Deuteronomy obligated a man to marry his widowed and childless sister-in-law, the wife of his recently departed brother (Deuteronomy 25:5–10). Under normal circumstance, brothers-in-law and sisters-in-law couldn't marry. But in a levirate marriage (from the Latin word, *levir,* meaning husband's brother), an exception was made because a childless widow had no one to support her, whereas other widows could depend on their adult sons to care for them. In this case, a widow could marry her brother-in-law.

Widows in both the Old and New Testaments were basically in a class by themselves. They were considered special not only because they had particular needs but also because their pain and loss came from an especially sad situation: the death of their husbands. Thus, showing them kindness wasn't considered pity but instead an act of mercy and charity that came from a real love of neighbor. Orphans and widows were given such preeminence in biblical times because, without a father, husband, or son, these two groups were considered very vulnerable.

Throughout the Bible, you'll find that widows receive special attention, respect, and even reverence. The Old Testament teaches, "You shall not abuse any widow or orphan" (Exodus 22:22). Psalms 68:5 says that God is a "protector of widows." The prophet Isaiah (1:17) exhorts people to "plead for the widow." Because women who have lost their husbands deserve care and concern, many people have long believed that blessings will come to those who honor and care for the widow.

Paul's first epistle to Timothy explicitly mentions widows. Paul says that a widow who has no relatives is truly a "needy" widow because she has no physical family to help her. By baptism, believers become part of the family of God and thus are considered brothers and sisters in Christ. That means a spiritual family relationship exists even if the physical, blood, or marriage relationships have disappeared. Paul asks Timothy to remind the faithful of their obligation as members of a spiritual family (the Church) to care for widows as they would if she had been a blood relative or one by marriage. Paul also warns that Christians who neglect their relatives have given up the faith (1 Timothy 5).

Meeting the Widows

In this section, we meet the widows, like the widow of Zarephath, the widow and Elisha, the widow in the temple, the widow and her dead son, and more. Some of them exhibit perseverance and patience, others show generosity and compassion, and all of them have to cope with disadvantages and setbacks, be it the death of a husband, the absence of children, or just simple poverty. We look at these women and see how they handle their respective situations in life and how others respond to their plight.

Widow of Zarephath

When a woman decides to take her husband's surname as her own, she is often identified as Mrs. so-and-so or as Mr. so-and-so's wife. But some women in the Bible don't even have this much to distinguish them. The widow of Zarephath is a case in point. We know neither her name nor the name of her husband, which in those days was critical because it determined the woman's position in society. What we do know is that the widow of Zarephath lived in the ninth century BC in the northern kingdom of Israel. We find her mentioned in 1 Kings 17:9–24.

The widow of Zarephath also is known more for her deeds than by what she is called. Zarephath was a small Phoenician town in an area that was a bastion of pagan religion known as Baal worship. Baal was the primary male deity in Phoenicia, and the priests of Baal were the archnemeses of the prophet Elijah. These guys forced their pagan religion on most of their neighbors and were considered intolerant bigots who used their religion, especially human sacrifices, for their own political agenda.

One of the greatest sins a Jew could commit during that time was to practice idolatry and to worship a false god. But to engage in Baal worship was considered the ultimate blasphemy. No greater insult could be made against God than to opt for Baal rather than the Lord.

Divine irony is such that the prophet Elijah, who will later have a spectacular showdown with the priests of Baal (1 Kings 18:20–40), will first encounter and be aided by a Phoenician woman living in the heart of that kingdom of darkness and evil.

This widow demonstrates that God rewards people's faith, especially when they're open to his teachings. The story also demonstrates that God doesn't discriminate — anyone can reap the rewards of his love whether rich or poor, widow or wife, man or woman, or Jew, Christian, or Phoenician.

Risking her last morsel

When Elijah first meets the widow of Zarephath, he asks for some water, which she willingly fetches. Even though they are worlds apart as individuals, the woman sees the prophet as a fellow human being who deserves hospitality. The ancient world held good hospitality in high esteem because it showed an awareness that even a stranger is a kindred spirit. You never knew when you yourself would be in need of some food or drink, clothes, or shelter, so people extended the courtesy to everyone in the hope that others would reciprocate.

When the widow returns with a drink, Elijah asks for some food as well. She painfully admits that she has no bread, only a little flour and oil. Because a severe drought had plagued the area, she and her son were going to use these as their last meal before starving to death (1 Kings 17:12).

Elijah assures her, however, that if she makes some bread for him, she will have enough for her and her son, and even more so. "The jar of meal will not be emptied and the jug of oil will not fail until the day that the LORD sends rain on the earth" (1 Kings 17:14). Doing as she is instructed, the widow of Zarephath discovers that her jug of oil and jar of flour miraculously sustain the three of them throughout the three-and-a-half-year drought. This is God's first miracle through Elijah in Zarephath.

Putting faith in God and Elijah

The widow comes on hard times when her only son suddenly becomes deathly ill. She fears that God may be punishing her for her initial hesitation when Elijah asked for food. Even though she explained that she had only enough flour and oil to provide a last meal for herself and her son before they died, the fact that she had to be reassured by Elijah that giving him hospitality would be rewarded (which it was) could have been interpreted as a sign of a lack of faith or trust. Many people in those days equated any and all suffering as a punishment for sins and transgressions against God.

She therefore begs mercy from the prophet in case her suspicions are correct. Neither Elijah nor the Bible affirms this theory of a universal cause-and-effect relationship between sin and suffering. However, Elijah does pray over the boy who has collapsed, and the widow's son is then restored to full health. This event is often viewed as Elijah's second miracle in Zarephath.

Despite her imperfections, weaknesses, and frailties, the woman professes, "Now I know that you are a man of God, and that the word of the LORD in your mouth is truth" (1 Kings 17:24). In fact, the widow of Zarephath becomes so well known that Jesus uses her as an example in the Gospel of Luke. When he returns to his hometown of Nazareth to preach, the audience gives him a cool reception. "Isn't this the carpenter's son?" they moan. He rebukes them by reminding them that during the time of Elijah there were many Jewish widows in Israel during the severe famine and drought, but that Elijah was sent to a widow in Baal-worshipping Zarephath instead (Luke 4:25–26).

This woman could have easily dismissed Elijah's request, considering her dire straits due to famine and drought. Instead, she extends hospitality to the holy man. When her son nearly dies, she again comes to a crossroad where she must make a choice: She can either blame God and become bitter or ask for divine assistance and seek a miraculous cure for her son. The Bible exalts her courageous decision to trust in God.

Although she isn't mentioned again, the generosity of the widow of Zarephath — albeit offered hesitantly at first — and her trust in the prophet's promise that God would provide make this nameless widow most memorable and admirable.

The widow and Elisha

Another widow in the Bible shows what happens when you pay attention to the prophet of the Lord. This widow of the ninth century BC encounters the prophet Elisha (a protégé of Elijah), and this time it is the widow who asks for help from the man of God. At wit's end, almost desperate, she pleads not for herself but for her two sons. They have been threatened with indentured servitude to pay off the debt of their now-dead father.

Up until the twentieth century, it wasn't uncommon for people to be jailed or to be sold into indentured servitude for unpaid debts. Declaring bankruptcy wasn't a possibility, as it is today. You paid your debts one way or another, even if it meant selling your own flesh and blood into slavery.

Elisha instructs the widow to gather empty vessels, even from her neighbors, and then shut the door behind her and her children. Then she is to pour the little bit of oil she has left in the house into all the empty containers. As bizarre as the orders seem, she dutifully fulfills them to the letter, and miraculously, the oil is multiplied, giving her enough to pay off her debts (2 Kings 4:2–7).

Like the widow of Zarephath, this widow is forced to make some choices. She chooses to ask for help from the prophet and to listen to his advice, even if it sounds strange at first.

Although her compliance with Elisha's order wasn't a monumental act of faith — she had little to risk — for a widow on the very brink of losing her sons into slavery, it is no light matter. The response isn't exactly a spectacular special effect found in an Arnold Schwarzenegger movie, but the outcome is still important. A small miracle saves her boys' freedom and preserves her family.

Not all miracles are stupendous occurrences, but even a small act of faith can be rewarded. The widow who approaches the prophet Elisha isn't asked to perform some huge demonstration of faith, but she does fulfill what is asked of her. Often faithfulness in small matters indicates the person is probably reliable in greater ones (see Luke 16:10). If you've ever been in debt, especially if you've reached your credit limit and you're a few days, weeks, or even months behind in your bills, you know what kind of stress this poor woman experienced. Instead of despairing, however, she survives, and from the viewpoint of the Bible, her faith is what preserved her. She isn't mentioned again after this.

The widow in the Temple

Both Mark and Luke, in their respective gospels, tell of the scene in which Jesus notices a poor widow in the Temple of Jerusalem (AD early first century). The story begins when Jesus observes the widow making an offering of two copper coins in the Temple. Jesus knew that the widow had little money and few possessions.

Then he called his disciples and said to them, "Truly I tell you, this poor widow has put in more than all those who are contributing to the treasury. For all of them have contributed out of their abundance; but she out of her poverty has put in everything she had, all she had to live on."

—Mark 12:43–44

Her two cents

In the story of the widow in the Temple, the Gospels of Mark (12:41–44) and Luke (21:1–4), which were written in Greek, use the word *lepton*, which is sometimes translated as *mite*, the equivalent of the penny of the day. It was the smallest coin in use, made of copper and worth about ⅕ cent ($0.002). One hundred twenty-eight mites or leptons equaled one Roman *denarius* (a silver coin) or one Greek *drachma*. Six thousand of these silver coins equaled one *talent*. The very rich would have used silver or gold talents for commerce, whereas the poorest of the poor had only copper mites.

The lesson of "the widow's mites" (the two copper coins that the poor widow offered at the Temple) is that giving alms isn't an option of convenience but instead a call to authentically living one's faith.

Jesus understands that this woman, as a widow in ancient times, needs every penny she has. Her extreme generosity shows the depth of her faith. She believes that God will somehow provide, and she gives from her want (*husteresis* in Greek) as opposed to the hypocrites whom Jesus says give only from their surplus (*perisseuo* in Greek).

Very often, Christ denounced the hypocrites who performed religious acts, like making donations, just to impress others. These people made token gifts that were a mere fraction of their discretionary income. On the other hand, the Bible makes the point that the widow in the temple actually gave much more — not in the actual amount, but in the degree of her sacrifice. While others gave only symbolically or for the wrong reasons (to win the esteem of others), her donation was a real demonstration of generosity and sacrifice to God.

This nameless widow shows that neither the amount nor the size of the gift is what counts; what matters is the love with which it is given. She showed her love for the poor by giving all she had. The accumulation of all the small donations from people of modest means may not equal the large contributions of the very wealthy, but as this woman demonstrates, quality is more important than quantity. This is the last we hear of her in the Bible.

The widow of Nain and her dead son

Another nameless widow is one who recently lost her son. The story of this woman, who lived during the time of the public ministry of Christ (AD 30–33), is told only in the Gospel of Luke. (See the sidebar "The gospel of women" in this chapter.) The encounter between this widow of Nain (a town six miles southeast of Nazareth) and Jesus takes place immediately after Jesus cures the servant of a Roman centurion. (In Luke 7:1–10, Jesus is asked to cure the servant of a centurion who is friendly to the Jews. But because the Roman officer feels unworthy to have Christ under his own roof, he merely asks that Jesus just verbally give the order "be healed" instead of bothering to come all the way to his home. The centurion shows great faith in the words alone of Christ and doesn't need to see the miraculous healing to believe it will happen. He takes Jesus at his word, and Christ compliments the great faith shown by the Roman.)

In this story, Jesus affirms the impenetrable bond between mother and son and acts to relieve a mother's grief. Her situation touches Christ in such a way that he is full of compassion in its true sense. The word *compassion* comes from two Latin words, *cum* (with) + *pati* (to suffer). Thus *compatior* means "to suffer with (someone)," or to empathize with their pain.

In Nain, Jesus meets a widow who is in the process of burying her only son. The scene moves him so much that the Bible says, "He had compassion for her" (Luke 7:13). Jesus approaches the casket and commands the young man to get up. At that very moment, the dead son sits up and starts talking. Jesus then "gave him to his mother." (See the account of this incident in Luke 7:11–15.)

The author accentuates the bond between parent and child by explicitly saying that Jesus "gave him to his mother." This is the first but not the only time Jesus raised the dead to life, and the reunion of a widowed mother and her recently deceased only son is touching. The crowd that watches this incident is filled with awe and gives glory to God.

The story demonstrates how Jesus broke the artificial barriers that discouraged Hebrew men from interacting with women in public — at least by Luke's account. We don't hear about the widow of Nain any more in the Bible, but her interaction with Jesus that resulted in the raising of her son from the dead remains a poignant moment nonetheless.

The widow and the judge

We find out about the persistent widow and the dishonest judge through a story that Jesus himself tells as an example of what patience and perseverance can do. (See Luke 18:1–5 for more details.) Her story, found only in the Gospel of Luke, is relevant because of the lesson Christ conveys through her.

The story goes something like this: A corrupt official makes rulings based only on the amount of bribes he receives. A widow of little means comes along and refuses to succumb to the dishonest judge's extortion. Rather than bribery, she resorts to perseverance through faith.

The gospel of women

The Book of Luke is often referred to as "the gospel of women" because it includes stories that demonstrate Jesus' compassion toward women. During his time, the local men and women did not interact socially except on rare occasions. Luke's Gospel, however, shows Jesus not only conversing with women as freely as he does with the men but also engaging in some heavy spiritual talk with the women. Jesus shows compassion by listening to the women who come to him, and he performs many miraculous cures and healing for Hebrew, Samaritan, and Gentile women alike. Many of these stories don't appear in the other three Gospels (Matthew, Mark, and John). Luke, a Gentile by descent and a physician by training, is much more sympathetic and empathetic to women in general than his Jewish or Roman contemporaries.

Jesus tells this story, and Luke includes it in his writings to demonstrate how Jesus encourages his followers to persevere in prayer. The parable shows the value of not giving up. The corrupt official never does receive a bribe payment from her, and the widow gets justice by wearing him down with her persistence:

> But later he said to himself, "Though I have no fear of God and no respect for anyone, yet because this widow keeps bothering me, I will grant her justice, so that she may not wear me out by continually coming."

—Luke 18:4–5

This widow, who could have given up and surrendered to discouragement, teaches us that patience is a virtue and perseverance produces results.

Greek-speaking widows

Stemming from the Babylonian captivity (586 BC) and the Diaspora (see Chapter 10 for details), tensions ran high between the Jewish minority (the Hebrew-speaking Jews in what was then called Palestine) and the Jewish majority (the Greek-speaking Jews scattered around the ancient world). Both sides claimed to be the authentic vestige of the Israelite religion, from Abraham and Moses to David and Solomon. When Christianity first entered the world in the middle of the AD first century, most of the early Christians were, in fact, Jewish converts. In the early years of the Christian church, however, there were more Hebrew-speaking Jewish converts to Christianity than Greek-speaking Jewish converts.

Those who spoke Greek didn't get along well with those who spoke Hebrew and vice versa. In one instance documented in the Acts of the Apostles, the Greek-speaking Christian widows complain that they are being overlooked by the Hebrew-speaking Christians. They felt snubbed in deference to the Hebrew-speaking widows.

Acts 6 explains how the apostles decided to resolve the matter. They selected and ordained seven deacons whose mission it was to care for the temporal needs of the widows, orphans, and the poor. The work of the deacons freed the apostles, their successors, and bishops to devote themselves to prayer and to ministry of the Word, while the widows would still be cared for. After the deacons start ministering equally to the Greek-speaking Christians and the Hebrew-speaking Christians, the problem disappears. Eventually, the quarrel between these two groups of widows ends. We don't hear about these women again.

The Hebrew word for widow, *almanah,* is *chera* in Greek and *vidua* in Latin. Usually the word referred to a woman whose husband had died, but occasionally it implied a woman abandoned by her husband.

Nameless but Significant Women

Some women of the Bible can't be described with modifiers, such as wives, mothers, daughters, or widows because their marital or family status may not have been known. Yet their stories are still relevant, and you can still learn from their examples — good or bad. These nameless but significant women are included in the following sections.

Women at the temple

Exodus 38:8 mentions some women (possibly between the eighteenth and thirteenth centuries BC) who served at the entrance of the tent of a meeting. Unlike their contemporaries (ancient Egyptians, Babylonians, Assyrians, Greeks, and more), the Hebrews didn't have priestesses for public worship, nor did they have the equivalent of the Roman vestal virgins. They did have pious women who frequented the Temple, however. Instead of ministering, these holy women prayed and taught by setting a good example and provided a beneficial service in terms of their religious devotion. Their prayers and hymns encouraged fellow Hebrews to imitate them in public piety, the external practice of one's religion (as opposed to spirituality, which is the internal practice of one's religion.)

These women can be compared to modern-day cloistered nuns. Although their ministry isn't one of authority, they do minister prayer and show witness to God. Although they're not mentioned again in the Bible, the women of the Temple who spent their time praying, fasting, and maintaining the house of worship inspire people today. Though no one today actually lives in their local synagogue, mosque, or church, many women of all faiths spend time praying and working (for the upkeep of the holy place in praise of God).

The wise woman of Abel Bethmaacah

In the book of Samuel, Joab, the military commander for King David, has just treacherously murdered his former rival Amasa and is about to lay siege on the city of Abel Bethmaacah in the tenth century BC. Before he does so, a wise woman seeks him out and asks him to spare the town; she reminds him that Abel is known for being a peaceful place. To spare the innocent citizens from slaughter, she agrees to hand over the head of Sheba (the new rival) at Joab's request. Sheba was of the tribe of Benjamin (same tribe as King Saul), whereas David was of the tribe of Judah. Soon after the death of King Saul (the first king of Israel), Sheba participated in a civil war among the 12 tribes of Israel in a failed effort to prevent David from taking the throne.

The wise woman tells Joab that the decapitated head of his current enemy (Sheba) will be thrown over the wall if he agrees to spare the town from being sacked. She then tells her compatriots to get the head of Sheba to have it tossed outside (2 Samuel 20:21–22). She is called "wise" (*chakam* in Hebrew), and it appears that through her intervention, she spares the city from ruin. All too often, the innocent suffered more than the guilty in time of war, and Joab had no hesitation in obliterating an entire town of men, women, and children, just to secure the death of his previous archenemy Amasa. The wise woman of Abel Bethmaacah, however, is the one person in that town who was willing to approach and speak to Joab. She enlisted the help of her fellow citizens whose own lives were on the line as well to get the head of the one responsible for this dire predicament.

We don't hear about her again, but the people of Abel Bethmaacah sure didn't forget her too easily. This woman demonstrates courage in a time of crisis and the ability to seek out and remove evil.

The woman with a hemorrhage

The story of the woman with a hemorrhage, found in the Gospels (Matthew 9:20–22, Mark 5:25–34, and Luke 8:43–48), describes an encounter between a very sick woman and Jesus. This woman of the AD first century demonstrates that through faith all things are possible.

The woman had been plagued with a menstrual blood hemorrhage for 12 years, wiping out all her financial resources while she was seeking a cure. No doctor or physician could heal her, and she was desperate for help. At that time, Mosaic law declared that women were ritually unclean during their menstrual periods, and men had to avoid them until the flow of blood stopped. To defy this law was to risk being barred from entering the Temple.

Because this woman understands her status as ritually impure, she anonymously approaches Jesus and merely touches the hem of his garment, instead of being touched by him. The very instant she touches the edge of his clothing, she is miraculously cured of her ailment. Jesus then asks, "Who touched me?"

Peter remarks to Christ that, with such a large crowd encircling them, they can't possibly know. But Jesus persists in asking, and the woman finally confesses her identity.

This nameless woman shows great personal faith by believing that the mere touch of Christ's garment would cure her. Jesus responds by asking her to acknowledge publicly what she had done discreetly. By encouraging her to come forward and own up to her act of faith, Jesus encourages others never to hide their faith. In the Bible, giving witness is what is asked of all true believers. She doesn't appear again in scripture.

Ten bridesmaids: Wise and foolish virgins

Using a parable, Jesus tells the tale of five wise virgins and five foolish virgins (Matthew 25:1–13). An old wedding custom involved a groom going to his bride's home to make a marital agreement with her father. Then the groom brought the bride home, and the wedding feast commenced.

Custom dictated that the bridesmaids (also called virgins) were to greet the happy couple as they approached. In response to this custom, the five wise virgins come prepared, in case of the groom's delay, with enough lamp oil to accommodate a wait. But the tale of these foolish virgins tells of their presumption that all will be well, so they make no such provisions for sticking around to wait.

Caught off guard, the foolish virgins run out of oil and leave to buy more. When the groom finally arrives, the sensible women who had brought enough oil are prepared to meet him and accompany him home. Meanwhile, the foolish ones who scurried off to buy more lamp oil return too late. After the door is shut, the five late bridesmaids are refused admittance.

"Always be prepared" isn't just a motto for scouting. It's a biblical imperative for believers to do regular and frequent housecleaning of their souls. The wise virgins used the gifts and talents they were given, while the foolish ones squandered and wasted the blessings and the time given them. Jesus used the story to make an analogy to a person's spiritual life and each human being's gift of a limited amount of time, talent, and treasure. To use these gifts wisely in this life affects an individual's situation in the next life.

The parable also teaches that vigilance and watchfulness are qualities to strive for. Being prepared for what you must or may do and staying alert to what is happening are two ideals for any believer. The parable of the wise and foolish virgins shows what happens when you don't pay attention and keep watch. At the same time, attentive observation is not enough. You should also be prepared and equipped for the work God has given you to do.

"Certain women" of the New Testament

The phrase "certain women" (*tines gynaikes* in Greek) is used several times in the New Testament to describe otherwise nameless women (AD first century) who appear conspicuously with the 12 apostles. They're mentioned in Luke 8:2 in the company of Christ and the apostles, and in Luke 24:22 after the Resurrection at the empty tomb. Finally, they're mentioned in the Acts of the Apostles:

> *When they entered the city, they went to the room upstairs where they were staying, Peter, and John, and James, and Andrew, Philip and Thomas, Bartholomew and Matthew, James son of Alphaeus, and Simon the Zealot, and Judas son of James. All these were constantly devoting themselves to prayer, together with certain women, including Mary the mother of Jesus, as well as his brothers.*
>
> —Acts 1:13–14

Some of these anonymous certain women have been cured of evil spirits and ailments (Luke 8:2) The Bible also mentions that they supported the apostles in their work by providing them with personal resources, such as money, food, clothing, and shelter (Luke 8:3).

These women freely chose to be present as witnesses to God, as opposed to those who were there by accident or happenstance. That they are mentioned along with the faithful apostles speaks of their significance. Although we hear of them no more in the Bible, their invaluable support helps the infant church survive and later thrive as more people come to know the Christian message — thanks to the work of these "certain women."

Part VI
The Part of Tens

The 5th Wave

By Rich Tennant

"Reading about the sinful women in the Bible really makes you think. It makes you think about repentance, forgiveness and what a great series on HBO their lives would make."

In this part . . .

Want to know what woman in scripture has been portrayed by artists more than any other? Wondering about the women shown in some of the most famous masterpieces hanging in museums and galleries around the world? This part is for you. Here is where we also discuss the ten most misunderstood women of the Bible and the ten most influential women in the Bible.

Chapter 22

Ten Most Misunderstood Women of the Bible

. . . .

In This Chapter

▶ Looking at some less-than-holy behaviors

▶ Understanding the motives behind trickery and deceit

▶ Examining the actions of some brave women

. . . .

Many women of the Bible remain — to this day — misunderstood, mysterious, and enigmatic. Though readers may try to understand them and scholars may continue to debate them, these women are not easily pigeonholed, nor are they easily stereotyped.

In this chapter, we discuss Mary Magdalene, probably the most misunderstood of the ladies in the Bible, along with Salome, Rebekah, Tamar, and more. The ten women here represent the most misinterpreted and misrepresented of the bunch. Most have an unknown or hidden past, and what isn't said about them in scripture is sometimes said elsewhere, such as in apocryphal (nonbiblical books of questionable authenticity) or fictional writings; such sources only contribute to the mystery.

Mary Magdalene — Married?

Mary Magdalene (the focus of Chapter 7) is the subject of much conjecture, speculation, innuendo, and countless rumors. Yet sacred scripture doesn't actually say that much about her; she is mentioned only 12 times in the New Testament, and more attention historically has been given to what is *not* said about this woman. Many of these issues have captured the active imaginations of controversial authors, scholars, and historians.

Even her name is misunderstood. Magdalene was not her last name in the same way Smith is one of today's common surnames. Magdalene, instead, referred to her native town, Magdala — just like today someone from New York City is termed a New Yorker, or from London, a Londoner. Jesus himself is often called the Nazarene because Nazareth was his hometown. To distinguish this Mary from the several other Marys in the Bible, she is called Mary Magdalene, after her hometown.

Debating her profession

Mary Magdalene's role during the time of Jesus is often discussed and debated. Although she has been referred to as a prostitute throughout the ages, the Bible never explicitly mentions her name in relation to this profession. Some people speculate that she is the unnamed woman caught in adultery in the story in John 8:1–11 or that she is the repentant prostitute in Luke 7:36–50. However, in neither instance is Mary Magdalene mentioned by name.

Nevertheless, two very different scholarly opinions exist about Mary Magdalene's role in Jesus' time. The first school of thought insists that Mary Magdalene has been viciously maligned since medieval times by being wrongly identified as a harlot. These scholars believe that an ulterior motive existed to label Magdalene a former prostitute, namely, to discredit any possible status or influence she or other women may have had in the ancient Church.

The other position maintains that she was indeed a prostitute and that she is important because she abandoned this life to become a disciple of Jesus, making a dramatic conversion. After all, if she had been forgiven for a horrible sin like adultery and/or a life of prostitution and if she had been close to being stoned to death for her sins — and then was saved spiritually and physically by Jesus — would she not be the most grateful person on earth? If Mary had such a notorious past and lurid skeletons in her closet, perhaps her being forgiven would show that no sin and no sinner are beyond the mercy and forgiveness of God. A repentant sinner can be as good as, if not better than, a disciple who never fell so hard or so deep.

The debate continues, and yet the Bible neither affirms nor denies that Mary Magdalene was a recovered call girl.

Looking at her relationship with Jesus

A number of books have recently alleged that Mary Magdalene and Jesus of Nazareth were romantically involved and that they were either married or had an illicit sexual relationship. Despite the absence of any biblical and historical evidence to support this belief, there is still some interest and curiosity in these extremely controversial claims. A few people even speculate that the alleged offspring of Jesus and Magdalene became the ancestors of European monarchies and aristocracies. Still, no credible scholarly evidence from archeology, history, or biblical theology has ever even alluded to or suggested any kind of romance between the two, let alone that they had any children, either.

Sultry Salome?

Who is Salome? Her name never actually appears in the Bible, but that fact doesn't stop people from guessing about her and her actions. Many Christians say that she is the woman who helped plot the beheading of John the Baptist. Some people also speculate as to whether Salome's dancing in front of her stepfather was sexually provocative or innocently sweet. (See Chapter 17 for her complete story.)

Matthew 14:6 and Mark 6:22 identify the woman who plotted John's death only as the daughter of Herodias, the illicit wife of Herod Antipas — and never by the name Salome. The name Salome is first mentioned by renowned Jewish historian Flavius Josephus in the first century AD to identify this woman, even though scripture never calls her that. Flavius Josephus is the most-quoted non-Christian historian of the early Christian era (AD 37–100).

The 1893 Oscar Wilde play and the 1905 opera (opus 54) by Richard Strauss, both by the same name: *Salome,* portray Salome doing the dance of the seven veils. This dance has virtually become synonymous with Salome of the Bible, who danced before her stepfather, Herod, to gain influence with him. Though scripture merely says she "danced" (Matthew 14:6; Mark 6:22), common assumption remains that it was a dance of seduction.

The Bible *does* make it clear that after the dance, Salome was promised anything by Herod, even half his kingdom. She in turn asks her mother, Herodias, what she should request. At this point, modern entertainers take license with the story. The 1953 movie *Salome,* starring Rita Hayworth and Stewart Granger, portrays Salome's intent as an effort to win the release of John the Baptist, not demand his head on a platter, as some say the Bible suggests.

No one knows whether Salome was merely being fiercely loyal to her mother, Herodias, who hated and detested John the Baptist because he publicly criticized her adulterous and illicit marriage to Herod. (She was previously married to Herod's brother Philip, who was still very much alive.) Or perhaps Salome made this gruesome request to show her contempt for her stepfather,

Herod, who had shown lustful eyes for her and who she knew would be reluctant to kill John the Baptist, because scripture says he had previously shown interest in John's teachings. Although we don't know Salome's motivation, we do know that she danced — and that she shares at least some of the responsibility for John the Baptist's death, because she requested his head on a platter.

Ruthless Rebekah?

Rebekah, who was the wife of Isaac (the son of Abraham and Sarah), is often misunderstood and maligned for her scheme to help her younger son, Jacob, steal the birthright from his older brother, Esau. (See more on this story in Chapter 9.) Were Rebekah's actions simply a case of playing unfair favorites? Or did she believe that Jacob simply would make a better candidate to carry out God's covenant with the Hebrews? Her motives are still cause for speculation today.

After 20 years of being barren, twin sons Esau and Jacob were born to Rebekah. Esau, born first, was to inherit the lion's share when daddy Isaac passed away. But Jacob was the apple of Rebekah's eye. She conspired with Jacob, encouraging him to impersonate his elder brother just before the blind Isaac is about to cash in his chips, in order to get Isaac's blessing for the birthright. The scheme works.

Some interpret Rebekah's motives as merely playing favorites. You know how everyone teases mothers about showing favoritism to a child. Perhaps, Rebekah was just favoring the younger son over the elder one, just as their father Isaac seemed to favor Esau over Jacob.

Scholars point out, however, that when her twin boys were born, Esau did come first — but his brother, Jacob, was grasping his heel as he followed from the womb. Perhaps this serves as a biblical symbol of things to come, that the younger would be grabbing what belongs to the elder.

Other scholars think Rebekah may have had good reason to skip over Esau's birthright. Esau had disappointed both Isaac and Rebekah when he married two foreign wives, who made life bitter for his parents (Genesis 26:34–35). In addition, Esau willingly gave up his birthright when Jacob asked for it from him in return for a bowl of porridge (Genesis 25:29–34). So some people insist that Rebekah simply felt that Jacob was the twin more qualified to carry out God's covenant because Esau treated the inheritance so cavalierly.

Despite the reasons for Rebekah's decisions, others believe good came of her actions. They say her actions contributed to saving the Hebrew people, because Jacob was the son who later was named Israel by the Lord, and whose 12 sons became the origins of the 12 tribes of Israel. The lineage of Abraham would therefore continue though Isaac and then Jacob and eventually to King David and his descendants. Jacob is considered a patriarch along with Abraham, his grandfather, and his dad, Isaac.

Tricky Tamar

Tamar has a run of bad luck when it comes to husbands and children. Her first husband, Er, dies before she can have a child. According to custom, she is allowed to marry her husband's brother, Onan, to fulfill the family birthright and continue the lineage. However, he, too, meets an unexpected death before she can conceive. Only one brother-in-law, Shelah, is left as a potential third husband. But Shelah isn't old enough, and after he is of age, his dad, Judah, refuses to let him marry Tamar (whom you can read more about in Chapter 9).

Her next course of action shocks some people. Tamar disguises herself as a prostitute and entices Judah, her father-in-law, to sleep with her. Three months later, she is with child, and people tell Judah that she is pregnant as a result of prostitution. Not knowing that she was the woman he had "visited" three months before, Judah orders her brought before him so he can turn her over to be burned at the stake. When she arrives, she shows him his personal artifacts that he left her after spending the night with her earlier. He quickly realizes that the woman he spent the night with was in fact his own daughter-in-law — and the unborn child is his own son.

Incest and deceit are charges that could be leveled against Tamar, but the Bible never accuses her of these things. She is mistreated by Judah when he goes back on his word to give her the third son, Shelah, as a husband. Judah knows that Tamar, a childless widow, is totally vulnerable economically, socially, and even physically. She has no means to support herself, let alone protect herself. (See Chapter 21 for more info on biblical widows.) Judah knowingly seals her fate when he refuses to keep his promise to allow Shelah to marry her.

Was Tamar's behavior entrapment or desperation? The Bible merely tells us what Tamar *did* and what Judah *did* — not what they intended or thought. These unknown factors are what lead to the controversy about whether Tamar was ingenious or unscrupulous. However, her union with Judah did produce twin sons — Perez and Zerah — and from Perez the lineage of King David and the Messiah come forth.

Some scholars evaluate Tamar's action (impersonating a prostitute to sleep with her father-in-law) as an immoral means to achieve a moral end, namely, the birth of her sons. They point out that classical ethics and morality insist that the ends never justify the means. Other experts point out that Tamar craftily took advantage of the existing religious customs of her time, and it would be unfair to take her actions out of context. They see her not as a sinful opportunist or a vengeful widow but as a resourceful person who used her wits to undo an injustice previously done to her by her father-in-law.

The debate goes back and forth between moral theologians and ethicists on one hand and biblical scholars on the other. Just because the Bible reports what a person did doesn't mean that their actions are condoned or approved. At the same time, while the objective morality of actions can be evaluated by using criteria like the natural law or Ten Commandments, the subjective guilt or culpability of a person requires knowing not only *what* they did but also what did they *know* and what did they *intend.*

Bathing Bathsheba

The Bible describes Bathsheba (whom we discuss in Chapter 16) as a gorgeous woman who takes an afternoon bath on the roof of her penthouse apartment, just within the vision of King David from his royal palace. When he sees her, he invites her to the palace, and she becomes his adulterous lover (her husband, Uriah, is away fighting the enemy). When she becomes pregnant with their child, David arranges for the "accidental death" of Uriah.

Bathsheba is sometimes believed to be a cheap woman who willingly enters an adulterous tryst while her soldier husband bravely defends the homeland from the enemy. But some people speculate that perhaps she was seduced or coerced by the most powerful man in the kingdom.

More speculation insists that she must have known that King David could see her bathing on her roof — after all, he lived in the highest building in town, and she may have been able to see him, too. Could she have been naïve enough to think no one would see her? Or did she knowingly put herself into a compromising situation?

Regardless, she does consent to the affair, although some people claim that no one in her right mind would refuse a royal request (if she wants to save her own life, that is). On the other hand, another woman in the Bible, Susanna, was propositioned by two respected religious leaders but resisted and refused their advances (see Chapter 11).

The debate continues today. The Bible doesn't indicate why Bathsheba was unfaithful to her husband, Uriah. We don't know if she was naïve, promiscuous, afraid for her life, or just taken advantage of at a vulnerable moment.

Misunderstood Miriam

The actions of Miriam, Moses' sister, in the later years of her life are the subject of controversy and misunderstanding, when she and her brother Aaron nearly mutiny against Moses' authority while in the desert.

On the one hand, Miriam supports her brother Moses, who is busy on Mount Sinai getting the Ten Commandments from God, by refusing to help create — let alone worship — a pagan idol. Her elder brother, Aaron, however, succumbs to some of the men who pressure him into making a golden calf from the gold they took as booty when they left their former masters in Egypt. Miriam and the other women allegedly do not contribute their gold to be melted down, nor do they worship the pagan idol (the golden calf), unlike many of the men who did. Miriam remains faithful to God by not participating in idolatry.

But on the other hand, Miriam opposes her brother Moses after he comes down from Mount Sinai. She and Aaron then become envious of Moses' position and authority, and she shows a darker side to her personality. Miriam and Aaron complain, "Has the LORD spoken only through Moses? Has he not spoken through us also?" (Numbers 12:2).

Although she is called a prophet in Exodus 15:20, she also attracts controversy. She resents the wife of Moses (either Zipporah, or perhaps his second wife, a Cushite) and, more important, she resents the honor bestowed on Moses by God Himself to be leader of the people, as opposed to herself. As a result, Miriam is struck with leprosy as punishment (see Numbers 12:10). Ironically, Moses is the one who prays to the Lord for her recovery, and after seven days, she does fully heal. (For Miriam's story, see Chapter 10.)

Did she think Moses was too big for his britches, or did she resent his popularity and leadership? The controversy has never been settled, and to this day, scholars debate her motives and rationale, charging that she held too much selfish pride (because she wasn't boss) or needlessly feared public scandal (because Moses' wife was a foreigner).

Zealous Zipporah

Zipporah, who is identified as the wife of Moses, and the daughter of Jethro (a priest of Midian), is the subject of three main points of controversy and misunderstanding: Bible scholars question whether she was Moses' only wife, they ponder her reaction to circumcising her son, and they wonder why she and Moses led separate lives for a time. (You can read more about Zipporah in Chapter 10.)

At one point in the Bible, Moses' siblings, Miriam and Aaron, show resentment for Moses' wife, whom they describe as a Cushite (see Numbers 12:1). Because the Bible never explicitly says Zipporah is a Cushite, some people speculate that Moses may have had one or two additional wives. Flavius Josephus, the Jewish historian, believed that Moses first married an Ethiopian (sometimes also known as Cushite) princess, Tharbis, and later on married Zipporah, the Midianite.

Because the Bible isn't precisely clear, Zipporah's origins and her treatment by her in-laws are the subject of much speculation and misunderstanding. Some scholars believe that Miriam and Aaron could have used the term Cushite in a pejorative sense. Zipporah — who was from Midian — could have had darker skin, unlike her Hebrew contemporaries, thus resembling a Cushite. So it's unclear whether Aaron and Miriam disliked Zipporah or another wife. And if Zipporah was Moses' only wife, then what was the source of the angst between her and her in-laws? Again, the answer isn't clear.

The second source of controversy surrounds the details of the circumcision of Zipporah and Moses' son, Gershom. As described in Exodus 4:24–26, to prevent the Lord from striking Moses dead, Zipporah performs the circumcision herself, a practice never performed by a woman. She flings the foreskin at the feet of her husband. Does this action reveal that she did what had to be done because Moses didn't do it himself, or was she inferring that, because this Hebrew custom wasn't part of her culture, she resented doing it? Scholars continue to debate her reaction.

Finally, the last area of misunderstanding concerns why, at one point, Zipporah separates from Moses. When her husband goes to Egypt to argue with Pharaoh for the release of the Hebrews, Zipporah takes her sons to stay with grandpa Jethro. They're later reunited in the wilderness, after the Exodus, but the Bible doesn't specify whether Zipporah stays away as a safety measure or whether this separation was a marital timeout after a quarrel — perhaps a quarrel about the circumcision.

Risqué Rahab

Rabbinic tradition (teachings of the rabbis over the ages, given respect and consideration by many Jews) says that Rahab was one of the four most beautiful women of the Hebrew Bible (what Christians designate as the Old Testament). In Joshua 2:1, Rahab is described as the town prostitute in Jericho during the time when Moses was leading his people to the Promised Land. Jericho was the last city standing in the way of the Hebrew people, now led by Joshua. Rahab ends up helping Joshua's Hebrew spies by hiding them while they stake out

Jericho. In return, these same men spare Rahab and her family, who become the sole survivors of the Battle of Jericho. (For more info on Rahab, see Chapter 10.)

Rahab's motives are often misunderstood. She wasn't actually unpatriotic and a traitor to her own people. Instead, the Bible says she believed that the God of the Hebrews is "the" God. Despite her colorful and risqué lifestyle, she is described as risking her life for this God and hiding the spies to help cover for them.

But some people speculate that she allegedly acted courageously for reasons other than her belief in the Hebrew God. These commentators consider Rahab an opportunist, hiding the spies merely to spare her life (which was a nice by-product of housing the Hebrew spies).

An interesting aside: The Bible points out that the story doesn't end when she saves herself and her family. She later becomes the wife of Salmon and the mother of Boaz, who eventually marries Ruth. They in turn had a son, Obed, who was the father of Jesse, the father of King David, and ancestor of Jesus. So Rahab helps create the Messianic lineage — an important role in the history of salvation.

Hagar — An Innocent Victim?

Bible scholars consider Hagar, the maidservant of Sarah and the mother of Ishmael (through Abraham), to be an enigma. (Check out Chapter 15 for more on Hagar.) The debate over Hagar involves two points:

- ✔ Whether she is an Egyptian princess offered to Abraham by Pharaoh
- ✔ Why Hagar becomes hostile toward Sarah after giving birth to Ishmael

The Bible merely says that Hagar is an Egyptian servant, but she becomes a key player when Sarah suggests that Hagar become Abraham's concubine, because Sarah had been unable to bear children after many years. (See Chapter 9 for more on Sarah.)

Some nonbiblical sources claim that Hagar was an Egyptian princess offered by Pharaoh to Abraham as atonement. Pharaoh had earlier taken Sarah, Abraham's wife, under the false pretense that she was Abraham's sister, not his wife. Possibly Hagar was given to Abraham by Pharaoh as a peace offering.

Hagar soon becomes pregnant and grows contemptuous of her mistress, Sarah. The Bible doesn't explain why Hagar scorns Sarah at this point. Some people theorize that after she produced an heir for Abraham in Ishmael, Hagar rose too high and may have forgotten her place as a maidservant.

But the story changes again when Sarah herself finally becomes pregnant and gives birth to Isaac. The conflict continues between the women, and the last straw occurs when Isaac is an infant and Ishmael a teenager. Something happens between the half-brothers that sets off Sarah's fuse. Sarah requests that Abraham exile Hagar and Ishmael into the desert, and he complies.

Whatever Hagar's minor flaws or weaknesses, Sarah and Abraham treat her badly. The Lord rescues her and her son, however, and he becomes the ancestor of a great nation (Ishmaelites). She is a pawn and a victim, and yet for a brief moment, she is at the top of the heap. If she hadn't become conceited when she was pregnant with Ishmael, perhaps Sarah wouldn't have abused her. By complying with the initial request to become a concubine, Hagar simply does what she is told, but maybe Sarah detects that Hagar likes her job a little too much.

Hagar is remembered and known for being the mother of Ishmael, the first son of Abraham but not the one to continue the lineage — that happens through Sarah and her son Isaac. Ishmael is the ancestor of the Ishmaelites. Paul later uses Hagar as an analogy of the Hebrew religion in contrast to Sarah, whom he sees as a symbol of the Christian faith (see Galatians 4:24–26).

What Hagar's background and motives, thoughts, and feelings were, we don't know. She remains a debatable mystery today.

Judith: Battling the Stereotype

Judith has a deuterocanonical/apocryphal book named after her (see Chapter 2 for more on the deuterocanonical books, or Apocrypha), but her heroic actions are sometimes misunderstood. Although no man was able to achieve what she did at the time, her character and actions sometimes are still questioned.

A wealthy and beautiful woman, Judith lived at the time when King Nebuchadnezzar sent General Holofernes to chastise the nations who refused to join the Assyrians in their war with the Medes. The Israelites were on his hit list. When Holofernes cuts off their water supply to coerce them to surrender, spirits decline and morale weakens.

Judith, an Israelite, reprimands her downcast Israelite leaders, reminding them that God's people cannot be conquered *unless* they sin. The Israelites are about to surrender, so Judith takes matters into her own hands. She infiltrates the enemy camp, pretending to be a defector to the Assyrians, and gets into Holofernes' tent. Gorgeous and brilliant, Judith impresses the general with her wisdom and beauty. She fools him into thinking she really wants to defect and help Nebuchadnezzar conquer her own people.

She notices that Holofernes has his eye on her, so she lets him think he can seduce her. All the time she is plying him with strong wine. When he is drunk, she takes his own sword and cuts off his head. She hides the head in her luggage, walks out of the camp, and returns to Jerusalem to show the elders what she has done. (See Chapter 8 for more on the story of Judith.)

People have different viewpoints of Judith's actions. Justifiable homicide, national defense, tyranicide, or murder? The Bible never evaluates or judges the morality or ethics of her deed. She kills the enemy, that's for sure, and she saves her people in the process. The absence of any punishment or moral outrage, however, indicates that Judith wasn't guilty of grave evil.

Nevertheless, some Bible scholars still consider Judith a murderess who helped her people by eliminating their enemy — yet used immoral means to do it. They point out that God never told her to kill Holofernes. She decided to do that on her own. Other scripture experts point out that Judith acted only after the military and religious leaders failed to act. Executing a tyrant — when there are no other alternatives to ending the evil — has always been an acceptable last resort. Judith showed more courage and bravery than many of the men who were supposed to protect and defend the Hebrew nation. When the Jewish leaders were ready to surrender, it took someone like Judith to show them that God would deliver their enemies into their own hands if they kept the faith. Many scholars, therefore, see her not as an assassin or a vigilante but as a patriot and devout believer.

Chapter 23

Ten Most Famous Women of the Bible in Art

In This Chapter

▶ Depicting some notorious Old Testament women

▶ Illustrating admirable Old and New Testament figures

▶ Portraying the Virgin Mary, the most recognized woman in art

Medieval and early Renaissance art was heavily oriented to Biblical themes. Stories in the Bible were not only popular but also profitable. Many of the wealthy wanted to show off their riches by having works of art in their estates. The poor who were illiterate also depended on religious art to teach them what was in the Bible. Church leaders supported the arts to assist in educating the believers, whether through stained glass, wood panels, or frescoes, as long as the image accurately portrayed what was written in the Bible.

Women in the Bible have always been a favorite subject for artists, from painters and sculptors, to authors and composers alike. This section looks at the ten most famous women of the Bible depicted in art. Most of them have been preserved for posterity in oil on canvas, but other media have also been used, such as Michelangelo's sculpture, the *Pietà,* or the aria *Ave Maria.* We point out to you the various masterpieces and the central female characters from Scripture who are the subjects of each work of art.

Judith

Judith, discussed in the deuterocanonical book, or Apocrypha, under the same name (see Chapter 2 for more on the Apocrypha), is depicted in no less than 15 masterpieces, spanning the fifteenth to eighteenth centuries AD. She is the subject of five operas and oratorios and several poems and plays. The scene of Judith with the severed head of Holofernes — which she herself cut off with his own sword — is most dramatic. Artists often depict her as demure, young, beautiful, and elegant, while her nemesis, Holofernes, is shown as either grotesque or at least very intimidating. Check out Chapter 8 for more on Judith's story.

Figure 23-1 shows a painting of Judith standing on top of the severed head of Holofernes. She stands in a casual pose, nonchalantly looking down as if seeing a piece of rubbish on the ground. Giorgione portrays Judith as a very young, beautiful, and dainty woman holding the masculine sword that decapitated the general. The artist contrasts this unlikely and uneven pair: the elegant and graceful Judith and the powerful and menacing Holofernes (whose name is spelled one of two ways, the other being Holophernes).

Following is a list of some of the most famous depictions and performances based on Judith:

- *Judith and Holophernes* by Giorgione (1504), painting
- *Judith and Holophernes* by Sodoma (real name: Giovanni Antonio Bazzi) (1477–1549), painting
- *Judith and Holophernes* by Donatello (1460), bronze statue
- *Judith and Holophernes* by Boticelli (1472), painting
- *Judith and Holophernes* by Johann Martin Schmidt (Kremser-Schmidt) (1718–1801), painting
- *Judith and Holophernes* by Michelangelo (1509), Sistine Chapel ceiling, fresco painting
- *Judith and Holophernes* by Artemisia Gentileschi (1612), painting
- *Judith and Nebuchadnezzar* by Lucas Cranach the Elder (1530), painting
- *Judith and Holophernes* by Jan Massys (1543), painting
- *Judith and Holophernes* by Andrea Mantegna (1495), painting
- *Judith and Holophernes* by Cristoforo Allori (1613), painting
- *Judith and Holophernes* by Tintoretto (1550), painting
- *Judith and Holophernes* by Francesco Solimena (1733), painting
- *Judith und Holofernes* by Leopold Kotzeluch (1799), opera/oratorio
- *Giuditta* by S. Levi (1844), opera/oratorio
- *Giuditta* by Salvadori and Gagliano (1626), opera/oratorio
- *L'Amor insanguinato* by Beccau (1720), opera/oratorio
- *Juditha Triumphans* by Antonio Vivaldi (1716), opera/oratorio
- *Judith* by Martin Opitz (1635), drama
- *Judith* by W. Schmeltzl and Hans Sachs (1542), poem

Figure 23-1:
Judith with the Head of Holophernes by Giorgione (1504). Located in Hermitage, St. Petersburg, Russia.

Scala/Art Resource, NY

Delilah

Delilah is the most famous biblical femme fatale of them all. After all, she used her feminine wiles to seduce the secret of Samson's strength out of him, only to betray him. After she figures out how to defeat her lover, she cuts his hair while he's asleep in her bed, rendering him vulnerable — and allowing his captors to gouge out his eyes and restrain him. Samson's hair eventually grows back, enabling him to destroy 3,000 Philistines and probably Delilah as well. See Chapter 16 for more on Delilah. Her story is portrayed in the opera by Camille Saint-Saens titled *Samson et Dalila* (1877), and several paintings depict her, usually showing her with a pair of scissors.

Figure 23-2 shows Delilah snipping the hair of Samson while he sleeps. She does so carefully so as not to awaken him. Cignani captures the intimacy of Samson falling asleep in the lap of his lover, while she gingerly robs him of his super strength.

Scala/Art Resource, NY

Figure 23-2:
Samson and Delilah by Carlo Cignani (1628–1719). Located in Pinacoteca Nazionale, Bologna, Italy.

Following are some of the most famous depictions of Delilah:

- *Delilah Cuts Samson's Hair* by Albrecht Durer (1493), woodcut
- *Samson and Delilah* by Peter Paul Rubens (1609), painting
- *Samson and Delilah* by Lucas Cranach the Elder (1529), painting
- *Samson and Delilah* by Sir Anthony van Dyck (1620), painting
- *Samson and Delilah* by Adrien van der Werff (1659–1722), painting
- *Samson Betrayed by Delilah* by Rembrandt (1630), painting

Salome (and Her Mother, Herodias)

Another favorite female subject in biblical art is Salome. Salome was encouraged by her mother to influence her stepfather with a seductive dance, which eventually led to John the Baptist's beheading. Operas and paintings depict the infamous dance that Salome performed for her stepfather and also the grisly scene of the head of John the Baptist on a platter that's presented by Salome to her mother, Herodias. Head to Chapter 17 for more on this story. The best-known opera is *Salome* by Richard Strauss (1905), which was based on the play of the same name by Oscar Wilde (1893).

Figure 23-3 shows Salome, the daughter of Herodias, holding a platter with the head of John the Baptist. She looks away from the grisly sight, possibly showing detachment from the heinous crime that has been committed.

Here are some other famous depictions of Salome:

- *Salome with the Head of the Baptist* by Caravaggio (1609), painting
- *Salome* by Alonso Berruguete (1516), painting
- *Salome* by Titian (1515), painting
- *The Apparition* by Gustave Moreau (1826–1898), painting
- *The Dance of Salome* by Benozzo Gozzoli (1462), painting
- *Salome with the Head of John the Baptist* by Jacob Cornelisz van Oostsanen (1524), painting
- *Herodias* by Bernadino Luini (1531), painting
- *Daughter of Herodias Receiving the Head of John the Baptist* by Gustave Dore (1865), engraving
- *Herodias' Revenge* by Juan de Flandes (1496), painting
- *Herodias Receiving the Head of John The Baptist* by Giovanni del Biondo (1370), painting

Figure 23-3:
Salome Holding the head of Saint John the Baptist by Bernardino Luini (c.1475–1532). Located in the Louvre, Paris, France.

Erich Lessing/Art Resource, NY

Esther

Queen Esther has captured the imagination of many artists through the centuries. She was the Hebrew woman who married the Persian king and saved her people from destruction by exposing the evil and corrupt second-in-command (Haman), who plotted to destroy all the Jews in the kingdom. With the help of her uncle, Mordecai, Esther used her position as queen and her relationship as the beloved wife of King Ahasuerus to save her people. Typically, she is shown with royal attire, her crown, and throne. Turn to Chapter 8 for the story of Esther.

Figure 23-4 shows Esther flanked by two servants, while she appears to be daydreaming. This painting probably depicts her preparation for marrying the King of Persia and her subsequent coronation as queen. Esther's youth and beauty are quite evident in this depiction by Chasseriau.

Some famous depictions of Esther include the following:

✔ *Queen Esther* by Andrea del Castagno (1450), painting

✔ *Esther* by François-Léon Benouville (1844), painting

Figure 23-4:
Esther at her Toilette
by Theodore Chasseriau (1819–1856). Located in the Louvre, Paris, France.

Scala/Art Resource, NY

✔ *Esther Made Queen* by Julius Schnorr von Carolsfeld (1860), engraving

✔ *Esther and Ahasuerus* by Bernardo Cavallino (1650), painting

✔ *Ahasuerus, Haman and Esther* by Rembrandt (1660), painting

✔ *Esther before Ahasuerus* by Peter Paul Rubens (1620), painting

✔ *Esther before Ahasuerus* by Nicolas Poussin (1640), painting

✔ *Esther before Ahasuerus* by Claude Vignon (1624), painting

✔ *Gantze Histori der Hester* by Hans Sachs (1530), play

✔ *Esther* by George Friedrich Händel (1718), opera/oratorio

Bathsheba

Bathsheba (see Chapter 16) inspired King David to break many a commandment. Although married to Uriah, she had an affair with King David when her husband, Uriah, was away in battle. And when she became pregnant with David's child, the king arranged for Uriah's "accidental" death so he could marry Bathsheba and avoid scandal. Although her first child with David died as a result of their sins, their second son, Solomon, became the third and last king of the unified kingdom of Israel.

Figure 23-5 shows Bathsheba in a painting by the famous Peter Paul Rubens. Here Bathsheba at the fountain shows off, revealing her beauty. Some people believe that — in the upper left corner of this painting —King David is luridly looking at Bathsheba from his palace.

The following famous works of art portray Bathsheba:

✔ *David and Bathsheba* by Raphael (1519), painting

✔ *Bathsheba at Her Bath* by Rembrandt (1654), painting

✔ *Bathsheba at the Bath* by Sebastiano Ricci (1720), painting

✔ *Bathsheba at the Fountain* by Peter Paul Rubens (1635), painting

✔ *Bathsheba* by Giovanni Battista Naldini (1570), painting

✔ *David and Bathsheba* by David (Frederick) Barlow (1969), opera/oratorio

Queen of Sheba

The Queen of Sheba (discussed in Chapter 12) came from the farthest corner of the earth to listen to the wisdom of Solomon. Although she's never given a proper name in the Bible, her appearance at the court of King Solomon is nonetheless still memorable. The Queen of Sheba tested him with questions, puzzles, and riddles to learn if he was truly the wisest man in the world. Jesus even remarked that the queen of the south (Sheba) shall rise up in judgment on his generation, because the people didn't appreciate his wisdom like Sheba did Solomon's. In art, she is almost always shown with Solomon as an equal peer or colleague, unlike the other people at court.

Figure 23-6 shows the Queen of Sheba embracing King Solomon. Raphael also includes the royal tribute (the four and a half tons of gold and spices and precious stones mentioned in 1 Kings 10:1–13) that the Bible says the Queen of Sheba brought with her to give to the king of Israel.

Important works of art that depict the Queen of Sheba include the following:

- ✔ *King Solomon and the Queen of Sheba* by Konrad Witz (1435), painting

- ✔ "Arrival of the Queen of Sheba" from *Solomon* by G.F. Handel (1748), opera/oratorio

- ✔ *King Solomon and the Queen of Sheba* by Konrad Witz (1435), painting

- ✔ *Queen of Sheba and Solomon* by Julius Schnorr von Carolsfeld (1860), engraving

- ✔ *Seaport with the Embarkation of the Queen of Sheba* by Claude Lorrain (1648), painting

- ✔ *Solomon and the Queen of Sheba* by Giovanni Demin (unknown), painting

- ✔ *Solomon Receiving the Queen of Sheba* by Gustave Dore (1865), engraving

- ✔ *Solomon and Sheba* with Yul Brenner and Gina Lollobrigida, United Artists (1959), movie

Figure 23-6:
The Meeting with the Queen of Sheba, school of Raphael (1483–1520). Located in Logge, Vatican Palace, Vatican State.

Scala/Art Resource, NY

Martha and Mary

Jesus spent a great deal of time with Martha and Mary, the two sisters of Lazarus. These sisters are very different; Martha is a type A personality who is concerned about the details of hospitality, whereas Mary is a type B — more relaxed, informal, casual, and adaptable. Martha represents the active life of a Christian, whereas Mary is the personification of the contemplative. Both personalities and spiritualities are important. You can read more about them in Chapter 13.

Figure 23-7 shows Jesus in the home of Martha and Mary, depicting the two sisters with their different attitudes. Martha is busy with the details of hospitality, so the artist shows her holding a tray of drinking glasses, while her sister Mary takes time to attentively listen to Christ as he speaks. Mary also holds an alabaster jar of costly oil, which she will use to anoint his feet (John 12:3).

These two women have been portrayed in the following major works of art:

- ✔ *Martha and Mary Magdalene* by Caravaggio (1598), painting
- ✔ *Christ in the House of Martha and Mary* by Peter Paul Rubens (1628), painting
- ✔ *Christ in the House of Martha and Mary* by William Blake (1805), painting

Figure 23-7:
Christ in the House of Mary and Martha by Alessandro Allori (1535–1607). Located in Kunst- historisches Museum, Vienna, Austria.

Erich Lessing/Art Resource, NY

 ✔ *Christ in the House of Martha and Mary* by Tintoretto (1575), painting

 ✔ *Christ in the House of Martha and Mary* by Jan Vermeer van Delft (1655), painting

 ✔ *Christ in the House of Martha and Mary* by Diego Rodriguez de Silva Velazquez (1618), painting

Mary Magdalene

No other biblical woman claims as much notoriety or misperception as Mary Magdalene (see more on this in Chapter 22). One of the female disciples of Christ, she is best known for her conspicuous presence at the foot of the cross when Jesus was crucified, and she also was the first to visit the empty tomb on Easter morning after Jesus had risen from the dead. She is often depicted in art either at Calvary with the Virgin Mary and St. John the Apostle or at the empty tomb. She is also portrayed as a repentant sinner — sometimes as a reformed prostitute. Head back to Chapter 7 for Mary Magdalene's complete story.

Figure 23-8 shows Mary Magdalene holding an alabaster jar of oil, presumably to anoint the feet of Jesus. Medieval artists often depicted Mary Magdalene as the public sinner who washed and anointed the feet of Jesus (Luke 7:37–38). Bacchiacca also shows her in elegant clothing and wearing red, possibly indicating her former profession. During the Middle Ages, it was commonly thought that Mary Magdalene was a reformed prostitute, possibly the woman caught in adultery in John 7:53–8:11. Today, scholars debate her profession, her background, and whether she anointed the feet of Jesus at all.

Some important works featuring Mary Magdalene include the following:

 ✔ *Mary Anointing Jesus' Feet* by Peter Paul Rubens (1618), painting

 ✔ *Risen Christ Appearing to Mary Magdalene* by Rembrandt (1638), painting

 ✔ *St. Cecilia with Ss. Paul, John Evangelist, Augustine and Mary Magdalene* by Raphael (1516), painting

 ✔ *Christ between the Virgin Mary and St. John the Evangelist, with John the Baptist and Mary Magdalene* by Rogier van der Weyden (1450), painting

 ✔ *Penitent Mary Magdalene* by Titian (1560), painting

 ✔ *St. Mary Magdalene* by El Greco (1585), painting

 ✔ *Mary Magdalene Speaking to the Angels,* by Giotto (1320), fresco

 ✔ *Martha and Mary Magdalene* by Caravaggio (1598), painting

 ✔ *Crucifixion* by Raffaello (1503), painting

 ✔ *The Crucifixion with the Virgin, Saint John, Saint Jerome, and Saint Mary Magdalene* by Perugino (1485), painting

 ✔ *Crucifixion* by Salvador Dali (1954), painting

Alinari/Art Resource, NY

Eve

The first woman, the first wife, and first mother of the human race is Eve. Genesis tells us that God created her from the rib of her husband, Adam — which is why Adam referred to her as "bone of bone and flesh of my flesh." Tempted by the serpent, Eve ate of the forbidden fruit and enticed Adam to do likewise. For their disobedience, they were expelled from the Garden of Paradise. Eve then had two sons, Cain and Abel, until the former killed the latter. After Cain murdered his brother, he became an outcast, and Eve and Adam had another son, Seth, who would continue the lineage. Head back to Chapter 5 for more on Eve.

Eve has been the subject of art for millennia because all three monotheistic and Abrahamic religions (Judaism, Christianity, and Islam) acknowledge her existence. She is often depicted without clothes in the Garden of Eden before the Fall, and with fig leaves or animal skins after the Fall.

Figure 23-9 shows Eve, the first woman and the wife of Adam, holding in her hand the forbidden fruit from the tree of knowledge. The wily serpent lurks in the background, dangling on the branch of the tree where he had just tempted Eve to take a sample of the fruit. Eve also appears to be offering the fruit to Adam, after she has eaten a piece. Medieval artists universally used an apple in their depiction of the fruit from the tree of knowledge of good and evil, yet the Bible never mentions what kind of fruit it actually was.

Major works of art that feature Eve include:

- ✔ *Creation* by Franz Joseph Haydn (1732–1809), opera/oratorio
- ✔ *Paradise Lost* by John Milton (1667), poem
- ✔ *Eve* by Andrea del Castagno (1450), painting
- ✔ *Eve and the Apple* by Giuseppe Arcimboldo (1578), painting
- ✔ *Fall of Adam and Eve* by Giovanni Bon (1410), painting
- ✔ *Adam and Eve* by Lucas Cranach the Elder (1533), painting
- ✔ *Rebuke of Adam and Eve* by Domenichino (1626), painting
- ✔ *Adam and Eve* by Albrech Durer (1504), engraving
- ✔ *Eve* by Paul Gauguin (1890), sculpture
- ✔ *Creation of Eve* by Michelangelo (1510), painting
- ✔ *Adam and Eve Banished from Eden* by Raphael (1519), painting
- ✔ *Eve Eating the Apple* by Rodin (1885), sculpture
- ✔ *The Expulsion of Adam and Eve from Paradise* by Benjamin West (1791), painting

Figure 23-9:
Eve by Lucas Cranach the Elder Cranach (1472–1553). Located in Museum der Bildenden Kuenste, Leipzig, Germany.

Erich Lessing/Art Resource, NY

Virgin Mary

Writer G.K. Chesterton once remarked that although the face of Helen of Troy adorned a thousand ships and the face of Queen Victoria was printed on thousands of coins and currency throughout the British Empire, only the face of Virgin Mary is better known and more recognized and has been universally loved throughout the ages.

The mother of Jesus has been depicted in more works of art than any human being in all of human history. Spanning two millennia, this woman of the Bible is the most readily identifiable female person even among non-Christians and nonbelievers. No other woman has had as many paintings, stained glass pieces, sculptures, frescoes, mosaics, poems, plays, hymns, arias, churches, or cathedrals named in her honor. Typically, the Virgin Mary is depicted with the baby or child Jesus, as the Sorrowful Mother at the foot of the cross at Calvary, or being assumed body and soul into heaven after her death. Read Chapter 6 for more on her story.

Figure 23-10 shows the Virgin Mary nursing the baby Jesus with Anthony of Padua on the right and Mary Magdalene on the left. Mary Magdalene is holding the alabaster jar of oil to anoint the feet of Jesus. Neither Magdalene nor Anthony of Padua, however, would have been present when Jesus was an infant, because Mary Magdalene was a contemporary of Jesus and would have been too young, if born at all at that time, and Anthony of Padua was a Franciscan friar who lived in Portugal during the thirteenth century (Jesus lived during the first century).

Following are just a fraction of the works dedicated to the Virgin Mary's image:

- Cathedral of Notre Dame, Paris (finished in 1250), church

- National Shrine of the Immaculate Conception, Washington, D.C. (finished in 1959), church

- Basilica de Guadelupe, Mexico City, Mexico (several versions have been on this spot since 1531), church

- Basilica di Santa Maria Maggiore (Saint Mary Major), Rome, Italy (432), church

- *Ave Maria* (Hail Mary), hymn; 15 composers have written their own versions of this prayer based on the passages from Luke 1:28–42: Bach and Gounod; Bizet; Brahms; Giulio Caccini; Cherubini; Donizetti; Franck; Gordigiani; Mozart; Rachmaninoff; Saint-Saens; Shubert; Tosti; Guiseppe Verdi

- *Virgin Annunciate* by Fra Angelico (1430), painting

- *Virgin of the Annunciation* by Botticelli (1490), painting

✔ *Virgin Mary* by Titian (1522), painting

✔ *Madonna and Child* by Giovanni Bellini, (1510) painting

✔ *Virgin of the Lilies* by William-Adolphe Bouguereau, (1899) painting

✔ *Madonna with the Child* by Donatello (1448), sculpture

✔ *Virgin and Child in a Church* by Jan van Eyck (1437), painting

✔ *Madonna Litta* by Leonardo da Vinci (1491), painting

✔ *Granduca Madonna* by Raphael (1504), painting

✔ *Mater Dolorosa* by Artus Quellin (1650), woodcarving

✔ *Assumption of the Virgin* by Nicolas Poussin (1650), painting

✔ *Madonna and Child* by Peter Paul Rubens (1625), painting

✔ *Pietà* by Michelangelo (1499), sculpture

Figure 23-10:
Madonna and Child with Saints Mary Magdalene and Anthony of Padua by Lo Spagna (c.1450–1528). Located in Pinacoteca, Vatican Museums, Vatican State.

Scala/Art Resource, NY

Chapter 24

Ten Most Influential Women of the Bible

In This Chapter

▶ Looking at the influence of matriarchs

▶ Understanding the influence of brains and beauty

*T*his chapter looks at the women in the Bible who were most influential. Some of them, through their actions, provided a direct and obvious influence, but others were influential in a more indirect way. No matter what the case, these women altered salvation history, and their stories continue to be told.

Eve

The first woman of the human race is certainly one of the most influential women of the Bible because she is considered "mother of all living" (Genesis 3:20). Eve (discussed in depth in Chapter 5) is considered to be of influence on mankind in two ways:

✔ Spiritually, Eve and her husband, Adam, are the prototype human beings who represent all humankind — for better or for worse.

✔ Physically, according to the Bible, all human beings descend from one woman — Eve.

The original rebel

When Eve disobeys God and eats the forbidden fruit — and her husband does likewise — their rebelliousness becomes what Christians historically call original sin or the sin of Adam and Eve. Because Eve was the first woman representing all human beings, the Bible tells us that Eve's sin also becomes ours, and all humans suffer the same punishment and guilt she did. This infamous credit also goes to Adam, the first man, because he disobeyed God (by eating the forbidden fruit) as much as Eve did.

So Eve influences human nature by scarring it from the beginning, but humans make matters worse by committing their own sins. Theologians have speculated for centuries about what would have happened if our first parents hadn't sinned. Without original sin, a Redeemer or Savior wouldn't have been necessary. So the big question that many religious scholars debated in the Middle Ages was whether Christ would have come to earth if there had been no first sin. This great mystery has never been resolved.

She has a lot of kids

Many people speculate that Eve is the universal mother of the human race, not just spiritually but also naturally. Mitochondrial DNA (something every human being has) studies have shown that every man, woman, and child who lived, is living, or will live, is related to and descended from one human female that scientists affectionately call Eve. Studies like these may help to show that all people actually do belong to one global family of humankind.

As the first source in humanity's gene pool, Eve (with Adam) passed to her descendants traits such as two hands, two arms, two legs, two feet, two eyes, two ears, and so on. She helped give everyone who came after her the biological capability of walking upright, speaking, using tools, thinking and reasoning, reading and writing, and so on. Had Eve breathed water rather than air, you and I would be living in the sea instead of on dry land. Her digestive, circulatory, and respiratory systems and all five senses were bequeathed to us as a biological inheritance.

Sarah

Sarah (formerly called Sarai), the wife of Abraham (formerly called Abram), is looked upon as influential in two ways:

- ✔ She was one of the first matriarchs of the Hebrew religion. Not only is she the mother of Isaac, the grandmother of Jacob (later known as Israel), but she is the great-grandmother of his 12 sons (who gave their names to the 12 tribes of Israel).

- ✔ She is considered the spiritual mother of the Hebrew religion just as her husband, Abraham, is the father in faith. Followers of other religions, including Christianity and Islam, also see Sarah as having influenced their beliefs for the better.

Matriarch matters

Through Sarah and Abraham and their descendants, the Hebrew nation was established, as well as a dynasty that included the likes of King David and King Solomon. She is part of the covenant between God and the Jewish people. Born Sarai, she is the only woman in the Bible whose name is changed by God (to Sarah), just as her husband's name was changed (from Abram to Abraham), a sure sign of her significance and influence. Although she is barren for most of her adult life, in her twilight years God blesses her with a son, Isaac, who becomes one of the founding ancestors of Judaism.

Respect from the religions

Sarah (see Chapter 9) is influential in the three monotheistic religions of the world: Judaism, Christianity, and Islam. Judaism owes a debt of gratitude to Sarah for her role in establishing the Hebrew faith, and Christians are equally appreciative. Because Jesus also comes from her lineage, Sarah has influence over Christianity. The Christian Messiah was a Jew and came from the Hebrew faith, as did his early followers. So Sarah is revered as a holy woman by Christians and by Jews.

Sarah even influenced the Islam religion. That's because in her barren years, she requests that Abraham sire a child with her maidservant, Hagar. Although her choice to promote an Arabic (Egyptian) servant as surrogate mother wasn't an easy one, she fears that her husband will have no one to establish the dynasty if she can't have a child. Later, after Isaac is born, bad blood develops between these women, and Sarah requests that Hagar and her son, Ishmael, be exiled. That unfortunate turn of events allows Ishmael to establish his own dynasty, separate from the Hebrew one of Isaac. Muslims (followers of the religion of Islam established by the Arab prophet Mohammed in AD 610) see themselves as children of Abraham via the Ishmaelites.

Although her actions were unintentional and not altruistic, Sarah still influences Islam by being the catalyst that results in Abraham's fathering a son with an Egyptian servant. Sarah's initial suggestion that her maidservant Hagar have a child (Ishmael) with Abraham started a chain reaction of events that influenced the future.

Rebekah

Rebekah, the wife of Isaac, has influence much like her mother-in-law, Sarah:

✔ Rebekah, like Sarah, is also considered a matriarch — in her own right — with influence over those around her.

> ✔ Though her intentions are questionable, Rebekah also influences salvation history by helping her younger son, Jacob, cheat her elder son, Esau, of his birthright. Without her assistance, the 12 sons of Israel wouldn't have become the foundation of the Hebrew religion, because the lineage (and *covenant,* the sacred oath between God and the Hebrew people) would have gone through Esau instead of his younger twin.

Rebekah disguises Jacob so he can impersonate Esau and fool the elderly Isaac into giving the birthright to the younger son. Had she not interfered, the sons of Esau would have established the dynasty rather than the sons of Jacob. They could have been Edomites (Edom was the son of Esau) rather than Israelites (Israel was the new name God gave to Jacob), and such influence is not negligible. Although the name of the Hebrew nation (Israelite or Edomite) may not be critical, the actual lineage is absolutely important. It is through Jacob (Israel) and his descendants that King David and ultimately Jesus of Nazareth would come, not through Esau and his son Edom.

Tamar

Tamar is influential in that she is an integral part of the ancestry of King David and, ultimately, Jesus the Messiah. Her significance, however, is also due to her perseverance and her intelligence, which allows her to outwit her father-in-law, Judah. (See Chapter 9 for the story of Tamar.)

Tamar is important for two reasons:

> ✔ Her maternal abilities (and wants) help to continue the lineage that will lead to Christ himself. Her influence goes beyond her biological reproduction capabilities, however.
>
> ✔ The difficult choices she makes influence how the lineage continues. She uses her smarts and guts, thereby eventually changing history.

Her first husband, Er, dies before they have any children. Then, according to custom, she marries his brother, Onan. Unfortunately, he dies just as suddenly — well before any little ones arrive. Only one brother, Shelah, is left, but he is too young to marry at the time.

Tamar patiently waits as her biological clock ticks. She's in a difficult situation. People in those days depended on their adult sons and daughters to care for them in their old age. Judah, the father of three sons, had promised Tamar his last son when he was of age. But Judah doesn't fulfill his promise. Tamar is left childless and also a widow two times around. Her fate is bleak until she outsmarts her father-in-law. Pretending to be a prostitute, she lays a trap for Judah, who sleeps with her, thinking she is a common harlot.

After his visit, she wisely keeps some of his personal belongings. And after she discovers she's pregnant, she uses his possessions as proof that he is the father. Tamar's plan works, and Judah owns up to his responsibilities. Twins Perez and Zerah are born, the first being a direct ancestor of King David and of Jesus as well.

Bathsheba

Bathsheba (discussed in Chapter 16) is influential for several reasons.

- ✔ Her tremendous beauty catches the lustful eye of King David.
- ✔ Her complicity in adultery leads to her illicit pregnancy, which becomes a catalyst for the king, who is her lover, to plot the death of her husband.
- ✔ Although her first child dies, she has another son after becoming the legitimate wife of King David — a son none other than the wise King Solomon.
- ✔ She inadvertently exposes the plot of Solomon's half brother, Adonijah, to usurp the throne after King David's death. Thus, she eliminates him and secures the crown for her son, Solomon, once and for all.

Second time's a charm?

Bathsheba is both gorgeous and brilliant, and although she's no saint, she's not a demon, either. The Bible doesn't reveal what, if anything, she knew of David's successful scheme to have her first husband, Uriah, bumped off while in battle. But it's certain that Bathsheba's very presence and beauty are influential on King David, and her later agreement to commit adultery and her subsequent pregnancy lead the king to plot the murder of her first husband. Bathsheba also influences her dying second husband, King David, by making him keep his pledge that their son, Solomon, will become his successor as king of Israel, despite Adonijah's attempted seizure of the throne.

Mother to a king

Bathsheba has a great influence on her second son — Solomon — as she raises him, and he becomes the wisest man on earth. Bathsheba finally seals Solomon's fate when Adonijah tries to use her to get Solomon to give over Abishag, the former concubine of David. By making this bizarre request to Solomon on behalf of Adonijah, Bathsheba thus reveals (perhaps unintentionally) the never-ending scheming of Solomon's half brother to steal the crown.

Bathsheba protects the lineage from King David, her husband, to King Solomon, her son, and through Solomon the line will continue to Jesus of Nazareth. Even though the kingdom will divide into two separate kingdoms — Israel and Judah — Bathsheba's influence to preserve the dynasty is still successful. Unfortunately, she isn't able to prevent her son in his later years from breaking the law of God and becoming an idolater, worshipping the false gods of his many wives. She does, however, keep Solomon on the throne, and according to the Bible, that's enough to continue God's plan for his people.

Miriam

Miriam, the sister of Moses, affects history in a number of ways. Despite her imperfections, her influence is positive, and she ultimately emerges as a faithful servant of the Lord. Her participation in the life of her brother Moses is influential from beginning to end, which, in turn, changes the history and lives of the Hebrews. (For more details about Miriam, check out Chapter 10.)

Her brother's keeper

She is sent by her mother to guard the infant Moses as he makes his journey down the Nile River. After the daughter of Pharaoh discovers Moses, Miriam persuades the princess to have the baby nursed by a Hebrew woman — Moses' own mother, Jochebed — although the princess remains unaware that she is turning the baby over to his rightful mother.

The good and the bad of it

Miriam also influences the Hebrews in two ways (by doing good, as well as by showing her rebellious side) during the Exodus — when the Jews leave the bondage of slavery to escape across the parted Red Sea. Miriam, the prophetess, is able to persuade the fleeing Israelites to joyfully and faithfully obey and follow her brother Moses, who is leading the Chosen People from Egypt into what ultimately becomes the Promised Land. When the people are wandering in the desert, she and brother Aaron complain that Moses has too much power. Her prideful act of rebellion results in a brief state of leprosy, but her sin and its consequence show others the repercussions of mutiny. She is cured when Moses prays to God on her behalf after her brief period of shame.

Zipporah

Zipporah, a daughter of Jethro and wife of Moses, is another influential woman of the Old Testament (see more about her in Chapter 10). Zipporah catches Moses' eye as he heroically protects her and her six sisters from a bunch of thugs who are harassing them. She soon becomes Mrs. Moses.

Sibling (in-law) rivalry

Zipporah may have indirectly influenced Aaron and Miriam, who complained that she was a foreigner (specifically an Ethiopian). Whether or not she was Ethiopian (the jury is still out), the Bible suggests that Zipporah could have been the scapegoat that Miriam and Aaron needed in their attempted coup against the authority of Moses. Zipporah was perhaps the unknowing and inadvertent catalyst that incites Miriam and Aaron to rebel against their brother. But instead of staging a successful mutiny, Miriam and Aaron fail in their attempted overthrow, resulting in punishment (Miriam's temporary leprosy) and thus probably discouraging future attempts by other Hebrews to oust Moses.

She's good with a knife

Zipporah's greatest influence probably stems from her actions in Exodus 4 — actions that change the course of history for Moses. Because Moses has not circumcised his son, he offends God so much that the Lord is about to smite him (the biblical way of eliminating a problem). Zipporah saves the day by circumcising their boy herself and throwing the foreskin at the feet of Moses. Whether Moses had inadvertently neglected doing this procedure or intentionally refrained from doing it, circumcision was nevertheless the sign of the covenant (the sacred oath between God and the Hebrew people).

Zipporah's action is so influential that it actually saves Moses' life that day, enabling him to continue on to Egypt, confront Pharaoh, and secure the release of all the Hebrew slaves.

Rahab

Rahab, the town prostitute of Jericho, gets a spot on the most influential list for hiding the spies of Joshua in the city of Jericho. As these agents are gathering intelligence on the town's defenses before going into battle, their presence is revealed. Rahab gives them safe passage on the condition that she and her family will be spared when the Israelites attack the next day.

Faith influences her actions; she realizes that the God of the Israelites is the true God and that his people would conquer Jericho. Rahab's bravery in hiding these notorious fugitives (if they had been discovered, it would have meant certain death for her) influences the outcome of the Hebrews' battle at Jericho, helping secure their journey into the Promised Land. Rahab also influences salvation history by marrying Salmon. Their son, Boaz, is the great-grandfather of King David. Thus, she saves the Israelites through her act of courage and secures the lineage through her marriage to a Hebrew man. We discuss Rahab in greater detail in Chapter 10.

Hagar

Hagar, the maidservant to Sarah and the concubine to Abraham, makes the cut of influential women because she gives Abraham his first son. Although Hagar (discussed in Chapter 15) gives Abraham a healthy boy, Ishmael, she also begins to treat Sarah rudely. Sarah reacts by abusing Hagar right back.

After Sarah gives birth to her own son, Isaac, her patience wears thin with Hagar. Sarah convinces Abraham to send Hagar and Ishmael into the desert as exiles. God, however, spares them and assures Hagar that her son will be the father of his own nation, the Ishmaelites. Her influence as a matriarch to these people — today called the Muslims — is vast, because they now regard her as an ancestor of their prophet, Mohammed.

Virgin Mary

Mary, the mother of Jesus, is a highly influential woman of the Bible. Not only does she give birth to the Christian Savior and Messiah, but she also provides a great example of Christian discipleship. (We devote all of Chapter 6 to a discussion of Mary.)

The example's been set

Her influence begins as she reacts to the angel Gabriel's news that she will soon become a mother, despite the fact that she is a virgin. The heavenly messenger assures her that she'll conceive by divine — not human — intervention. After Mary finds out that the Holy Spirit will overshadow her (she will conceive by the power of God and without the cooperation of a human father) and the child she is to mother will be called holy, the Son of God, she gives a reply that influences countless future generations: "Be it done unto me according to your word" (see Luke 1:38, King James Version). These can be considered the best words spoken by any disciple of the Lord; she is basically saying let it happen as God wills (and not her will), a sentiment of many people who practice their faith. Although she could have said no — like Eve did in response to God's request — she instead places herself into the service of God by submitting to his will.

Mary also influences future disciples by her example of humility. Even though she is to be the mother of the Savior, as soon as she learns that her elderly cousin, Elizabeth, is with child, she goes in haste to be of service to her. Rather than stay home and take care of herself now that she is pregnant, Mary instead puts her cousin Elizabeth first; Elizabeth's needs outweigh Mary's wants, at least in Mary's heart. Her example of putting others first serves as an inspiration to all Christians as to what it means to be a disciple today.

Mother knows best

Mary also influences her son, Jesus, as most mothers do. Although he is divine in nature, he is also human. That means that he has to learn how to walk, talk, and tie his shoes, and guess who taught him: mom.

Jewish boys spent their infancy and early childhood with their mothers until the age of 13, when they were bar mitzvahed. Thus, Hebrew boys and girls learned their faith and other aspects of life from their mom.

During Jesus' adult life, Mary influences her son, even if only with a nudge. At the wedding feast of Cana, Mary is the one who mentions to Christ that the wine is all gone. Who but a mother would notice such a detail? Her request is followed by Jesus' first public miracle, turning gallons of water into vintage, premium wine. After this event, mother and son no longer lead a quiet life, and Jesus begins his public ministry, teaching and preaching for the next three years. Mary's influence is also expressed at the foot of Calvary as Jesus is dying on the cross on Good Friday. Right before he dies, Jesus tells the Apostle John (also known as the Beloved Disciple), "Here is your mother" (John 1:27), and to Mary he says, "Woman, here is your son" (John 19:26). As his last will and testament of sorts, Jesus leaves his most precious possession, his mother, to the care of John the Apostle, the one whom he loved as a best friend. Some biblical scholars believe that John also represents the Christian church in that the personal relationship Jesus had with his mother would now extend to his mystical body, the Church. Sometimes, you can't do anything for the ones you love, especially when they're suffering and you are powerless and helpless, unable to offer any relief. Yet your very presence often is enough in these situations.

Likewise, Mary could say or do nothing to lessen the agony of her son, Jesus, but her mere presence at the cross when he needed her most is appreciated and influences Jesus to entrust his mother to John and through him to the entire church.

Pious and always present

Mary is also present, along with the apostles, at the descent of the Holy Spirit 50 days after the Resurrection of Jesus, an event called Pentecost. She is the only one who already "knows" the Holy Spirit, because it was by this power that she conceived a child without the biological cooperation of any human father. The one biological connection to Jesus is his mother, Mary, and the apostles stay close to her at least from the death, burial, resurrection, and ascension of Jesus until the coming of the Holy Spirit at Pentecost. Remember, the apostles didn't have any photos of Jesus to help them remember him, but they had his mom, who reminded them of her son.

Mary is also believed to have influenced Luke, the gospel writer. Because he wasn't one of the original 12 apostles, and because his gospel contains much information about her, scholars believe that Luke may have gotten his information directly from her. Jews and Christians consider scripture to be the revealed Word of God, so Christians consider anything and everything Luke wrote in his gospel to be inspired. Luke based some of his writings on what he learned from the mother of Jesus, who thus made an important contribution to Luke's work as an evangelist (gospel writer). What he in turn wrote influenced those who read and preached those same words in the years (and centuries) to come.

Paint me a picture

Even after her death, Mary's influence in the early and medieval church is enormous. No other woman is the subject of as many poems, hymns, sculptures, paintings, and other artistic works. She influenced thousands of artists, poets, musicians, and theologians over the past two millennia. Medieval and renaissance artists did more than simply depict or represent the Virgin Mary as the subject in their works. They often sought to also honor her as sons and daughters might try to honor their own earthly mother.

Although Jesus remains the central and essential person of salvation for Christians, the mother of Jesus for centuries has had a special place in the hearts of many poets, authors, composers, and painters. The plethora of different images, poses, and titles of Mary found in these works of art can boggle the imagination. For more on Mary's presence in the world of art, see Chapter 23.

Appendix

Alphabetical List of Women in the Bible

• •

*T*his alphabetical list contains the names of women in the Bible, many of whom we discuss in detail elsewhere in this book. Some are just barely mentioned in the Bible, with no other information, and others are described in more detail and in more verses. In some cases you'll notice that more than one woman has the same name. This list includes the Bible verses that mention them so you know where to go to read about them.

Abigail: (1) Widow of Nabal, one of David's wives, and mother of Chileab. 1 Samuel 25, 27:3, 30:5; 2 Samuel 2:2, 3:3. (2) Sister of David and mother of Amasa. 1 Chronicles 2:16–17; 2 Samuel 17:25.

Abijah: Mother of King Hezekiah of Judah. 2 Kings 18:2; 2 Chronicles 29:1.

Abishag: Concubine to King David. 1 Kings 1:1–4.

Abital: Wife of King David and mother of Shephatiah. 2 Samuel 3:4; 1 Chronicles 3:3.

Achsah: Daughter of Caleb and wife of Othniel. Joshua 15:16–17; Judges 1:12–14.

Adah: (1) Mother of Jabal; one of the wives of Noah's father, Lamech. Genesis 4:19–20. (2) Wife of Esau. Genesis 36:2.

Ahinoam: (1) Wife of King Saul. 1 Samuel 14:50. (2) Wife of King David; mother of Amnon. 1 Samuel 25:43, 27:3, 30:5; 2 Samuel 3:2; 1 Chronicles 3:1.

Anna: (1) Wife of Tobit. Tobit 1:9, 20. (2) Prophetess in the temple at baby Jesus' presentation. Luke 2:36–38.

Asenath: Wife of Joseph; mother of Manasseh and Ephraim. Genesis 41:45, 50, 46:20.

Athaliah: Daughter of King Omri of Israel. 2 Kings 8:26.

Basemath: Wife of Esau and mother of Reuel. Genesis 36:3, 17.

Bathsheba: Wife of Uriah, the Hittite; wife of King David; mother of King Solomon. 2 Samuel 11:2–5, 12:24; 1 Kings 1:11, 2:13.

Bathshua: Wife of Judah and mother of Er, Onan, and Shelah. Genesis 38:2–5; 1 Chronicles 2:3.

Bernice: Eldest daughter of Herod Agrippa I; heard Paul testify before Festus. Acts 25:13, 23, 26:30.

Bilhah: Maidservant to Rachel and mother of two of Jacob's sons, Dan and Naphtali. Genesis 29:29 and 30:3–6.

Chloe: Woman who informed Paul of the divided state of the Corinthian church. 1 Corinthians 1:11.

Claudia: Female Christian mentioned by Paul. 2 Timothy 4:21.

Cleopatra: Daughter of Ptolemy VI Philomotor and wife of King Alexander and King Demetrius. 1 Maccabees 10:57–58, 11:12.

Cozbi: Midianite woman killed by Phinehas. Numbers 25:6–15.

Damaris: One of the first Christian converts in Athens. Acts 17:34.

Deborah: (1) Prophetess, Judge, and wife of Lappidoth. Judges 4:4–9, 5:1–31. (2) Nurse of Rebekah. Genesis 35:8.

Delilah: Mistress of Samson who betrayed him to the Philistines. Judges 16:4–20.

Dinah: Daughter of Jacob and Leah; raped by Prince Shechem; her brothers Levi and Simeon retaliated by massacring Canaanites. Genesis 30:21, 34:1–27.

Dorcas: Greek for Tabitha; raised from the dead by Peter. Acts 9:36–41.

Drusilla: Third and youngest daughter of Herod Agrippa I; wife of Felix, Roman procurator. Acts 24:24.

Edna: Wife of Raguel, mother of Sarah. Tobit 7:2–8, 15.

Eglah: Wife of King David; mother of Ithream. 2 Samuel 3:5; 1 Chronicles 3:3.

Elisheba: Wife of Aaron; mother of Nadab, Abihu, Eleazar, and Ithamar; daughter of Amminadab; sister of Nahshon. Exodus 6:23.

Elizabeth: Wife of Zechariah, mother of John the Baptist, and cousin to the Virgin Mary. Luke 1:1–57.

Esther: Queen of Persia; saved her Hebrew people from massacre. Book of Esther.

Eunice: Mother of Timothy; Jewish Christian. 2 Timothy 1:5; Acts 16:1.

Eve: First woman; wife of Adam; mother of Cain, Abel, and Seth. Genesis 3, 4.

Gomer: Harlot wife of Hosea. Hosea 1:2–3.

Hagar: Egyptian slave of Sarah and mother of Abraham's first son, Ishmael. Genesis 16, 21:9–21; Galatians 4:24.

Haggith: Wife of King David and mother of Adonijah. 2 Samuel 3:4; 1 Kings 1:5, 11, 2:13; 1 Chronicles 3:2.

Hamutal: Mother of Kings Jehoahaz and Zedekiah. 2 Kings 23:31, 24:18; Jeremiah 52:1.

Hannah: Mother of prophet Samuel and wife of Elkanah the Levite. 1 Samuel 1:1–28.

Hephzibah: Mother of King Manasseh of Judah. 2 Kings 21:1.

Herodias: Daughter of Aristobulus and Bernice, wife first of Herod Philip I and then his brother Herod Antipas, and mother of Salome. Matthew 14:3–11; Mark 6:17–25.

Hoglah: Daughter of Zelophehad the Gileadite; responsible for allowing heritage to pass on to daughters if no son was born. Numbers 26:33, 27:1-8, 36:11; Joshua 17:3–4.

Huldah: Prophetess; discovered by the high priest Hilkiah. 2 Kings 22:14–17; 2 Chronicles 34:22–24.

Jael: Wife of Heber the Kenite; killed Sisera, the captain of Jabin's army. Judges 4:17–22, 5:24.

Jecholiah: Mother of King Azariah of Judah. 2 Kings 15:2; 2 Chronicles 26:3.

Jedidah: Mother of King Josiah of Judah. 2 Kings 22:1.

Jehosheba: Daughter of King Jehoram (Israel); saved King Joash of Judah as an infant. 2 Kings 11:2; 2 Chronicles 22:11.

Jemimah: First of three daughters born to Job after his prosperity had been restored. Job 42:14.

Jezebel: Daughter of King Ethbaal of Sidon; wife of King Ahab of Israel; notorious evil queen. 1 Kings 16:31, 18:4, 19:1–2, 21:5, 23; 2 Kings 9:30–37.

Joanna: Wife of Chuza, steward of Herod the Tetrarch; among the women who discovered Jesus' empty tomb. Luke 8:3, 24:10.

Jochebed: Wife of Amram; mother of Moses, Aaron, and Miriam. Exodus 6:20; Numbers 26:59.

Judith: (1) Widow from Bethulia who beheaded the Assyrian general Holofernes. Book of Judith. (2) Wife of Esau. Genesis 26:34.

Julia: Probably wife of Andronicus; sister of Nereus. Romans 16:15.

Keturah: Second wife of Abraham after death of Sarah. Genesis 25:1–4; 1 Chronicles 1:32.

Leah: Daughter of Laban; wife of Jacob; mother of Reuben, Simeon, Levi, Judah, Issachar, Zebulun, and Dinah. Genesis 29:16–35, 46:15, 49:31.

Lois: Maternal grandmother of Timothy. 2 Timothy 1:5.

Lo-ruhama: Daughter of Hosea and Gomer. Hosea 1:6, 2:23.

Lydia: Dealer in purple; Gentile woman who converted by preaching of Paul in Philippi. Acts 16:14, 15, 40.

Maacah: (1) The concubine of Caleb. 1 Chronicles 2:48. (2) Princess of Geshur; wife of King David; mother of Absalom and Tamar. 2 Samuel 3:3. (3) Daughter of Absalom. 1 Kings 15:2; 2 Chronicles 11:20–22.

Mahalath: (1) Granddaughter of Abraham; daughter of Ishmael; one of the wives of Esau. Genesis 28:9. (2) Wife of King Rehoboam of Judah. 2 Chronicles 11:18.

Martha: Sister of Lazarus and Mary; friend of Jesus. Luke 10:38–41; John 11:1–39, 12:2.

Mary of Nazareth: Mother of Jesus; wife of Joseph; cousin of Elizabeth. Matthew 1:18–25, 2:11, 14, 20, 21, 12:46–48, 13:55; Mark 3:31–32, 6:3; Luke 1:26–56, 2:5–19, 34, 48, 51, 8:19–20; John 2:1–5, 12, 6:42, 19:25–27; Acts 1:14.

Mary Magdalene: Woman from whom Jesus had expelled seven demons; follower of Jesus; went to Jesus' empty tomb on Easter. Matthew 27:56, 61, 28:1; Mark 15:40, 47, 16:1, 9–10; Luke 8:2, 24:10; John 19:25, 20:1–18.

Mary of Bethany: Sister of Lazarus and Martha; friend of Jesus. Luke 10:39–42; John 11:1–45, 12:3.

Mary, wife of Cleopas: Relative of the Virgin Mary; mother of James the Less and Joses; was at the foot of the cross with the mother of Jesus. Mark 15:40, 47, 16:1; Luke 24:10; John 19:25.

Mary, mother of John Mark: Provided room for Christian worship. Acts 12:12.

Merab: Elder daughter of King Saul. 1 Samuel 14:49, 18:17–19.

Mehetabel: Wife of King Hadar of Edom. Genesis 36:39; 1 Chronicles 1:50.

Meshullemeth: Mother of King Amon of Judah. 2 Kings 21:19.

Michal: Daughter of King Saul; wife of King David. 1 Samuel 14:49, 18:20, 28, 19:11–17, 25:44; 2 Samuel 3:13–14, 6:16–23.

Milcah: (1) Daughter of Haran; wife of Abraham's brother, Nahor; mother of Bethuel, father of Rebekah. Genesis 11:29, 22:20–23, 24:15. (2) Daughter of Zelophehad. Numbers 26:33.

Miriam: Prophetess; daughter of Amram and Jochebed; sister of Moses and Aaron. Exodus 2:4, 6:20, 15:20; Numbers 12:1–15, 20:1, 26:59; 1 Chronicles 6:3; Deuteromy 24:9.

Naamah: Wife of King Solomon; mother of King Rehoboam. 1 Kings 14:21.

Naomi: Wife of Elimelech of Bethlehem; mother of Mahlon and Chilion; mother-in-law of Ruth and Orpah. Book of Ruth.

Nehushta: Mother of King Jehoiachin of Judah. 2 Kings 24:8–15.

Oholibamah: Wife of Esau. Genesis 36:2.

Orpah: Wife of Chilion; daughter-in-law of Naomi. Ruth 1:4, 14.

Peninnah: Wife of Elkanah. 1 Samuel 1:2, 4.

Persis: Christian woman in Rome to whom Paul sent greetings. Romans 16:12.

Phoebe: Deaconess; Christian woman of the church at Cenchrea. Romans 16:1.

Priscilla: Wife of Aquila; Paul was a guest in her home. Acts 18:2–3, 26; Romans 16:3–4; 1 Corinthians 16:19; 2 Timothy 4:19.

Puah: Egyptian midwife who refused to kill Hebrew male newborns. Exodus 1:15.

Rachel: Wife of Jacob; mother of Joseph and Benjamin. Genesis 29:6–31, 30:1–25, 31:4–35, 33:1–7, 35:16–24, 48:7; 1 Samuel 10:2; Jeremiah 31:15.

Rahab: (1) Prostitute in Jericho who hid Joshua's spies in her house. Joshua 2:1–21, 6:17–25; Matthew 1:5; Hebrews 11:31; James 2:25. (2) Wife of Salmon; mother of Boaz. Matthew 1:5.

Rebekah: Daughter of Bethuel; wife of Isaac; mother of Esau and Jacob. Genesis 22:23, 24:15–67, 25:20–28, 26:7, 35, 27:42, 35:8, 49:31.

Reumah: Concubine of Nahor, Abraham's brother. Genesis 22:24.

Rhoda: Maid in the home of Mary, mother of John Mark. Acts 12:13.

Rizpah: Daughter of Aiah, concubine of King Saul, mother of Armoni and Mephibosheth. 2 Samuel 3:7, 21:8, 10.

Ruth: Widow of Mahlon; daughter-in-law of Naomi; wife of Boaz; mother of Obed, grandfather of King David. Book of Ruth.

Salome: (1) Follower of Jesus; witnessed Crucifixion; at the empty tomb. Mark 15:40, 16:1. (2) Daughter of Herodias and Herod Philip; asked for head of John the Baptist. Matthew 14:6; Mark 6:22.

Sapphira: Wife of Ananias; she and her husband withheld money and lied to Peter about it. Acts 5:1–11.

Sarah: (1) Originally called Sarai, wife of Abraham, mother of Isaac. Genesis 11:29, 12:5–20, 16:1–8, 17:15-21, 18:6–15, 20:1–18, 21:1–12, 23:1–20, 25:10, 49:31; Romans 4:19, 9:9; Hebrews 11:11; 1 Peter 3:6. (2). Daughter of Raguel, had seven husbands before becoming wife of Tobiah. Tobit 3:7, 17.

Shelomith: Daughter of Dibri and mother of Shelomith who blasphemed the Lord's name and was stoned to death. Leviticus 24:10–14.

Shiphrah: Egyptian midwife who refused to kill Hebrew male newborns. Exodus 1:15.

Susanna: (1) Heroine of Chapter 13 of the Book of Daniel; falsely accused of adultery. Susanna 1:1–63. (2) Benefactor and supporter of Jesus and the apostles. Luke 8:3.

Tabitha: Aramaic for *Dorcas,* raised from the dead by Peter. Acts 9:36–41.

Tamar: (1) Wife of Er; mother of Perez and Zerah through her father-in-law, Judah. Genesis 38:6–24; 1 Chronicles 2:4; Ruth 4:12; Matthew 1:3. (2) Daughter of David raped by her half brother. 2 Samuel 13:1–32. (3) Sister of Absalom; daughter of King David. 2 Samuel 14:27.

Taphath: Daughter of King Solomon; wife of Ben-abinadab. 1 Kings 4:11.

Timna: Concubine of Esau's son, Eliphaz; mother of Amalek. Genesis 36:12.

Tryphaena: Christian woman of Rome greeted by Paul. Romans 16:12.

Tryphosa: Christian woman of Rome; traveled with Tryphaena. Romans 16:12.

Vashti: Deposed Persian Queen; replaced by Esther. Esther 1:9–19, 2:1–4.

Zebidah: Mother of King Jehoiakim of Judah. 2 Kings 23:36.

Zeresh: Wife of Haman the Agagite. Esther 5:10,14, 6:13.

Zeruah: Mother of King Jeroboam I of Israel. 1 Kings 11:26.

Zeruiah: Daughter of Nahash; sister of King David; mother of Joab, Abishal, and Abishel. 2 Samuel 2:18; 1 Chronicles 2:15–16.

Zibiah: Mother of King Joash of Judah. 2 Kings 12:1.

Zillah: Wife of Lamech; mother of Tubalcain and Naamah. Genesis 4:19–23.

Zilpah: Maidservant of Leah; concubine to Jacob; mother of Gad and Asher. Genesis 29:24, 30:9–12, 35: 26, 46:16–18.

Zipporah: Wife of Moses; daughter of Jethro; mother of Gershom and Eliezer. Exodus 2:21–22, 4:25, 18:1–6.

Index

• •

• *N* •